GEN Z, EXPLAINED

Gen Z, Explained

THE ART OF LIVING
IN A DIGITAL AGE

Roberta Katz,
Sarah Ogilvie,
Jane Shaw &
Linda Woodhead

THE UNIVERSITY OF CHICAGO PRESS

Chicago and London

The University of Chicago Press, Chicago 60637
The University of Chicago Press, Ltd., London
Published 2021
Paperback edition 2022
Printed in the United States of America

31 30 29 28 27 26 25 24 23 22   1 2 3 4 5

ISBN-13: 978-0-226-79153-1 (cloth)
ISBN-13: 978-0-226-82396-6 (paper)
ISBN-13: 978-0-226-81498-8 (e-book)
DOI: https://doi.org/10.7208/chicago/9780226814988.001.0001

Library of Congress Cataloging-in-Publication Data

Names: Katz, Roberta R., author. | Ogilvie, Sarah, author. |
    Shaw, Jane, 1963–, author. | Woodhead, Linda, author.
Title: Gen Z, explained : the art of living in a digital age / Roberta Katz,
    Sarah Ogilvie, Jane Shaw, and Linda Woodhead.
Description: Chicago ; London : The University of Chicago Press, 2021. |
    Includes bibliographical references and index.
Identifiers: LCCN 2021016935 | ISBN 9780226791531 (cloth) |
    ISBN 9780226814988 (ebook)
Subjects: LCSH: Generation Z. | Generation Z—Attitudes. |
    Social change. | Social values. | Technology and youth.
Classification: LCC HQ799.5 .K37 2021 | DDC 305.242—dc23
LC record available at https://lccn.loc.gov/2021016935

♾ This paper meets the requirements of ANSI/NISO Z39.48-1992
(Permanence of Paper).

For Margaret Levi
dear friend and colleague

Contents

Introduction

Gen Zers, also called postmillennials, Zoomers, or iGen-ers, are the first generation never to know the world without the internet. The oldest Gen Zers, now in their midtwenties, were born around the time the World Wide Web made its public debut in 1995. They are therefore the first generation to have grown up only knowing the world with the possibility of endless information and infinite connectivity of the digital age.

Gen Zers are shaped by and encounter the world in a radically different way from those who know what life was like without the internet; they seamlessly blend their offline and online worlds. They have had to navigate this new digital world largely without the guidance of their elders, and so they have learned how to make their way within this fast-moving, digital environment on their own. This has led to a range of daily practices that are distinctive to them—though increasingly adopted by others, a trend that was accelerated during the COVID-19 pandemic, when so many more aspects of everyone's lives went online. The COVID Age is a digital age; it marks the moment when the rest of society began to catch up with Gen Zers who, with their tech savvy, lead the way.

This book is about the distinctive ways of being, values, and

1

worldview that are shared by many Gen Zers. It tells their stories in their own words, their memes, and much more. We do not claim that this is a definitive study of this generation; it is, rather, a snapshot of some Gen Zers' lives in the years 2016–2020, exploring who they are and how they go about their daily lives. It also uses the lens of Gen Z to think about the issues facing our world today, including the paradoxes and pressures we all encounter, by looking at what Gen Zers see as the big concerns and how they address them. In that sense, it is also a book in which we hope not only to reflect Gen Z lives but also to understand how they are seeking to mend so many broken aspects of our world.

HOW WE CAME TO WRITE THE BOOK

All four of us work at universities, and over a conversation one afternoon on the Stanford campus in spring 2016, we found ourselves sharing anecdotes about our experiences of postmillennial students. We had all noticed that, in recent years, incoming students were strikingly different from those from a few years before. They had a new vocabulary for talking about their identities and their places of belonging; they were hardworking but also placed an emphasis on their well-being and self-care; and they engaged in activism in a distinctively nonhierarchical, collaborative manner.

By the end of that conversation, curious about the distinctly different ways in which postmillennials express themselves, we decided to engage in our own collaborative work. We would use the combined methods of our fields of anthropology, linguistics, history, sociology, and religious studies to devise a study that would collect data, establish facts, and shed light on the broader historical context to understand better just what was going on with "kids these days." We then immersed ourselves in the worlds of eighteen- to twenty-five-year-olds through interviews and surveys in both the US and UK. We also created the "iGen Corpus," a seventy-million-word collection of the language used by Gen Z. Out of that collaborative work came this book.

Using their own words, we show how Gen Zers have gone beyond navigating this new world to harnessing it to achieve a workable co-herence of beliefs and values, identity and belonging. We show how they use the vast expansion of information and options on the inter-net to find like-minded people with whom to cluster and, through such exploration, discover, refine, and create their own identities. We explore the values they have forged to guide them in this new and uncharted territory, and we show how important those values are to maintaining the stability and security they seek. We uncover their preferences for new ways of relating and acting when authority has seemingly become dispensable and the distinction between offline and online has become obscured. Finally, we discuss the tensions and pressures that Gen Zers are experiencing as they move through this world in transition, along with their fears and hopes about the future.

Ultimately, what we first noticed in our work on campuses rep-resents something far more significant than a mere shift between generations. The story of the Gen Zers that we narrate here serves as a focusing lens; it crystallizes and reveals changes and tensions that have been present in society for some time. The postmillennials and the culture they are creating reflect back to us how they are—in their distinctive way—struggling with the innovations, failures, and contradictions of our society, many of which are inherited from the latter half of the twentieth century and affect all of us.

The experience of Gen Zers is therefore often paradoxical, even contradictory. They have more "voice" than ever before (e.g., a meme or a YouTube or TikTok video can reach hundreds of thousands, even millions), but they also have a sense of diminished agency "in real life" (e.g., institutions and political and economic systems seem locked, inaccessible to them, and wrongheaded). They are often opti-mistic about their own generation but deeply pessimistic about the problems they have inherited: climate change, violence, racial and gender injustice, failures of the political system, and little chance of owning a home or improving on their parents' level of affluence.

Gen Zers navigate these paradoxes using the new—usually digi-tal—tools that they have at hand. We highlight three main strate-gies. First, they are very clear about who they are, and they use that clarity of identity to self-define and push back against unwanted pressures and demands (e.g., "no, that's not appropriate to who I am"). Second, they join (mainly online) communities that fit, support, and help refine their personal and collective identity, purpose, and (for some) activism. Third, they reject hierarchy and embrace wider distributions of voice and power on the basis of equality and collaboration and having a clear set of values.

Nevertheless, as we lay out in this book, Gen Zers carry a heavy burden: namely, how can we all live in this dramatically changed world? Postmillennials are demonstrating much of what is at stake for humanity in the face of a digitally defined, network-oriented society that moves with unprecedented scale, scope, and speed. It is increasingly clear that massive social rebuilding is needed and that the job is going to require all to participate. So far, postmillennials are effective at modeling alternatives, often, though not only, within the limited spheres in which they operate. Obvious examples are online moderation and student activism on campus, both of which we discuss. However, they do not always understand or know how to operate within or change existing institutions and hierarchies, and this can sometimes lead to standoffs with their elders. This can happen even when they and their elders have similar values and aspirations because Gen Zers' ways of doing things have been so profoundly shaped by digital technology, leading to new methods of working, connecting with others, activism, and so much more. In turn, Gen Zers might argue that many existing institutions, with their related hierarchies and outmoded, largely analog modes of doing and being, are incapable of being the sites of change that the world needs.

As much as postmillennials have to learn, they also have much to teach. They are trying to humanize an intractable, inhuman world that seems to be headed for disaster. Their skills are complementary to predigital generations. Those of us who are older—and we include ourselves in that cohort, of course—need to work with postmillennials and learn from their alternative ways of being and doing things, and postmillennials need to work with other generations to embed the change they are modeling in their own spheres of action in wider, more lasting ways. They have great insights for the rest of us; however, there are limits on what they can achieve alone. Perhaps we can turn "OK Boomer" into a term of collegiality instead of the epithet it has become, so that we can work together to rebuild our crumbling industrial age social institutions into something that better reflects the needs of digital age humans.

A crisis looms for all unless we can find ways to change. As this book attempts to show, Gen Zers have ideas of the type of world they would like to bring into being. By listening carefully to what they are saying, we can appreciate the lessons they have to teach us: be real, know who you are, be responsible for your own well-being, support your friends, open up institutions to the talents of the many not the few, embrace diversity, make the world kinder, live by your values. In the pages ahead we share not only what we can learn from and about Gen Z, but why we believe even more significant social changes could occur as members of this generation move further into adulthood and the public sphere.

Our goal throughout our research and the writing of this book is neither to pathologize nor to idealize Gen Zers, but rather to understand them in and on their own terms, and as inheritors of problems we all face. We have tried to observe their methods of addressing those problems and to listen with critical respect to their solutions. For those of you (older) readers who are puzzled by postmillennials, we hope this book will enable you to understand them better and without immediate judgment. For those of you readers who are postmillennials, we hope that you will find at least some aspects of yourselves accurately represented here and that you will find the study useful in reflecting on what you and your peers might especially contribute to the world. We are all in this together, and as this book shows, we have important things to learn from one another across the generations.

HOW WE RESEARCHED AND WROTE THE BOOK

Our aim throughout has been to understand and present the Gen Zers we have studied in their own terms, and in particular in their own words, showing how they are distinctive. It took us some time talking together to work out exactly how we were going to do that. The open-mindedness of our funders, the Knight Foundation, and the support of our institutional host, the Center for Advanced Study in the Behavioral Sciences at Stanford, gave us the freedom to work collaboratively and to grow the project organically, adjusting our approach as findings brought into question some of our initial ideas and introduced new themes. Our topic spilled over disciplinary boundaries and required the expertise we each brought to the project. We learned from colleagues in social psychology and communication studies, as well.

In 2017, we began with a series of interviews with eighteen- to twenty-five-year-old postmillennial students, mostly but not only undergraduates, whose words are central to the texture and narrative of this book. We trained student research assistants to do the interviews, on the grounds that we—and they—thought that such peer-to-peer conversations would elicit more interesting and more honest responses. The interviewees were asked about their use of technology, how they see themselves in the world, their values, and how they relate to others, including their families, friends, and acquaintances. We kept the questions as broad and open as possible and ensured that we had a cross-section of students from a diverse range of socioeconomic backgrounds, cultures, races and ethnicities, and religions. We also supplemented the interviews with some focus groups, engendering conversation among students from different groups across each campus. We should note here that when we quote from the students, we assign different names to anonymize them. We deliberately do not use their identity markers (e.g., ethnicity, gender, sexual orientation, nationality), nor do we note which campus they came from, unless relevant to the topic being discussed, to protect those identities and to ensure anonymity.

The interviews were generally conducted on three campuses: Foothill Community College in Northern California, which largely caters to students seeking two-year associate degrees; Lancaster University, a public research university in the UK in the heart of declining manufacturing industries; and the top-ranking, private

Stanford University with its close ties to Silicon Valley and the tech industry. Each represents a distinctive type of higher education institution.

Within a few years, we had data from 120 formal interviews from the three campuses and from a handful of focus groups. The next step was to compare the findings from this qualitative research with their peers in the wider population, in particular including those who were not pursuing higher education. We did this in two ways, gathering quantitative data with linguistic and sociological methods.

First, based on the premise that language is a key to culture, we explored the language of postmillennials from a variety of sources. We created the iGen Corpus, a seventy-million-word collection of age-specific English language in the form of text, image, and video scraped from social media, time-aligned video transcriptions, memes, and our interviews. The iGen Corpus comprises postmillennial language from a variety of social media platforms: social (Twitter), gaming (Twitch), discussion (Reddit), imageboard (4chan), and video (YouTube). We applied machine-learning algorithms where necessary to extract the language of people in our age group. The iGen Corpus also includes memes, emoji, and copypastas (copied and pasted chunks of ironically edited text) from a variety of platforms, including Facebook and Instagram. This large collection of postmillennial language allowed us to compare the values and opinions of this cohort against the wider population (all ages) as represented by comparable collections of language such as the British National Corpus (BNC) in the United Kingdom and the Corpus of Contemporary American English (COCA) in the United States. As is evident throughout this book, this computational analysis enabled us to determine whether certain words and concepts had more salience, or "keyness," to postmillennials than the general population.

After we had concluded a large portion of the interviews and had some initial findings, we conducted two surveys of eighteen- to twenty-five-year-olds in general, both college-educated and not, in the US and the UK. The results allowed us to see how representative of the broader population our interview findings are, and to see the bigger picture. Together, the corpus and surveys serve the study like an establishing shot in a movie, pulling the camera out high and wide, to reveal the overall contours of the age group in question. The participant observation, interviews, and focus groups allow us to focus in more tightly, supplying depth, texture, and human richness.

Finally, we commissioned a series of short articles about this age group for an online social studies journal, *Pacific Standard*. We invited a cross-section of Gen Zers themselves, plus teachers, parents, journalists, academics, and higher education administrators, as well as others working in the arts, technology, science, and religion, to write about their perspective on what is distinctive about postmillennials, intergenerational relations, and much more.[1] Additional information about our methodology can be found in the appendix.

This raises the "generational" question. During the years we were busy gathering this material, a number of widely debated books about Gen Z, the iGen, and postmillennials appeared. They have shaped the conversation into which we now speak, even though our agenda is different. Generational studies assume that each generation—traditionally lasting about twenty years—is different from the one that preceded. Noticing significant differences between the youth and the millennials, also called "Gen Y," who were born around and after 1980, these studies concluded that we needed a new way to label those born around and after 1995. Consensus seems to be building around three such labels: Gen Z, postmillennials, and, most recently, Zoomers. As noted previously, this book is not a definitive study of Generation Z, but we do try to provide historical context for our findings. We draw on history to place Gen Zers' experiences and ideas, not least their adoption of finely grained identity, into a longer trajectory. We do from time to time provide Gen Zers' commentary and thoughts on the generations after (Generation Alpha, born in 2010 or after) and before them (Gen Y, Gen X, and boomers). Furthermore, this is not a definitive study of postmillennials around the globe: our sample does not allow for that. That said, we do hope it offers a snapshot of Gen Zers in the United States and Great Britain that will be both illuminating and useful.

We also hope it may inspire others to investigate Gen Z in other cultures and societies.

One of the first things we learned from Gen Zers is the high value they place on collaboration; in their words, they like to "collab." In keeping with this theme, this research project and the resulting book have been entirely collaborative. The four of us have written this book together, in one voice; we hope you enjoy reading the book as much as we have enjoyed writing it. We also hope that you learn as much about yourself and others from reading the book as we have from writing it.

1

Technology Shapes Postmillennial Life

> If you're thinking about either yourself or your social media, then you're online. No matter what, whether you're checking your phone or whatever—if you're thinking about it, you're online because it's really easy for you to check it. So even when you are in class, if you're thinking, "Oh my Dad is going to reply to me," you're mentally online at that moment. [Mei]

Technology is woven tightly into the lives of postmillennials. They take the internet and related digital networks and tools for granted; technology and online activities are incorporated into everything. As one of our interviewees put it, "For me, online and offline are one and the same, basically the same thing, integrated" [Jordan]. Others consistently repeated this view in their interviews, and it was reiterated by the results of our survey.

This should not surprise us: the oldest Gen Zers were born around 1995, the year the first browsers hit the global marketplace and the world began to explode with something called "websites." That was also the time when new online platforms started to appear— Amazon sold its first book online in 1995 —and digital devices began to proliferate. The journalist and historian W. Joseph Campbell, discussing (twenty years later, in 2015) the massive impact this "hinge moment" had on American society, described 1995 as the year the future began.[1] As the first group to grow up with network connections that were inconceivable to most people even twenty years before (except in science fiction), postmillennials were distinguishable from their elders, including the pre-internet generation usually called millennials or GenY, precisely because they have never known life without the internet.

It was only during the COVID-19 pandemic lockdown in 2020 that many who were born long before the internet was launched, who were used to separating online and offline activities, began to experience online/offline life as postmillennials do. Forced to use digital devices for various activities and communications that had been conducted in person before the lockdown, older generations began to understand more clearly how the line between online and offline could blur. In that sense, the pandemic has been a great accelerator of preexisting trends that Gen Zers were already living. While those who grew up in the twentieth century can still recall what life was like before smartphones and the internet, for postmillennials there was no life before these powerful, fast, connecting technologies. They have used software tools since they were very young to read, write, create, compete, understand, organize, interact, process, and interrogate—in other words, to be directly or indirectly in touch with others. They cannot imagine life without digital technology because they have never been without it; indeed, as one interviewee put it, "I wouldn't want to live without it" [Malia].

The tools of communication now available have fundamentally changed human interaction. Technology enculturates its users, who mirror its structures in their practice, language, and thought. Culture is changing and being shaped by technologies almost simultaneously, and it is the postmillennials whose daily habits of being demonstrate the unprecedented speed, scale, and scope of this change. An important key to understanding how and why so many Gen Zers do what they do and think what they think lies in appreciating how profoundly the new digital technologies have broadened the ways in which humans are able to interact and, especially, *communicate* with one another.

For the Gen Zers we interviewed, online and offline interaction with family, friends, and others is interchangeable. As one put it, checking her phone is an integral part of her life, and what she sees and reads on it is what her friends discuss when they are physically together, as well as on social media and in texts [Jordan]. Another interviewee noted that he uses social media as a way of interacting with people he knows in real life (IRL), and as a way of keeping up to date on their lives [Andy].

Growing up with the internet — and never knowing a world without it — has profoundly shaped the ways in which Gen Zers "do" life. Digital technology, with the constraints and freedoms it imposes, has affected and shaped not only their online habits of being but also their offline life and practices and the merging of the two. To illustrate, we look at three technology-driven themes that emerged in our interviews:

- the need to learn multiple social codes,
- collaborative modes of working together, and
- new behaviors and attitudes that have developed around the use of time.

SOCIAL CODES

Behavioral codes have always accompanied media use; for example, the twentieth century saw many rules regarding the "proper" times to place a telephone call. We authors agreed that none of us growing up would have dared phone a friend's home after 9:00 p.m. Now an abundance of *online* social codes have arisen that Gen Zers have had to become skilled at recognizing, developing, and putting into practice in their digitally facilitated interactions. At the same time, they still have had to learn how to behave in diverse offline spaces, from formal occasions such as weddings to informal events like visits with grandparents. And they have had to learn to change codes when they move from one location, activity, or context to another, whether online or offline, which requires a high degree of social dexterity. As danah boyd puts it in her study of networked teens, "Although navigating distinct social contexts is not new, technology makes it easy for young people to move quickly between different social settings, creating the impression that they are present in multiple places simultaneously. What unfolds is a complex dance as teens quickly shift between—and often blur—different social contexts."[2]

Gen Zers have become adept at quickly and easily delineating the codes and etiquette of different online sites, and what this means for their own online behavior, as this interviewee's words make clear:

> By the time I feel comfortable interacting with the group in a meaningful way beyond just browsing content, I usually already have a good sense of what the rules are, and you kind of pick it up based on what other people are doing in terms of sharing content in the comments, right, like inside jokes and stuff. . . . I guess since the things you talk about are different, it's hard to make comparisons, but the comparison is that in one of them you get really personal and you're supposed to just be unconditionally supportive, whereas in the other one, debate is in almost all cases encouraged unless it becomes a flame war. [Andy]

Another interviewee described the distinct etiquette associated with sharing memes by tagging (alerting someone to a post): "I only tag my closest friends in memes, so it signifies that they're a close friend and that I can joke with them. . . . It would be weird if I tagged a person I never talked to in a meme. . . . I don't actually know anyone who tags random people in memes, unless it's a spambot" [Malia].

Gen Zers articulate the difference between themselves and the members of older generations in terms of their recognition and observation of social codes online. The failure of older users to "get" these intricacies is the source of some postmillennial puzzlement. As one postmillennial said in a BBC interview in September 2019, "It's that lack of basic understanding of the etiquette of the internet that I often find with some people who are older than me [who] use a lot of hashtags on Instagram. It's just such a different way of using the internet. But it seems completely alien to us."[3]

New social codes and generational differences also emerged in email. For Gen Zers, emails, like business letters in the past, are for formal communications that require care over content and grammar, such as exchanges with professors and employers. Some students expressed an intense dislike of emailing, finding the composition of an email message—to a faculty member, for example—burdensome in its formality and too time-consuming. As one explained, "If it's a professor you don't have a close relationship with, you have to say, hi professor whatever, I'm in your class or I'm interested in this blah blah blah. You have to kind of frame it: why you are emailing them, and then say what you want, and you have to make sure it's respectful and it's not demanding too much of them. That takes some time!" Furthermore, the content of emails is often perceived as unduly long and wordy. "I feel I really don't email other people besides professors. Sometimes my dad will forward random stuff and I don't respond. He sends me articles from a website called Science Daily, and then whenever I talk to him, he's like, 'Did you read that article I sent you?' I'm like, 'No.' I've literally read one of the 300 that he's sent me" [Malia].

In contrast, Gen Zers favor texting and messaging and regard these modes as more spontaneous and especially suitable for communications with friends and family. The associated social rules are nuanced and intricate, as meaning is attached to the use of punctuation, capital letters, or numbers, as well as how and when a message is sent or responded to. Those texting and messaging nuances can also reveal intergenerational differences, as an interviewee observed: "Old people tend to use more punctuation [in texts], lots more, like all caps to emphasize words. . . . When I want to emphasize words, I put asterisks on either side of the words that are meant to be emphasized. So to me, when I read all old people's written comments, they just read more awkwardly, so you can kind of tell because the capitalization and especially all caps really tip me off, because young people generally don't capitalize anything" [Andy]. Similarly, a period (full stop) at the end of a sentence or after an abbreviation might indicate that the writer is angry with the intended recipient. Failure to respond immediately to a text or message might also be read as evidence of some hostility.

As technology evolves, so do associated social codes and behaviors. People who used SMS texting on the first mobile phones in the 1980s and 1990s became familiar with "textspeak" slang in which numbers replaced letters, such as *c u l8r* (see you later), *gr8* (great), and *2mrw* (tomorrow), and emoticons appeared as :-) and :-/ (note the use of "noses," a distinct sign of the era). Words were often shortened to a single letter and numbers were used for certain sounds when young kids were learning to message each other on flip phones, which required clicking a number keypad several times to get to certain letters. With the subsequent adoption of Blackberry phones, which had full keyboards, and then touchscreen-equipped iPhones, these mechanical shortcuts were no longer needed, and the social rules about using numbers to replace words became unfashionable.

The rapidity with which digital technologies and their associated social codes evolve can make the intergenerational differences all the more glaring, as any parent of a Gen Zer has learned when trying to text *okay* to their child. Should the communication be *okay*, *ok*, *K*, *kk*, *k*, or something else? To a postmillennial, these five responses have come to communicate drastically different messages. A response of *k.* means "you're in big trouble" for two reasons related to perceived intentionality. First, the letter is lowercase, indicating that the sender took the time to "undo" the capitalization that would have automatically occurred (given that the phone capitalizes the first letter of a text), and second, there is a period (full stop) after the letter. If a sender took the extra time to "personalize" the response in this way, it must mean that they were not happy. In contrast, *kk* has a positive, cheerful connotation; it is understood as a quick, low-effort way to soften the curtness of the single letter.

Given that text-based communication lacks many of the cues we are accustomed to in face-to-face conversations, like tone and body language, Gen Zers have adapted, perfecting typographical tones of voice. As one interviewee boasted, "I can express myself way better—even tonally—through text" [Elijah]. Mindful that their texts and messages can easily be perceived as sarcastic, rude, or confrontational, postmillennials have devised strategies that avoid "shouty" caps, commas, and full stops. They use smiley emoji as a softener and social lubricant; employ ~tildes~, XML closing tags </s>, winking emoji, and *asterisks* for sarcasm and irony; and use lol (laugh out loud or lots of laughs) in a variety of ways to express irony, softening, or passive aggression with different implications depending on where it occurs in a sentence.[4]

Rapidly changing digital technologies will continue to drive even more change in social codes and influence daily life practices. A kindergarten teacher in California, who has been teaching for twenty years, reported to us that she had recently noticed a difference in how her five-year-old pupils speak to her—curtly, directly, devoid of respect, courtesy, or politeness.[5] She believes this change has occurred because they now see her as a "human Alexa"—an information provider akin to Amazon's Echo (Alexa), Apple's Homepod (Siri), or Google Home (Google Assistant). The early-stage technology in these new devices, which struggles to deal with the messiness of natural speech (accents, pauses, hedging, and cultural politeness), is such that it requires users to speak more directly and clearly, in a manner that in other contexts could be considered rude and discourteous.

COLLABORATION

The desire for collaborative ways of working and problem solving is widespread among postmillennials. They like to "collab together" to address problems [Sunita].[6] This preference became clear to us early in our research project, sparked by the comment of a student on one of our American campuses who said she would choose her college major based on where she could most readily work in collaboration with other students. For her, it was so much more rewarding and enjoyable to learn and problem solve with others, rather than having to work alone.

Digital technologies have been instrumental in the push toward collaborative activity. Postmillennials became comfortable with group assignments—and group grades—in their precollege classrooms, and many had been exposed from an early age to software and websites that promoted joint efforts. They became accustomed to using digital tools like GroupMe, Google Docs, Office, Facebook Messenger, and Skype to create documents jointly, engage in group chats, and share calendars, and they became familiar with "crowd-sourcing," "crowdfunding," and other communal action through prominent websites like GoFundMe, Kickstarter, Patreon, Change.org, Indiegogo, Wikipedia, Zooniverse, and Amazon Mechanical Turk. Offline, digitally enabled ridesharing, couch surfing, and community organizing have reinforced the idea of sharing.

Gen Zers also learned that collaborations could lead to exciting results. The internet itself and various wikis are collaborative projects, created without top-down management; blockchain technologies (based on a decentralized database system) are being created through consensus and decentralization; and open-source software is valued precisely because it is built and refined by a large body of volunteer developers from around the world. The entrepreneurial companies of Silicon Valley mirror this "flat organization"—at least ostensibly if not always in practice—and some startups begin as crowdsourced or crowdfunded projects before being spun out.

The term *collab* is used to signify any collaborative enterprise among postmillennials, such as "collab days" (days on which Tik-Tokers will arrange to meet up to collaborate with other content creators) and "collab houses" (virtual or physical houses for group content creation). Most collab houses are now virtual groups, but the notion began as actual physical houses rented especially for the purpose of bringing social media influencers together for living and creating content with a shared aim of boosting their number of followers. Collab houses became popular in 2018 when a group of YouTubers formed the Clout House in Hollywood Hills and the following year when a group of nineteen TikTokers, YouTubers, and Instagrammers set up the Hype House in Los Angeles.

The range of ways in which postmillennials choose to contribute to group efforts, sometimes without any expectation of personal recognition or reward, is striking. Even in the context of the factory assembly lines that characterized the industrial age, there was a cultural expectation that each person's contribution would be recognized as such. But now, for the Gen Zers in our study, simply being able to participate in something new and worthwhile can be satisfying in its own right. A good example is the website Wattpad, described as a "hub for young people drawn to its interactive approach to the written word," with 65 million monthly users.[7] Novelists can use Wattpad to propose thoughts and ideas to that large community, and the users will then offer the authors advice on how to develop their plots and characters. Similarly, fan fiction has become an important creative arena that is reshaping the nature of authorship and allowing fans to become active participants rather than passive consumers. For example, you can find more than 85,000 stories at HarryPotterFanFiction.com, a website on which fans have used *Harry Potter* characters, settings, and plots to reimagine the franchise. Such fandoms are evidence of the new "participatory culture" that the internet has brought into being.[8] One interviewee, a product design major, uses a site called Dribble where he uploads his own graphic designs for others to use: "You can like it, put it in your bucket, save it to collections. I often use [Dribble] for inspiration. Well, inspiration and to copy off of, so I can improve my interface design skills" [Tran]. Another collaborates on Simutrans, an open-source transportation game. "It's crowd built so all the graphics, all the programming is just done by this community of loosely organized volunteers who just have time to kill." He explained how they "paint little pictures of trains and buses and plug them into the game which somehow just became the largest scaled game out there because there are so many people building assets for it." He clarified the game's collaborative purpose: "It's a purpose-built community. You know, we were all on this forum not to socialize with each other. We're here to build this game in contrast to social media and meme groups, which are about social connection. I would, for example, upload this bus I painted and then people would give comments. I would adjust, like, here's a revision. Everyone, good? Good. Okay, here is the final file. Feel free to put it into your game" [Andy].

Modularity and flexibility are two important aspects of contemporary collaborative work. A recent graduate of one of our three campuses, now employed at a large tech company, told us he simply did not know how work could be accomplished without collaboration. When his *team*—a word that is typically used for today's work units and reinforced through office-working software—found it needed additional expertise to solve a particular problem, members would search the company rosters for someone with that expertise. Once identified, the expert would join the team on a temporary basis to help address the issue at hand. In other words, his modern workplace, typical of Silicon Valley, is built with flexible structures that can support modular work groups that are not static but transform from time to time as needed.[9] This graduate's story sheds light on how Gen Zers approach collaborative work in several ways. First, it underscores that collaboration is based on the idea that each contributor has a unique role to play within the group. Second, it illustrates that collaborations are generally project-specific and thus require flexible work structures. And third, it shows that collaborations can reconcile flexibility and stability: a flexible structure allows for stable, even if temporary, modular work groups that can meet unique work challenges as they arise.

This distinctive form of collaboration also underpins student activism (a topic we return to later in the book). One interviewee used the metaphor of "links in a chain" to explain her experience of collaborative work in an activist context: "There's a person who does the theory, and then there's the person who writes the twenty pages of theory. There's a person who writes on the twenty pages of theory. Then, there's the organizer who reads the person who wrote on the twenty pages of theory and comes up with an organizational strategy. Then, there's another person from that" [Ayotunde].

In spring 2016, Who's Teaching Us? (WTU), a coalition of Stanford students who self-identified as coming from marginalized backgrounds, sent a document with a set of demands to university administrators, asking that future faculty hires and the curriculum reflect their own experiences and teach their histories. It was a precursor to the current movements that have become prevalent in many US and UK universities and colleges, seeking to diversify the faculty and the curriculum. The issues around identity raised by such movements are important for understanding postmillennials, and we discuss these issues in subsequent chapters.

It was the *methods* employed by the WTU movement that most surprised the university administrators because they were strikingly different from those of previous generations of student activists. Students conducted all communications online via a shared, collaboratively composed Google document; there were no specific leaders; and when in-person meetings did take place between the students and the administrators, different students participated each time, so the administrators felt completely at sea in trying to negotiate an outcome that satisfied everyone. It also gave administrators the sense that the document of demands was somewhat "unyielding." For the Gen Zer students, it seemed entirely natural that their online collaborations would also shape their offline activities, but for the older generations of university administrators, this mode of being and working was initially bewildering.

Flexibility, modularity, and collaboration enable contemporary activists to mix online and offline activities seamlessly. Their modes of working and organization are in part shaped and determined by the constraints—or lack thereof—of technology. Their collaborations are fueled by the speed, scale, and scope afforded by digital networks and tools, but they also reflect new attitudes about how to get work done. That said, we recognize that the activists in the current Black Lives Matter (BLM) movement have deliberately chosen this collaborative mode, without overt national leadership and with local groups having more autonomy. As one of the BLM founders, Opal Tometi, notes: "We've structured ourselves in this decentralized way so that we could be more safe.... It's also to celebrate the organic leadership of everyday people in their local community."[10]

Not every Gen Zer relishes collaboration, and particular identities, abilities, disabilities, and inclinations may or may not play a role.[11] Among our interviewees, one student was a particular outlier; she did not see herself as collaborative and expressed her preference for being a leader rather than a follower, which was not echoed among her peers: "I would say I'm more of a leader. I'm not very comfortable with the idea of just following. And I always feel like I have to compete even, like, implicitly. And that's why I don't do well in group projects because I always feel like I have to lead right away, I can't be submissive" [Hiba].

TIME

Gen Zers experience time as more fragmented and "24/7" than was true in the past, when, for example, a nine-to-five workday was a widely shared cultural expectation. While society as a whole increasingly has a 24/7 sense of time, postmillennials grew up with an abundance of information, presented at ever-increasing speed by faster computers and faster networks, and therefore they had the possibility of being "on" all the time. Postmillennial life therefore can exemplify the tension that emerged from juggling offline and online time.[12] It was not surprising, then, that the organization and use of time was a recurring theme among our interviewees.

One undergraduate reported that she and her friends rarely go to lectures. They have calculated how long it takes them to cycle to the lecture, attend the lecture, and then cycle back to the dorm, and have decided instead to stay in their dorm rooms and watch a recording of the lecture. They watch it at triple speed: this is not only to save time, but also to help them stay attentive. When they watch the recorded lecture in triple time, they are forced to concentrate on the lecture and are not tempted to multitask and access social media.[13] This example illustrates how postmillennials have adapted their daily habits of being to organize their days and save time using the very digital tools that produce so much information—and this is only one way they use digital organizers.

Gen Zers regard time as a precious commodity. As one interviewee explained: "I treat attention as a currency . . . and you can spend it on whatever you like" [Ethan]. They are strongly oriented to the present moment, focusing their attention on what is immediately before them. Theorists such as Thomas Davenport have coined the phrase "the attention economy" and have demonstrated that attention is money.[14] Being savvy about the economics of digital platforms, many postmillennials understand that when they watch a

YouTube video, for example, their attention may translate into actual ad dollars for the video's producer.

This emphasis on attention, coupled with a sense of "being in the moment," must be understood in the context of multitasking and constantly moving from one activity to another. Postmillennials may have many different windows open on their screens at the same time, and they flip frequently between their apps and windows. In this regard, they are like other heavy users of digital technologies studied by Byron Reeves and his team, who observed the "screenomes" of 400 computer users in the US, China, and Myanmar with the aim of understanding the sequence of screens these users viewed and interacted with over time. Observing screenshots of the participant's devices every five seconds, they discovered that users switched screen activity every twenty seconds on average, and rarely spent more than twenty minutes on any one activity.[15]

If time is precious, a commodity even, then making the most of it is a priority: Gen Zers prefer texting and messaging to email because texts and messages are short and hold the promise of an instant response. They use the minutes between classes to check in with friends and family, or take a break to look at a newsfeed or video. Much of this is related to convenience — on the internet, everything is just a click away — and so the expectation of convenience bleeds into all aspects of life. Many Gen Zers can efficiently "diarize" their time, managing it for ultimate convenience.

The sheer scale of the information available via the internet means that postmillennials prioritize relevance. Rapidly sorting through data online, they look for what they believe will be especially useful to the issue or task at hand, dismissing any information that does not immediately appear pertinent. An emphasis on relevance seeps over into offline experience as well: students increasingly select majors or their main subject of study, as well as classes, in terms of relevance, selecting what they think will improve their job or income prospects. For example, lecturers who offer practical advice or provide material regarded as especially relatable receive high ratings for "relevance."[16]

Similarly, Gen Zers look for "relatable" content in their online communications. As one interviewee put it, online she feels she must figure out what will be most relatable to others to ensure that she will keep their attention, but offline she does not have that concern because the person is with her, clearly listening; she does not have to "keep" them, as she has to keep followers on her social media sites [Jordan]. This sentiment that online content has to be "relatable" or "relatable af" (af standing for "as fuck," a phrase often used as an intensifier, with high occurrence in our iGen Corpus) was frequently expressed. One engineering student reported giving up posting on Facebook and no longer tagging people with memes specifically because having to think up relatable content "got kinda old" [Henry]. Our iGen Corpus also revealed that the word relatable is far more common in the language of postmillennials than in general population usage.[17]

We do not yet know whether or to what extent habits emphasizing speed, relevance, and productivity will undermine deep thinking skills, but we do note here that various academics and commentators, from a range of backgrounds and fields, are raising concerns about changes to the mind and brain caused by the use of digital technologies and media. Journalist Nicholas Carr writes in his book The Shallows that "with the exception of alphabets and number systems, the Net may well be the single most powerful mind-altering technology that has ever come into general use."[18] Neuroscientist Susan Greenfield asks whether a "mentality of collecting isolated bits and pieces of information [will] overtake the formerly normal process of making use of these facts, of joining up the dots,"[19] and the literary critic Maryanne Wolf questions whether "we as a society [are] beginning to lose the quality of attention necessary to give time to the essential human faculties that comprise and sustain deep reading."[20] In the field of education, Sam Wineburg and his team are creating new K–12 curricula to teach digital literacy and reasoning skills after their research led them to find that "overall, young people's ability to reason about the information on the Internet can be summed up in one word: bleak."[21] While not disagreeing about the need for learning media literacy skills, other commentators are less worried about the changes that are occurring, with some, such as Mizuko Ito, even suggesting that "the current anxiety over how new media erode literacy and writing standards could be read as an indicator of the marginalization of adult institutions that have traditionally defined literacy norms (whether that is the school or the family)."[22]

The increasing focus of postmillennial students on what is relevant to their job and income prospects also raises concerns that they have an instrumental view of education—that they are learning simply to get a job instead of learning for the sake of learning—which can undervalue abstract thoughts and ideas such as those encountered in the study of philosophy or literature. Even salient information from history can be more readily dismissed as not immediately relevant. Many universities have seen dramatic declines in the number of students majoring in the humanities and social sciences in the past several years, not only because students and their parents assume better job prospects will follow from physical science and engineering degrees, but also because they do not see the significance of such subjects to their own lives. To counter this trend, some universities are actively working to explain to incoming students the contemporary value of the non-STEM disciplines. Many Silicon Valley companies are realizing the value of the humanities, especially (though not only) for the "front end" (the user interface) of the internet, and are increasingly advertising for humanities graduates. Indeed, universities in the UK and US are currently debating whether they are sufficiently responsive to the societal needs and challenges of the digital age.[23]

A few of our interviewees nevertheless articulated the problems with processing a lot of information for "relevance." One poignantly described how dealing with fragmented and shallow content, which he described as "ingrained" in modern life, had adversely affected his own habits of thought: "If I have an idea and I want to develop it like one, two, three steps away, there exists a point at which ... I'll be, 'eh, I don't feel like it—let's turn back.' ... It changes the number of degrees of freedom of your thought from ten or something to three; literally, if you graphically showed that, it'd be shallower" [Luke]. This comment, along with others that we discuss later, reveals that Gen Zers are aware that society's rapid adoption of new digital tools and networks, while beneficial in many ways, has also led to new paradoxes, difficulties, and concerns, as we explore in the next section.

ANXIETY ABOUT THE DIGITAL AGE

The telephone kept ringing, and Winifred answered it, bringing her mistress each time some redundant and unnecessary message for her or for Arnold or for both. Telephones. The sort of thing people *would* invent, so that even being in different houses shouldn't stop them talking to each other.

ROSE MACAULAY, *CREWE TRAIN* (1926)[24]

Some thinkers, notably Jean Twenge, have emphasized the downsides of the digital age and blamed its technologies for harming postmillennials, arguing that they are anxious, depressed, and lonely because they are too engrossed in their devices, too deficient in critical thinking skills, and (a negative for Twenge) too communal in their work habits.[25] This argument needs to be given some historical context.

Moral panic and technological advancement frequently go hand in hand. Today, we worry about social media, personal-information tracking, autonomous artificial intelligence, drones, virtual reality, uncontrollable automation, harmful robots, biomedical technologies, and self-driving cars. In the nineteenth century, people's anxiety was focused on the invention of electricity and trains. Electricity changed our relationship to time and space because suddenly large spaces could be lit by electricity, thereby changing cities and buildings forever. When homes were first supplied with electricity, homeowners worried that it would be dangerous for women and children because predators would see lights on and know that they were home; others regarded the lighting of large city spaces as making them safer. "[Electricity] rearranged the cityscape completely," according to anthropologist Genevieve Bell, who also notes that trains were initially considered dangerous; it was believed that women's bodies were not designed to go at 50 miles per hour because their uteruses might fly out of their bodies.[26]

In other words, we have long worried about the impact of technology on human interaction. The telephone was a game changer because it made communication immediate between two or more people who were not in the same place; before that, the fastest form of communication had been the telegram. Invented in 1876, by 1900 the telephone was being used in business in the US; by the 1920s and 1930s—marketed increasingly to women for social purposes— it had become fairly common for domestic use, especially in the US, but also increasingly in the UK, which meant that it was not only purposeful but also social, its use associated with a whole series of rituals and practices.[27]

The language of promise and the language of concern that we find in relation to digital devices and social media today were both there when people spoke about the telephone in the early part of the twentieth century. Some were concerned that the telephone was forcing people to be available constantly, and always on call, as the quotation at the beginning of this section, from Rose Macaulay's 1926 novel, *Crewe Train*, illustrates. Others worried that the telephone broke into the intimacy of family life and was damaging to real friendship. Yet others saw it as an invasion of privacy and a security risk, as exemplified in Kafka's *The Neighbour*, written in 1917, in which a character expresses his anxiety about his neighbor listening through the wall to his business conversations on the phone.[28] At the same time, there were those who thought that this new technology could extend friendships across great distances in a new and exciting way.

The first half of the twentieth century witnessed a gathering intensity of technological mediation of experience. The telephone was joined by the radio and talking pictures, both popular in the interwar years, and, by midcentury, television. Twentieth-century technological advances in communication were such that all the pieces were in place for the hyperconnected society that has been a hallmark of the early twenty-first century. In that sense, the current digital age is the outworking of a capacity for connection and information gathering that began at least a century ago.

So what has changed? It is the sheer speed, scale, and scope of

TABLE 1. Gen Z Survey, US responses

Do you think new technological innovations will make life better or worse, where 0 is a lot worse and 5 is a lot better?

0—A lot worse	3%
1	3%
2	10%
3	31%
4	24%
5—A lot better	18%
Not sure	10%

the new networks and technologies that is unprecedented, driving the profound changes in how we conduct our daily lives, both online and offline, in the past quarter of a century. This theme of the sheer speed, scale, and scope of the digital age recurs throughout this book.

Gen Zers understand both the potential and the downsides of technology; it would be surprising if they did not, given that they are necessarily engaged with it in every aspect of their lives. As one student put it, "Technology makes my life efficient, helps to save time and run our lives more efficiently, but advances in technology scare me because they're tied to corruption, power, like inappropriate uses of dominance" [Jordan]. Tables 1 and 2 illustrate the responses from our surveys of representative samples of postmillennials in the UK and US to the question, "Do you think new technological innovations will make life better or worse, where 0 is a lot worse and 5 is a lot better?"

Gen Zers express critical awareness about the technology that shapes their lives in several ways, but especially in their sense of its potential to cause social damage—the harmful parts of the internet, the bias baked into algorithms—and in their sense that face-to-face time with people gives them something that online connection does not. Alongside their pervasive reliance on technology and appreciation of its benefits, most of the Gen Zers we interviewed were aware of its potential for harm. One interviewee, a computer science major, cautioned that "technology is imperfect and while the goal of technology is actually to be better than human error,

TABLE 2. Gen Z Survey, UK responses	
Do you think new technological innovations will make life better or worse, where 0 is a lot worse and 5 is a lot better?	
0—A lot worse	1%
1	2%
2	8%
3	34%
4	29%
5—A lot better	16%
Not sure	9%

sometimes it can be actually really bad." She continued, "There's examples of people trusting technology or algorithms or software, and those have dire consequences. . . . The perception is often that technology is neutral, but it's not neutral actually, so you have to be careful. People should learn about these things" [Lily].

Other students—of various ethnicities and socioeconomic backgrounds—were aware of the racial and socioeconomic inequalities baked into algorithms, a topic recently explored by Safiya Noble in *Algorithms of Oppression* and Virginia Eubanks in *Automating Inequality*.[29] "I think technology is really cool and it's doing a lot of things. There's a lot of things that come with technology. Like if you're able to reach so many people at once, you have to be sure that you're not only reaching a certain type of people," said one student. Another explained, "For example, Facebook was given a lot of flak for their ad managers being able to target only white people for certain types of job applications. So I think with tech comes a lot of things, and we have to worry about those as well. But I think, overall, tech is pretty amazing" [Ryan]. Several commented on the need to bake ethics into code. "I think there should be more of an emphasis on reviewing technology from a sort of ethical standpoint, ethical and social, before rolling it out. I think that there's probably been a lot of harm done by how sort of recklessly we have proceeded forward with technology, but there's also a lot of capacity to do good" [John].

The August 2020 debacle in Britain around national high school (A level) results, which had been determined by an algorithm when final-year high school students could not sit the exams during the

COVID-19 pandemic lockdown, illustrated the awareness of the youngest postmillennials of the problems with such a method. The algorithm took into account the results of previous graduates of those subjects and schools to determine grades for the A levels, which resulted in about 40% of the year's A level results being lower than had been predicted by teachers. This led to many university offers, which had been made on the basis of predicted grades, being rescinded. Young postmillennials demonstrated, holding signs such as "Judge potential not postcode [zip code]." One eighteen-year-old writer, Jessica Johnson, had—before the fiasco—written a dystopian story about an algorithm that sorts students into bands based on class, and commented that she had "fallen into her own story." This story, "A Band Apart," about the myth of meritocracy in the education system, had won the 2019 Orwell Youth Senior Prize, the year before. In summer 2020, she found herself rejected by the University of St. Andrews because her algorithm-derived A level grades were lower than predicted and commented that it was "ironic to become a victim like one of her own characters." Her university place was later reinstated when the British Government made a U-turn, replacing the algorithm A level results with the grades predicted by teachers who knew their students' ability and potential. It is revealing that a young Gen Zer had more understanding of the bias baked into algorithms than Ofqual, the British Government Office of Qualifications and Examinations Regulations.[30]

Postmillennials are coming of age when techno-optimism is turning into techno-skepticism, as society is reeling from data breaches and evidence of deceptive practices and "surveillance capitalism" by technologists, and as we have come to realize that artificial intelligence and genetic engineering could be seriously disruptive to human society.[31] They are aware of bot-enabled blackmailing, hacking, and fake news; potential spying of home devices; and how facial recognition can be used for racial profiling. They have grown up becoming aware that the same technology can be used for good and for bad. Deepfake technology, for example, may allow a video to be dubbed or edited without the need for a retake, but it may also be used during class to superimpose a teacher's face onto a porn video. A drone may deliver a package for Amazon or drop cluster bombs on innocent civilians. Postmillennials exist in a media world fueled by fake news bots or "deepfakes for text" such as Grover AI, which may take a fake news article and expertly reword it an infinite number of ways, as a mechanism for spreading misinformation. Many interviewees were wise to these negative possibilities: "People should question everything you read on Facebook, question everything that you see. Even question like why—why do I like this social media so much? Like it's a habit. But you should question" [Lily]. They were also aware of the problems with garnering their news from social media only:

> I do know that Facebook has a tendency to only show you what they think you want to see. So from time to time, I would go to the home page of a news source, like BBC or *Washington Post*, because they're a middle-of-the-road, fairly nonbiased place and so seeing, like, what are the headlines on their home page gives me a sense of, okay—just make sure that the headlines I've been reading is, like, an accurate sampling of what's actually most important, what's going on right now, and not just, like, what Facebook thinks I want to think is going on, so overall, it usually works out to be that way. [Andy]

What is not surprising about this student's comments is that, even when reading a newspaper, postmillennials are doing it online. By 2015, just 6 percent of those aged eighteen to twenty-four years were getting their news from print.[32] The intrusive extent to which artificial intelligence could be integrated into their daily lives was real, and in some cases regarded as frightening:

> It scares me, all this stuff. . . . They're making stuff where they can set the music the second you walk in based on the heat that your body is giving off from your emotions. Like they could start playing, like, happier music when you're feeling sad because you are giving off more juice. Yeah, like right away, and I'm like, "I don't want you

to know all this about me." So that part I am genuinely, like, really scared [about], but I'm also really fascinated that oh my god there is something that can recognize my body heat and do all this. [Aarna]

Gen Zers' online behavior is conditioned by their awareness of the potential for harm to their privacy and security. "I have big problems with those platforms [Facebook and Twitter, which he reported using a lot] and how they are. Yeah, it's kind of part of the larger structure of technology in the modern age, but it's owned by this one person who makes—I'm talking about Facebook here—very large amounts of money selling our information, and it's basically moderated by people paid very low wages who aren't even interested in doing it" [Zach]. Most interviewees attempted to protect themselves from surveillance and safeguard their privacy to some extent: "I accept that it is forever on the internet so I never share sensitive financial information and I would not want to share my address, [because] they might break into my house; snapmaps [a feature of Snapchat that allows others to know where a person is geographically located at a given time] are only for my friends" [Alex]. They are much more savvy than their elders at detecting and safeguarding against scams such as "cramming" (unauthorized charges for add-ons on a mobile phone bill), "whaling" and "phishing" (emails purporting to be from official organizations with links to fake websites in order to extract personal information or credit card details), "pharming" (redirecting a user to a fake website in order to steal confidential information), "scareware" (a malicious computer program that tricks you into buying software to protect your computer from viruses), and "ransomware" (a malicious computer program that restricts or disables your computer, and then blackmails the user to fix the problem). Fear of "doxing" (tracing someone's identity and maliciously publishing it online, especially on anonymous sites) was a motivation for some of our interviewees to "lurk" but not actively participate on some platforms, such as on chans or on the dark web, on which it is not unusual for someone to be seduced into sharing personal information or taking naked videos or photographs, only to be traced and publicly shamed and exposed (and sometimes blackmailed) on their personal social media accounts.[33] One student talked about a lesson learned when she was fourteen; she had gone onto a video chat site that attracted people with similar interests, but the site had become overrun with people saying and doing inappropriate things, including giving her and her friends on the site a computer virus that caused their computers to be hacked. As a result, she now shares far less online [Zoe]. "I had that experience online," explained another. "When I was debating something with a microblogger, he has millions of fans, and he just posted my account in front of others, and trying to say that I was doing it wrong, my opinion is wrong, and his followers just came to my page really attacking me, abusing me, things like that. I was so embarrassed because maybe even 5,000,000 have seen that post. Oh my god. I shouldn't have said that. There's the reason why people are afraid to share their real opinions online because sometimes you can have really huge costs" [Jun].

Gen Zers also know that what they put online can have lasting impact. "I do not post political or medical information online because it could hamper my employment chances," said one student [Malia]. "I don't want people to be cynical and mistrustful of everybody," commented another. "I think that's also bad in its own way. But at the same time, people should be careful about what information they put out there" [Cyrus].

GOING OFFLINE

Gen Zers' understanding of the downsides of the internet, coupled with the pervasiveness of technology in their daily lives, means that, although their online and offline lives are integrated to a great extent, they nevertheless understand the value and security of offline time with others. One interviewee noted she liked face-to-face interactions best because "it's the most secure." She explained that she got her appreciation for in-person time and her awareness of the need for online security from her father, who was obsessed with security issues, had no mobile phone, was not on social media, and had told his children not to go on social media (they ignored him);

her mother, by contrast, "was clueless" [Malia]. Another interviewee who fully engages in online life in many ways described her offline time as her "truest" world, a place where "I'm just me and I don't care. I don't have to care about anything that people say" [Hiba]. Others spoke about online media as usefully supplementing and servicing their offline experience—for example, by helping them stay connected with others who were physically distant and arranging times to meet IRL. But they often insisted that there was something irreducible about being offline, especially for experiencing relationships fully. They valued and would schedule more time to hang out in person—sometimes, with the added rule of no one being allowed to use their phones unless it was for an emergency. One interviewee reported that she gets tired of being on the screen a lot, enjoys a break from it, and likes talking to people—of having what she called "a voice conversation," which might just as easily be a phone call as an in-person talk [Yun].

Face-to-face interactions are often preferred over other kinds of communication and for a variety of reasons. "It's faster and it is easier, both in terms of easier to participate in logistically, as well as easier to express what it is you want to say, I guess, just because text will never replace voice in terms of ability to communicate something that you want to communicate" [Henry]. "I prefer it so I can see people's reactions to the information I give them and, you know, their emotions in general" [Camila]. They noted that it is "harder to convey emotions" online [Luke], that "it creates more misunderstanding" [Sunita], that you "can't really go into detail" [Eve], that you "can't really get intention or inflection" on social media [Malia], and that "you can better understand [a person]" through facial expressions and body language when in person [Jun]. Some noted as well that it is easier to assess authenticity when you see someone face-to-face. The desire to be in the present moment, discussed earlier, can also be used for meaningful offline encounters: as one student said, she appreciates a friendship precisely because it "is just like really being in the moment and caring for other people, being a great support system, in the moment" [Eve]. Our interviewees' clear appreciation of spending time offline with friends jibes with what S. Craig Watkins found in his study of students at the University of Texas: young people "do not choose intimacy with their screens over intimacy with their peers."[34] As one of our interviewees summed it up, "I think that in real life, you get something that the internet can't give you, which is empathy and human connection, kind of everything like a human can give you, like touching. I think that there's definitely advantages that humans still have over technology and that sense of like for humanness" [Bella].

Online and offline remain integrated in making friends and forging deeper relationships with them, but offline time is essential to many for sustaining the most valued friendships. As one interviewee explained, she no longer has "only online friends" whom she rarely or never meets, regarding that as a "young person mindset" that is "phased out as you get older." She noted that she was different with those online-only friends; in particular, she was "less vulnerable," and therefore, her best friends were all those she could and did meet in person. This was despite the fact that, as a self-defined shy person, she would often speak up more often when online because she could hide behind the computer [Zoe].

This desire to spend more time in the physical presence of others can affect how postmillennials think about geographical space, as illustrated by examples from both Lancaster University and Stanford University. At Lancaster, the library, exemplifying a trend seen across many campus libraries, has become a hybrid work/social space. In a study of library usage there, we saw that students were gathering in the library in much the same way as in their dorms, creating cozy, personalized nests where they would not only study, but also eat, drink, chat with others, and use their laptops. The students wanted to study side by side, in a common physical space, rather than working in isolation in their rooms.[35]

While the Lancaster libraries integrated online and offline, at Stanford the students went one step further: they took the initiative to set up some new spaces devoted exclusively to offline social interaction. They said that the coffee houses, student unions, dorms, and other potential social locations on campus were not sufficient because those were places where students also brought their computers to study. The need instead was for spaces that would be devoted exclusively to social activities, away from computers and online interactions. The "IT (Information Technology) Center" of yesteryear is being replaced by the "SI (Social Interaction) Center." Considering that Gen Zers spend much of their days online, where work and play are experienced in a constant, seamless mix, the desire for a new kind of place that is not in any way associated with work and that emphasizes in-person socializing underscores an expressed desire to connect with others in a meaningful, authentic manner.

Gen Zers also make concerted efforts to cut back on their technology usage, particularly in the context of social media. Among our interviewees, they described tactics of deliberately leaving a phone at home, downloading a monitoring app to limit online time, making pacts with others not to look at phones during meetings or meals, and deleting certain platforms altogether for extended periods. The process of cutting back can be difficult, as one student explained: "I just began to notice how I didn't like how much time I was spending on it, so I'd move the Instagram app to the back app page, and my finger would just automatically go there and click it. And even when I closed the app, I would automatically click it again if I didn't have the conscious thought of what to do next, which is really freaky. So I just thought I'd delete it, which is helpful." Now, she went on to say, she is less distracted and "feels more in control of what I'm doing with my life, which is really important" [Alisha].

Gen Zers express concern about the ways in which the generation below them, Generation Alpha, use technology. Some of our interviewees spoke with dismay about friends or, especially, younger siblings who had become overly dependent on social media or gaming. One interviewee noted that she was scared about the accelerated rate at which younger people were acquiring the kind of technology that she and her peers did not have until they were older [Zoe]. These interviewees were also critical of the social media apps their younger siblings were using, adopting a tone that sometimes made them sound like much older adults. One worried about seeing five-year-olds with smartphones: "When I see younger children using technology, I've noticed that they tend to use [it] in a very self-centered way. . . . [They] go off into a corner during a gathering just to use their phone and they're isolated" [Santiago]. Another interviewee described a technological "divide" with younger kids: "They'll use this thing called musical.ly, which I don't get. It's ten-year-olds singing to a song ten-year-olds should not know . . . or they'll do stupid things, like the Tide POD challenge . . . because someone, on probably musical.ly, told them it was cool." Younger kids in her home communities "do not use Facebook and follow less original content. For me, individuality is important. I hate musical.ly!" [Malia]. In a similar vein, another interviewee said that some eight-year-olds had left her feeling "like a moron" because she didn't use the same apps; she then commented, "It's weird to see the kind of stuff that they're obsessed with" [Madison]. Yet another interviewee remarked that "The younger generation uses technology differently. I do not interact with the younger generation. Younger kids love musical.ly but it is bizarre" [Gabe]. What none of these Gen Zers could foresee was that postmillennials would soon be heavily using the platform, in a different guise, themselves. In 2018, musical.ly merged with TikTok, owned by the Chinese company ByteDance, and two years later it was the fastest growing social media app in the world, with over 620 million downloads in the first half of 2020 alone. Its popularity has shifted beyond younger children across all age groups, including postmillennials, who have found themselves easily seduced by, and addicted to, the results of the app's smart recommendation algorithm. In June 2020, TikTok users spent twice as much time on TikTok as they did on Instagram, WhatsApp, or Twitter.[36]

CONCLUSION: THE PARADOXES OF TECHNOLOGY

There is a sense among Gen Zers, articulated clearly by so many of our interviewees, that technology is here for good and/or ill, and it is their responsibility to ensure that it is used for good. One interviewee, fretting that technology is keeping us from "walking around," acknowledged "that there is no way technology is going away, so we've just got to find a way to make it better somehow" [Lina].

Digital technologies present paradoxes for and to all of us: the wonders of technological change are held as keys to a better future but none has yet brought utopia, and many have made life more precarious, all overshadowed by the as yet mostly unknown consequences of the development of artificial intelligence. While the internet brings access to a vast resource of information, contacts, networks, connections, and the possibility of more voice and agency, it also brings vulnerability as privacy and security are compromised. The Gen Zers in our study are especially aware of these paradoxes, having lived with them for their whole lives and, as we shall explore further, having often coped with them alone as they found their elders more at sea than they were with such rapid technological changes.

Tim Urban of the blog *Wait but Why*, popular with many of the Gen Zers we interviewed, articulates the issue clearly:

> Tech is a monster god that is on the horizon running towards us right now. And when the god gets here, it's either going to be a really good benevolent amazing god or a really bad god depending on what we do right now, so we should go into tech. The people who are in tech right now are the people creating that god and deciding what that god is going to be like when it gets here.... If you care about people, if you care about grandchildren, you should be focusing on this too.[37]

Every generation inherits a world they did not make, but Gen Zers are especially concerned about what they face, from faltering institutions to increasing inequality to climate change. They have no choice but to turn to the tools with which they have grown up—digital technologies and networks—to try to solve these problems. They are aware that the digital technology that causes problems might also offer some of the solutions.

We return to the issues raised by these paradoxes of digital technology, and to how postmillennials are addressing them, later in the book. We turn next to the ways in which identity formation is important to postmillennials and how the internet has come to play such an important role in the forging of identity.

2

Fine-Grained Identity

The poet Elizabeth Alexander opened her 2018 baccalaureate speech at Stanford with a description of her ten-year-old great-nephew:

> Maxie, who is Scottish and Eritrean, lives in Aberdeen, Scotland, and traveled to see his auntie get married. In the photograph, he wears a kilt in the plaid of his father's clan, and atop his head is a tartan yarmulke made specially for the occasion for him to wear in the temple. He has the sweetest shy smile you have ever seen, and he is learning to dance an Eritrean dance with the older men in the family.... I think he may be the only Scottish-Eritrean boy with a tartan skullcap in the whole wide world. But surely he is not the last.[1]

Alexander's story resonated with the Gen Zer graduates. Her description of her great-nephew as a *tribe of one* or a *unicorn* (someone with a unique combination of attributes) reflected their own adoption of finely grained identities.

Identities forged in this digital age are intricate individual mixes of attributes, the result of careful and ongoing discovery. The search for and articulation of a finely grained identity was reflected over and over again in our interviews with students across the three campuses. Consider, for example, an interviewee we met in Lancaster, England, whom we will call Marcus—a gay man, strongly religious, whose parents had come from China to settle in the UK. He spoke poignantly about his quest to discover and understand his identity during his teenage years. Through internet searches he found that his sexual leanings had a name and a community. He discovered other people of Chinese heritage who were gay, something that brought him a particularly deep sense of comfort. In addition, Marcus spent two years as a Muslim convert, after childhood friendships with British Muslims in his neighborhood piqued his interest in their religion. He then reverted to the Christian religion of his parents.

Marcus described the process of navigating this complex set of attributes. His Christian friends may not accept his sexuality, his gay friends may not accept his religiosity, and his white and Asian friends do not always understand him or each other; but by keeping up his association with lots of different communities, he can nourish each aspect of his identity. Some aspects he considers fixed; others, potentially more fluid, stand the test of time and remain; and still others change over time as he does. To his delight and amazement, his online communities eventually led to him meeting another person just like himself: gay, Christian, and of Chinese origin.

Identity here is largely the result of a moral process of personal discovery, potentially offering a person an inner stability that in the past might have come from family or workplace—institutions that postmillennials often regard with skepticism. Gen Zers hold on to and even cherish some of their inherited identity markers, while others are rejected: this process of selection and rejection reflects a critical interrogation of the labels that have been ascribed to them by family or society. Spirituality commentator Casper ter Kuile describes this process as "unbundling and remixing." Unbundling means that we separate out the different elements from a whole collection of offerings and then remix some or all of them to suit ourselves—to make them entirely personalized and fully authentic.[2]

Postmillennial identities are fine-grained because they encompass a specific set of attributes that are subject to change as the discovery process continues. This discovery process enables greater and greater precision to be given to their identities, which is often seen in the adoption of multiple markers—for example, Marcus's Christian and gay and first-generation Asian-British identities. We were repeatedly struck by how clearly interviewees articulated who they are. Their fluency is due in part to a widespread generational agreement about the attributes that matter most: gender, sexuality, race, and ethnicity are particularly salient for Gen Zers. But most important of all is how different grains of identity are refined and combined by each individual in the process of discovering, constructing, and communicating their unique selfhood. This self-discovered identity is closely tied to another highly valued quality: authenticity. Gen Zers feel the need to be honest and not hypocritical—especially (but not only) in relation to the ethnic and gendered communities with which they identify and therefore claim belonging. This theme of authenticity is a vital one for understanding Gen Zers, and we explore this concept more fully in the next chapter.

Postmillennials regard their identity formation as distinctive to their own generation, so how does their process of self-discovery fit into a longer history of identity discovery?

IDENTITY AS A SOCIAL CONCEPT

Since the middle of the twentieth century, identity has increasingly come to be seen as a social concept, reflected in what were then relatively static categories, like gender, race and ethnicity, religion, class, and nationality—categories that were usually the product of a person's perceived biology, family background, and affiliations.[3] But identity-based political movements, combined with changes in policy in immigration in both the US and UK, changed all that. The civil rights movement of the 1960s was closely followed by the women's liberation and the gay liberation movements, which flourished in the 1970s, and all these movements brought the subjugation of those groups to greater public attention, especially as they clarified and claimed their identities in the quest for their rights. These movements also questioned the "naturalness" of certain attributes that were ascribed to their identities in ways that were oppressive. We started to understand better how gender is culturally constructed. For example, the nineteenth-century ideal of the "angel in the house," which involved viewing women as pious, sympathetic, submissive, and necessarily linked to the domestic or private sphere, was a constructed ideal of femininity that emerged with growth of the middle classes and the advent of the industrial revolution.[4] Our Gen Zer interviews show that this discussion about the construction of gender has now widened to question the binary of *man* and *woman* and the possibility of sexuality being more fluid.

And it is no wonder that ethnicity and race have become important identity markers—the US and UK both reflect greater ethnic diversity than ever before. The Immigration Act of 1965 in the US abolished national-origin quotas, which had overwhelmingly favored immigrants from western and northern Europe. Whereas seven of ten immigrants to the US were from Europe in 1960, by 2010, nine of ten came from other parts of the world. The 1990 Immigration Act ended discrimination against prospective immigrants who were homosexual. In the UK, post–World War II (and postimperial) immigration policy in Britain sought to bring new (and needed) labor into the country and likewise introduced greater diversity to the population. The British Nationality Act of 1948 gave free entry to all Commonwealth citizens, and the arrival of the ship *Empire Windrush* in 1948 from Jamaica symbolized this new era. In the 1950s, 1960s, and 1970s, this act resulted in waves of immigration from the Indian subcontinent, as well as a range of African countries. In both the US and UK, the parents of postmillennials grew up in societies that were becoming increasingly ethnically diverse, and this ethnic (and often accompanying religious) pluralism is now the norm for our Gen Zer interviewees. As Western societies have become multicultural, the articulation of identity has become more significant.

Postmillennials have therefore inherited the idea of identity as a social concept to be claimed and individually worked out in relation to broader social groups. They feel an imperative to self-define. Though this working out of social, political, and policy trends began several decades before they were born, it has been reinforced by many aspects of socialization, both online and offline. This emphasis on identity formation is largely unquestioned by most of them and is often regarded as the continuation of "identity politics," especially as they emerged on campuses in the 1980s.[5] But that's not quite right. What we heard from the Gen Zers as they talked about identity was both more nuanced and fine-tuned than that and also a response to rapidly changing conditions. Postmillennials have inherited the process of identity formation, but they have greatly expanded and developed it.

INTERSECTIONALITY AND THE INTERNET

So what has changed? Identity has taken on a new urgency as the combined forces of population growth, globalization, and urbanization have created new questions about where a person fits into the world. But two things are especially significant, as the story of Marcus illustrates: first, an individual's identity is uniquely fine-grained, flexible, and "intersectional" (a term we shall explore in a moment); secondly, the internet plays a huge part in the process of identity formation. The digital has shaped how postmillennials think about their identity, offering a wide range of choices from which they can create and shape their unique identity, as well as the capacity to know, at least online, "people like me." In turn, the internet offers postmillennials the opportunity to display those identities through their curation on social media.

Many Gen Zers, especially but not only student activists, in forging their finely grained identities have embraced the notion of intersectionality, a term coined in 1989 by the feminist legal theorist and civil rights activist Kimberlé Williams Crenshaw to indicate how the many pieces of your identity interact to become more than the sum of each part, with tangible effects in how we are perceived and treated in society as a result of the specific interplay of those pieces. Crenshaw summed up the significance of the term like this:

> Intersectionality is a lens through which you can see where power comes and collides, where it interlocks and intersects. It's not simply

that there's a race problem here, a gender problem here, and a class or LGBTQ problem there. Many times that framework erases what happens to people who are subject to all of these things.[6]

Chelsea Miller, a postmillennial (2018 Columbia University graduate) and activist who cofounded the Freedom March NYC in summer 2020, articulates how and why the term resonated with her:

> The first time I heard the term *intersectionality* it resonated so much with me as a Black person, as a Black woman, as a first-generation American, as the daughter of immigrants. . . . I was finally able to put into words why I've been able to understand people's challenges without necessarily having experienced them. Having all these intersecting identities and experiences, I don't need to be Native American or to be from the LGBTQ+ community to empathize with their stories. When someone says, "I've been hurt, and this system has served to oppress me and silence my voice," it's mind-boggling that it takes generations for us to say, "I see you. You're human."[7]

This notion of intersectionality dovetails with the ways post-millennials seek ever more precise identity markers, as illustrated by the shift from the LGB (lesbian, gay, bisexual) movement to LGBTQ (adding trans and queer), and then LGBTQIA+ (adding intersex, asexual, and all other sexualities, sexes, and genders). This kind of fine-grained specificity, and a fine-tuned understanding of the politics it demands, is reflected in the growing number of student groups on our three campuses that represent the particularities and intersectionalities of identity (e.g., the Black Pre-Law Society, the Society of Latino Engineers, Women in Computer Science, Jewish Queers, Queer and Asian). These groups open up opportunities and provide encouragement to be who you really are, within a set of identity attributes that are unique, individual, and complex yet clearly communicable.

The internet especially facilitates the continued refining of identities. Some of these minutely defined identities start as "interest groups," but as the groups then take on shared vocabularies, in-jokes, memes, heroes, and behavioral expectations, they become a shared identity and, often, a shared culture. We see this in both offline and online clubs, as any review of social media will reveal. There are millions of subgroups found on Facebook, Reddit, and Tumblr. Consider one example, the self-identified "Numtots": over 200,000 people who found their way to, and then became identified with, a Facebook group called "New Urbanist Memes for Transit-Oriented Teens."[8] One of our interviewees explains: "It's one of the most niche things I could imagine. It's just about urbanism and transit. But because it's such a niche topic, people who are interested in these things I feel like don't really have opportunities in real life to find people to talk about it.... It's shockingly active in the sense that it doesn't stop, like new content keeps getting created and there's people in literally every single time zone in the world, so it literally never stops" [Andy].

GENDER AND SEXUALITY

Of all the identity attributes that the Gen Zers wanted to discuss in interviews and focus groups, gender and sexuality—intimately connected to each other but increasingly considered distinct categories—came up most often. Similarly, in our iGen Corpus of online language, the word *identity* is most frequently used in relation to gender: *gender identity* occurs twice as frequently as other identity expressions. The fluidity and diversity of gender and sexual identity are also central. As model and actress Cara Delevingne (born in 1992, and therefore a little older than the postmillennials) commented: "When I realized that gender is so much more fluid than 'masculine' or 'feminine,' it was a breakthrough moment for me."[9]

Both online and offline, students frequently introduce themselves in terms of one or more of their gender and sexual identities. Far from being a taken-for-granted "package," these aspects of identity are differentiated, with each one becoming a site of discovery and choice. Within each category, there is a plethora of choices, some with their own tag and identifying label, including *nonbinary* (identifying as neither male nor female), *cisgender* (someone whose gender identity matches the gender assigned at birth), *trans* (someone who changes from one binary gender to another), *gender nonconforming* (neither male nor female, but not necessarily identifying with another nonbinary gender), *gender fluid* (a type of nonbinary gender in which one's presentation and identity varies over time between maleness, femaleness, and androgyneity), *genderqueer* (identifying as neither explicitly masculine or feminine, but can be a combination of both), and *postgender* or *agender* (those who completely disavow gender as a social category).

The ever-increasing diversity of gender and sexual identification, and their relationship to romantic disposition and identity, is reflected in the dictionary of words that coauthor Sarah Ogilvie compiled with her linguistics class at Stanford, words that these Gen Zers considered unique or characteristic of their cohort.[10] The words—with definitions—encompassed the following:

ace	abbreviation of *asexual*
afab	acronym of *assigned female at birth*
amab	acronym of *assigned male at birth*
aromantic	experiencing no romantic attraction
biromantic	romantically (but not necessarily sexually) attracted to two or more genders
boi	a gender-nonspecific person who presents in a boyish way
deadname	to call a trans person who uses a new name by their birth name
demigirl	identifying as neither male nor female but with some inclination toward girl-ness
demisexual	experiencing sexual attraction only when a deep emotional bond is formed
enby	a nonbinary person (from the abbreviation *nb* of *nonbinary*)
femme	feminine gender or aesthetic presentation
going stealth	presenting as your gender assigned at birth, when transitioning, for self-protection

graysexual	an asexual who rarely experiences sexual attraction, except under certain conditions
intergender	nonbinary identity specifically for intersex people identifying as neither male nor female
intersex	born with sexual anatomy not fitting typical definitions of male or female
juxera	gender that is near female but distinctly separate from it (cf. **proxvir**)
masc	masculine gender or aesthetic presentation
misgender	to use the wrong pronouns or name for someone
OTP	abbreviation of one true pairing; a person's favorite relationship, usually romantic, within a work of fiction or real life
pansexual	experiencing sexual attraction to all genders
pass	to look like the gender with which you identify
polyamorous	interested in having multiple romantic or sexual partners
polygender	nonbinary gender identity in which you identify with multiple genders simultaneously
proxvir	gender that is near male but distinctly separate from it (cf. **juxera**)
sapiosexual	attracted to intelligence
skoliosexual	sexually oriented toward gender nonconformity
unicorn	a bisexual person, usually female, who noncommittally joins a straight couple for sex

Even with this plethora of labels and descriptors, frustration can still result when someone feels their unique identity has been ignored or misunderstood by others. One postmillennial Reddit user explains their path of discovering their identity amid pressures to conform to conventional expectations:

The best advice I can think of is to ignore labels and categories and express yourself however you want to. The map is not the territory. When I started coming out to family, friends and health professionals as trans I felt both internal and external pressures to conform to a binary gender.... Anyways, 5 years later I realized that binary wasn't working (shocker), so thought I may be nonbinary, which I believe is closer to the truth. However, moving into the nonbinary space can be just as fraught, so I ignored anything people said about my gender and developed enough confidence and security regarding my gender identity to not be affected by external factors. So whether people refer to me as male or female just does not matter to me anymore, as what is most important is how I feel about myself.[11]

One interviewee expressed his/their gender identity in fluid terms, as a journey of exploration. "I'm trying to figure [out] my gender identity. It's kind of a weird thing. I still identify as a man, like male. But I think my gender is kind of fluid or queer. I don't know how to label it all the way. But I pronounce. And that's what makes people comfortable. That's just who I am." Nevertheless, he expressed a certain hesitancy in expressing his fluid gender identity on a daily basis with markers such as clothing, preferring to wear "certain clothes" just to evening functions "when it's dark." But, he concluded, "we'll see. We're going to challenge it. We're going to see how my confidence is coming here" [Travis].

Surveys reveal that the majority of postmillennials accommodate gender-neutral pronouns. The Pew Research Center, using surveys carried out in 2018, reported that 35 percent of postmillennials (which Pew defines as those born after 1996) in the US know "someone who prefers that others use gender-neutral pronouns to refer to them." And nearly 60 percent of postmillennials stated that they believed that "forms or online profiles that ask about a person's gender should include options other than 'man' or 'woman.'"[12]

The selection of a label is only part of the story; what meaning someone ascribes to it is also essential, as we learned when we talked with students about a particular finding from our population surveys of postmillennials in the US and UK (representative samples of the whole generation in each country). Our survey found that the vast majority (91 percent), whether college-going or not, identify as male or female. Only 4 percent identify as "gender fluid or nonbinary" or "other," and 5 percent preferred not to say. The figures are virtually identical for both countries. In subsequent conversations with students about this finding, they pointed out that it does not tell us what respondents *meant* by "male" or "female." The interesting thing is therefore not just which label someone chooses but what meaning they ascribe to it and how they live it. We should also recognize that the numbers of people who identified as male or female in our survey might include some trans men and women: those who had transitioned in or out of those binary categories or were in the process of doing so.

The broadening of gender identities and increased gender fluidity are now accompanied by the introduction of new pronouns (e.g., *ze, ey, em, eir, sie, hir, they, them, their*) to refer to an individual. Many of our interviewees, after self-identifying by their gender category, told us which pronouns they favored for themselves, with the nonbinary students generally using *they* and *them*. Why have pronouns become such a prominent issue? One interviewee who identified as cis female suggested that it is because of a widespread desire among her generation to respect and care for all identities, whether majority or minority. As she said, "For non-cisgender people, it's something they have to do to ensure that people refer to them in the way that is consistent with how they feel. However, for cisgender people, saying your pronouns is not always considered 'necessary' but is rather seen as a sign of allyship — a way of making it easier for non-cis people or friends to then say their pronouns without having to be the first to say it" [Eve].

This theme of respect for minority identities, and the need to protect and proclaim them in order to counter hostility or opposition, was one we heard over and over again. Nor is it an exclusively liberal concern among postmillennials. A self-defined politically conservative male student from Ohio, in an interview in the *New York Times*, noted positively that he had grown up with gay and transgender friends and classmates, reflecting that "for over half my life, I've been shown the other side of sexuality and gender. . . . I don't care about their sex or gender; I just care about the individual."[13]

In an article in our Gen Z series for *Pacific Standard*, Phillip Hammack, a social psychologist who researches sexual and gender diversity, argues that members of this generation are bringing about a nonbinary revolution:

> It's important to remind ourselves that the revolution is underway. It's not complete. The *future* is nonbinary. The present is a state of flux. This nonbinary future isn't about indulging teenage rebellion or experimentation. It's about a new culture of collective appreciation for the differences among us. It's about opening up to creativity and authenticity in how we think, feel, and act in the world. It's about being able to look in the mirror and see reflected back what feels "right" in our minds.[14]

This proliferation of gender identities can be seen within a longer history. The articulation of sexual difference was innovative when introduced in the eighteenth century: this was the notion that there were two distinct sexes rather than one sex with superior (male) and inferior (female) versions, as so many of the classical and medieval scientific thinkers believed. This binary "sexual difference" became a central plank of identity in nineteenth-century Western cultures.[15] The twentieth-century women's movements began to question the "naturalness" of gender, suggesting that the characteristics we ascribe to women and men as "feminine" and "masculine" were culturally constructed; this movement initiated another phase in a long history of change and contestation. New developments in hormonal therapies, surgical techniques, and reproductive technology in the late twentieth and twenty-first centuries have also played a role. When Gen Zers work out in their own lives the idea that gender is not fixed or binary, and integrate it with other aspects of a fine-grained identity, they are taking another step in this evolving history.

While the recent unsettling of gender categories owes a good deal to second-wave feminism, generational differences are also leading to disagreement and controversy. Postmillennials grew up reading and enthralled by the *Harry Potter* books, so when *Harry Potter* author J. K. Rowling tweeted that "sex is real" and went on to defend her feminist understanding of the category of woman, many postmillennials were deeply disappointed; she was condemned by many of them as a TERF (trans-exclusionary radical feminist), and the hashtag #RIPJKRowling trended on Twitter.[16] Aja Romano, who writes on internet culture for *Vox*, commented: "Rowling masked obvious transphobia as a personal appeal to reason, rooted in her own experience as a woman and an abuse survivor. She asked for empathy and respect for her experiences while showing none for her targets."[17]

The reason for postmillennial anger against J. K. Rowling is bound up with disappointment that someone so important to this generation, who had defended women's rights and minority rights more generally, was, in relation to their values, so off key. As a video on YouTube by "Jammidodger" explains to Rowling and her supporters, "cis gender is merely an adjective used to describe someone who is not trans gender to save time. . . . Both of these terms fall under the umbrella of 'woman' . . . it is just an extra adjective." As such, a trans woman is no less a woman than a cis woman and no less in need of women's rights.[18] As Romano says, "It took me a very long time to figure out I was genderqueer, and when it finally clicked, one of my biggest revelations was that I'd spent years mapping my own identity onto fictional characters without realizing it—above all, Tonks in *Harry Potter and the Order of the Phoenix*. I vividly remember the visceral excitement I felt the first time I read the fifth *Harry Potter* book in 2003 and met Nymphadora Tonks, a shapeshifter with spiky pink hair, a punk-rock aesthetic, and an insistence on being called by her gender-neutral last name." Romano's reaction is not to repudiate this past but to think about how she might set the *Harry Potter* characters free: "to express themselves however they want, transition if they want, practice as much radical empathy and anarchy as they want. Harry Potter is Desi now [from the Indian subcontinent]. Hermione Granger is black. The Weasleys are Jewish. Dumbledore's Army is antifa [antifascist]."[19]

Postmillennials are used to including sexual orientation as one of the markers of their identity, as our interviews illustrated. For example: "Chinese American, female, straight" [Jenni]; and "Indian, my friends are Indian immigrants, queer, I have a dog, like field

TABLE 3. Gen Z Survey, US responses

If you had to choose, which one of the following would you say comes closest to how you would describe yourself?	
Gay/lesbian	5%
Mainly gay/lesbian	2%
Bisexual	9%
Mainly straight	12%
Straight	60%
No category	3%
Other	2%
Prefer not to say	6%

hockey, reading, and art" [Alisha]. A striking finding in our survey of representative samples of this generation in the US and UK is that only 60 percent of respondents, in both countries, identified as straight. This perhaps surprisingly low proportion can be explained by the way the question was formulated: we rejected existing standard survey questions because they did not reflect the categories we were finding in our on-the-ground research.[20] Instead of asking about categories of heterosexuality and homosexuality, we asked the question as shown in table 3, where we also display the full results for the US.

The figures are almost identical for the UK. There is virtually no difference between those who are college educated and those who are not, nor is there a difference by gender. Religious affiliation and political vote make some difference. For example, among US post-millennials who say they voted for Donald Trump, 62 percent describe themselves as straight, compared with 57 percent of those who voted for Hillary Clinton; 72 percent of US respondents who say they are Protestants identify as straight, compared with 56 percent of those who say they have "no religion."

Generational differences, with regard to gender and sexuality, were clearly articulated by the Gen Zer interviewees, who reported they felt they have freedom to explore their gender, sexuality, and romantic orientations with an openness that was not available to those who grew up in earlier decades. Many of our interviewees pointed to attitudes about sexuality and binary gender conformity as the biggest difference between their own values and those of their parents. One put it this way: "I definitely think a lot of where I see the disconnect is just not understanding where people are coming from. Like a lot of people don't understand the purpose of pronouns or a lot of things to do with gender identity and race, so I guess [the difference is in] being more open to that instead of just thinking … this generation are snowflakes." She went on to suggest that her age peers should reach out to "older people who aren't growing up in an age where their formative years are informed by discussions of gender or race or identity" to help them understand where younger people are coming from [Alisha]. As we discuss later, this is just one of several areas in which the interviewees articulated a sometimes exasperated, sometimes proud, but definitely heartfelt need to educate their elders.

RACE AND ETHNICITY

Black Lives Matter and similar movements, with their focus on current and historic racial injustices, have highlighted the multiple ways in which race remains a charged category of identity. In the US, for some of the African American Gen Zers we interviewed, this meant that being around like-minded Black students was a safer, positive thing for their identity, enabled by being in a large college community. As one put it: "I was happy the whole time last year. I met friends who I could relate to. I learned more about my identity, my racial identity, about issues within the Black community" [Jaden]. Another African American woman commented, when asked what causes were important to her, "To me, Black women are really close to my heart, not just because I am one, but because I think that the people, especially in my college years, who were always there for me were Black women. They were always the ones to show up. And often, I think, especially at Stanford, they're always the ones who are asked to show up and do the work, and then not acknowledged."

The same interviewee referenced Beyoncé as a role model, noting of one of her groundbreaking albums: "when *Lemonade* came out, it was great being a Black woman" [Ayotunde]. Other students clearly articulated their pride in their Black identity, like this male interviewee: "Being Black is very important to who I am" [Travis].

Halsey, the postmillennial artist, activist, and singer, defines her identity as biracial, bisexual, and bipolar.[21] Our interviewees similarly articulated an awareness of the interlocking, intersectional parts of their identities. Different aspects of an identity may be more salient according to the setting. A male student said:

> It is important to me that I'm Black. That's important to me that I'm queer. It's important to me here [at college] that I'm fli [first-generation, low income]. Outside of college, I don't really think about it. But I think, those, yeah, those are the three things that are most important to me. But I'm also Christian, I'm also a tennis fan. And just think I see identity as so much more than just this is me. I am this, this, this, this. I am all of those things, but I'm also all of these things. And I think they combine really well. [Jaden]

In contrast with the sense of flexibility that the postmillennials express with regard to their gender and sexual identity, the category of racial/ethnic identity is generally viewed as not subject to the same degree of personal choice or control, with only occasional caveats and exceptions. This is related to the profound importance of *authenticity* for postmillennials, a theme we discuss more fully in the next chapter. There is a sense of the "given-ness" of how race and ethnicity are assigned and interpreted in the broader society, and the consequent injustices and dangers that come with that. A Black student who also identifies as lesbian commented: "There are parts of my identity that make it more dangerous to walk through the world than others. I think there are a lot of parts of my identities, like class, my class background, the fact that I'm a US citizen, the fact that I went to Stanford, that make it much easier for me to walk through the world than even some of my cousins, or even some other people in the US or otherwise in the world" [Ayotunde].

In his book *Trans*, the sociologist Rogers Brubaker compares recent controversies about gender with those about race, noting the asymmetry between them. With the way prepared by feminist theory since the 1970s, recent generations have significantly developed notions of sex and gender, turning them into categories of intense negotiation and choice. Never has there been such openness about individual self-discovery in relation to gender and sexuality, with accompanying legal reforms and social change. Yet with race there is much greater hesitation about opening it up to personal exploration and self-discovery in quite the same way. This Brubaker attributes to the heavy ancestral load of race and ethnicity, along with histories of oppression and violence. He speculates about the possibility of a coming change, fueled by the increasing cultural salience of racial and ethnic mixing, DNA testing that reveals the hybrid backgrounds of so many individuals, and the role of popular media in highlighting the "artificiality, constructedness, and instability of racial and gender categories."[22] He might also have considered the online games familiar to many of our interviewees and their peers, in which players can select different "skins" to inhabit—but whether this online activity will develop into more fluid notions of race offline remains to be seen. We note later that our UK survey finds that 20 percent of postmillennials say that the ethnic identity of the child of the Duke and Duchess of Sussex will be a matter of choice, while in the US only 12 percent of postmillennials say the same. These low percentages likely reflect the fact that the accurate description of an ethnic identity for the sake of authenticity, and to avoid the dangers of appropriation (another theme we explore in the next chapter), is a high priority for postmillennials.

There was a strong sense among some of our interviewees of the ways in which various ethnic groups experienced racism differently. One of the students quoted previously articulated this when noting that he had chosen to write an activist article specifically with two other Black students. He said that there are many times in a political discourse when the term *people of color* is used, but "there are levels to racism, there's levels to prejudice, there's anti-Blackness even amongst people of color." In other words, this student observed, the oft-used binary of white and nonwhite does not work: "It's kind of like white and nonwhite, but not all nonwhite people are treated the same" [Jaden].

Postmillennials have a keen awareness of the power dynamics inherent in identity markers, and the concurrent respect that is owed to those with particular racial/ethnic identities. A Black female interviewee observed that her ethnic and gendered identity meant that she had no choice but to think consciously about her place in the world, something that she felt "grateful for": "I think I'm forced to—or rather encouraged to really—think about how the position I'm in and the space I'm in influences my view of the world, and to think about how that changes from person to person to person." This, she believed, is different for those whose identities have for so long been the unexamined norm: "I think that's something that's a little bit more difficult, say, if you're a white man. Not because white men are less capable of it inherently, but because you don't automatically get this label of subjective, or partial, or particular ascribed to you" [Ayotunde].

This finely grained labeling makes visible identities and associated privileges that were once taken for granted. Hidden, unexamined and "unmarked" identities are articulated. Those interviewees who self-identified as white talked self-consciously and sometimes apologetically about the "privilege" associated with their racial identity, acknowledging that they had had economic or social advantages not generally available to their ethnic minority and less affluent friends. One interviewee, when asked about identity, emphasized "being white, being affluent, being decently able-bodied, having citizenship status, all these things that help me move through the world safely and easily." However, they went on to say that the identities that mattered the most to them personally were those that were most marginalized: they "had to fight more to come into them, to inhabit them. Definitely being queer and nonbinary" [Taylor].

A female student told us that she "presents as white" but is in fact "mixed race," a position that enables her to see that a large part of white privilege is being able to ignore offensive things happening. She went on to say that those who do not understand their position of privilege can often be "really offended if you try to call them out on something." Both Lancaster University and a university in America she had attended before going to England are "pretty white," and "not all people like to acknowledge white privilege as it makes them uncomfortable." She experiences this as a "difficult topic that causes tension," so sometimes she tries to avoid such discussions, while recognizing that such avoidance is a privileged thing to be able to do [Julie].

Some reflections on race and ethnicity were embedded in references to shared cultural values and experiences, as when a Chinese American female student talked about the ways in which her parents were, she felt, typical Asian immigrants, wanting their children to do well. She had inherited their values of hard work and dedication to success, but she has added what she described as Chinese values of her own: relationships with other people and wanting to do good for other people and the world. There is a clash, she noted, when being successful in the world means you are not doing good in the world. She also acknowledged that, as a Chinese American cis female who is heterosexual, she had not had to face the hardships that her gay friends of various ethnicities endured [Jenni].

Interviewees who, as children of immigrants, were trying to keep one foot in their parents' culture and one foot in the American or British culture in which they had grown up were especially vocal about the interplay between race/ethnicity as a personal element of identity and as an element of cultural familiarity and belonging. A Mexican American student put it this way: "I feel like the values in my generation are one perspective I share, or I'm accustomed to, because I've grown up here in American society, but from my other culture, which is a much more family oriented, collectivist culture, it clashes a little bit." He talked about assessing the different values associated with his bicultural ethnicities, explaining that he needs to be "selective between what traditions and thoughts I want to hold onto from a collectivist culture and what I want to adopt from this individualistic culture" [Santiago]. This can result in a juggling act between those different attributes and the values associated with them. An Asian American interviewee at Stanford spoke about navigating clashing values after growing up in the Midwest of the United States: "In Indiana . . . commitment and respect are really highly valued. And that is not valued as much [here]," she explained. "I feel like I view the world very similarly to people at home, I mean, like, my close friends at home who also were Asian or of minority race basically. I feel like I met a lot of people here who haven't experienced as much prejudice in their life and so sometimes their values are less than mine because they can't understand what it's like to be prejudiced against, I guess" [Lily].

Other interviewees, embedded in their cultures of origin and embracing their ethnic identity, wished to criticize some aspects of that culture of their upbringing in ways that they believed only they and not outsiders could. One queer second-generation student from India reported that she and her best friends—also female Indian immigrants—often talked about the oppressive values of their mothers and female relatives who believe that a woman's primary duties are to do household chores and get married (to a man), whatever their educational status. This conflict between cultural values may be especially shaped by the fact that the students are second-generation immigrants [Alisha]. These conflicting cultural values play a key part in that process of unbundling and remixing, as ter Kuile describes it, in identity formation.

While many interviewees felt that they had learned more about their ethnic and racial identity since arriving at college and were proud and pleased about that, a few felt that they had been brought up without a sense of their specific ethnic identities and that this continued once they were students. This often put them at odds with their fellow students. For example, a cis woman who is interracial— Native American and African American—and grew up on the US East Coast, talked about the impact of her past experience on her present experience of identity:

> I feel like people in my generation are very into racial things. They think that white people all have some inherent privilege that we must destroy or mitigate somehow. I feel like I have a much more tame thought process about that. . . . Clearly there's lots of issues with race in this country that I think need to be addressed. . . . Back home I'm from a pretty white community. My family is pretty culturally white. . . . I went to a school that my parents sent us [to] because

they didn't emphasize race. It was just like they didn't want to make it an issue for us to have to think about. So I never really talked about it there.... I feel like, it's weird, but I'm more comfortable in a room full of white people than a room full of Black people. And I think that's just because I grew up with mostly white. I don't know even how to explain it. Like there are things about the upbringing, the experiences that most Black people have had that I haven't shared. So a lot of times I feel uncomfortable, like trying to relate to that because I can't. And then also, I feel uncomfortable when people just assume that I've had struggles or whatever because I'm Black. [Malia]

As with sexuality and gender, our interviewees were appreciative of the fine-grained textures of racial and ethnic identity that have come with increasing levels of migration and multiculturalism, interracial relationships, and the desire to honor a person's unique identity. As political scientist Lauren Davenport has shown, social, economic, and historical forces have led to the construction of multiracial identities in the US.[23] Our Gen Zer interviewees clearly illustrated that multiracial identification. We heard descriptions such as "interracial African American and Chinese," "Asian American," "British Muslim," and "third-generation Afro-Caribbean Jewish convert."

We asked in our survey how postmillennials would think about a child of Meghan, Duchess of Sussex, and Prince Harry, Duke of Sussex, with the choices being "Black," "White," "interracial/biracial," "other," and "up to the children to decide for themselves." In the US, 43 percent said the child would be interracial/biracial, 21 percent said they did not know, and 12 percent said it would be a matter of choice. In the UK, 55 percent said the child would be interracial/biracial, 12 percent said they did not know, and 20 percent said it would be a matter of choice. "Interracial/biracial" was the most popular choice irrespective of the respondent's own racial or ethnic identification but was even more popular with BAME (Black, Asian, and minority ethnic) respondents than white ones, the latter being more likely than BAME respondents to say it was up to the child to decide or they did not know.[24] As noted previously, more

British than American respondents said it was up to the child. Virtually nobody in either country said "Black," which would have been a
common choice in the US in previous generations in which children
of Black–white interracial unions were usually described as Black.
This is perhaps not a surprise given that, since 2000, it has been possible to self-identify with more than one race on the US Census, and
multiracial identifiers have become increasingly important over the
subsequent two decades.[25]

A group of Lancaster undergraduates working with coauthor
Linda Woodhead interviewed thirty-three fellow students aged eighteen to twenty-five years about issues of identity. Of these, three-
quarters were white British. Noting that "race or ethnicity is an identifying factor that comes with multiple complexities including the
issue of defining one's ethnicity . . . especially when a person can
have numerous ethnicities that society may view as in opposition to
one another," they found that among the thirty-three students they
talked with, those identifying as interracial or biracial were especially discomfited by the fact that others "felt the need to place them
into a racial box." The group concluded:

> Overall, race and ethnicity were understood by our participants as a
> spectrum of identity, leading to many different ideas of how it im-
> pacted their belonging. In comparison with other markers of iden-
> tity, race was explicit in the ability of others to define one's racial
> identity without a sense of consent. While there was a strong sense
> of ethnicity having the capacity to be a platform of belonging, only a
> minority of our participants actively engaged and preferred this plat-
> form. Many participants [the majority of whom identified as "white
> British"] used it as a complementary aspect of their identity rather
> than a central platform of belonging.[26]

What is striking here is the sense among the majority, identifying as
white British, that they did not need to make race a central marker of
their identity, precisely because they are the dominant ethnic group.

In general, there is a sense that communities do not coalesce
around "whiteness" per se. One white interviewee explained that

she did not "think there is a community around whiteness, so although that is technically an identifier, I would not call it a part of my identity" [Emma]. On the one hand, for these students, being white and in the majority offered too broad an association—too big a "tribe"—to find a meaningful sense of social belonging in a world of so many people and so many other, more sharply defined social groups. It is part of the privilege of the dominant ethnic group not to have to identify according to ethnic markers. On the other hand, there are also many white groups on and off campuses who mobilize around that identity, most notably the political "alt-right." And even they are crafting more finely grained identities, thinking about their particular kinds of ethnicity, gods, rituals, and heritage–for example, the association with Norse and Germanic pantheons by some alt-right groups. And a particular experience of white immigrants in the US has been to identify as part Scottish/German and so forth in their heritage.[27]

There was also discomfort among some of our interviewees that by taking on a certain kind of ethnic identity they might be thought to represent everyone to whom that ethnic category applied. A South Korean student succinctly made this point when she explained that her adoption of an "Asian" identity had social correlates that made her somewhat uncomfortable, because she emphatically did not want to "represent the whole culture" [Yun].

OTHER IDENTITY MARKERS: NATIONALITY, CLASS, AND RELIGION

Gender, sexuality, race, and ethnicity are not the only aspects of identity by which members of this generation discover and communicate who they are, even if they are the most commonly articulated. In addition to things that are specific to students (e.g., the subjects they are studying, dorms, societies, sports teams), nationality, class, and religion came up in some of our interviews. In the case of each one, however, there was usually more hesitation and ambivalence than might have been the case for previous generations.

In our iGen Corpus, the words *nation, national,* or *nationality* occur far less than they do in the spoken language of the general population of all ages in the UK and the US.[28] However, of our survey respondents, when asked whether they were proud to be American or British (whichever was their nationality), 72 percent of US postmillennials said they were proud, while 68 percent of postmillennials in the UK said the same. When it comes to highlighting this aspect of identity, however, the picture is mixed. Some students had vague or contradictory views about nationality, especially when compared with the clarity with which they talked about other facets of their identity. A white male British interviewee at Lancaster University, for example, disparaged nationalism as an element of identity, but nevertheless went on to talk positively about his connection to elements of his British heritage and his active involvement in national (but *not* nationalist) politics [Harry].

Issues of nationality often came up in clearer and more prominent ways for students whose circumstances served to highlight nationality as an aspect of their identity. This was often true of international students who had traveled to the US or UK to study, of second- and third-generation immigrants who may have juggled different nationalities all their lives, and, particularly in the US, of undocumented students. The student from South Korea quoted previously, when asked about how she identified herself, explained: "I think sometimes [I identify] as being Asian too, which I wouldn't have known can be an identity before coming to America, because everyone was Korean, but . . . I can see that's an identity and sometimes other people see me through it too" [Yun]. Other students have juggled different national identities all their lives, often traveling between those different countries. One, who is now a college student in the US, remarked that she was born in Houston of German parents and went to a German school in Denmark, whose schooling system she discussed at length. She described herself as "100 percent blood German" [Nicole]. Yet another interviewee described himself as a cis African American but noted that he grew up in Switzerland and speaks many languages and therefore might also describe himself as European American [Adam].

First-generation students often experience national differences because their nationality impinges on their identity formation as they negotiate the values, expectations, and customs of the new country. One Mexican American student, now at college in the US, whose parents came to the US from Mexico before she was born, explained that she clashes with her father about schoolwork, because her father has no experience of being at school in America "because obviously, school in Mexico is a lot different from here. And so I told—sometimes I tell him that 'oh, I'm really tired. I have so much homework to do,' and he's like, 'Yeah, I understand that,' but come on." The student reflects: "I know it's doable, but it's obviously much more work than what in Mexico it was, because obviously Mexico was a lot easier for them in a way. And for us, it's just kind of like, we have to handle different things at [Foothill]—you know?" She uses her Instagram page to learn about issues around undocumented students on her campus and any planned protests or marches: "I follow them because I am able to be more aware of what's going on, and maybe if there's some in my community, I can join in" [Maya]. Some children of immigrants have particular investments in the articulation of their own and their extended families' national identities, especially at a time when immigration is a vital global issue.

Class, a significant identity marker in past decades, appears at first glance to be disappearing as a salient category for postmillennials. Our interviewees rarely mentioned the word, and the words *class, privilege,* and *status* are unusually infrequent in our iGen Corpus when compared with data banks of broader language use.[29] Furthermore, many of the students told us that two topics they rarely discuss are class and religion.

However, as with nationality, so with socioeconomics: those interviewees who are in a situation in which they need to be aware—or are made aware by others—of their socioeconomic status articulated it, even if they did not use the word *class*. This happened prominently in relation to being *fli*—a first-generation, low-income student. As one white interviewee articulated his identity: "I am twenty years old. I almost said nineteen, freshly twenty. I am queer. . . . I'm a sophomore from a low-income background. I'm a first-generation college student. So neither of my parents went to college" [Gabe]. He then went on to say that his parents run a fast-food restaurant together, which for a long time they expected him to take over, "but now I'm here, sort of doing my own thing. And hopefully I will be going to law school in a couple of years." Another student described himself as "a nineteen-year-old male, Black college student.... I'm a first-generation and low-income college student." He enjoys his work on campus with prospective students and newly admitted fli students: "And just to see all those kids come here, and experience Stanford, and take up space was so amazing. And it's what I'm most hopeful for." He contrasted his own awareness and activism with his family situation:

> They weren't exposed to problems. She [my mother] didn't know about things. They lived in Black neighborhoods with Black people. My mom didn't meet a white person until she was in fifth grade. And so she is not actively in an environment where she's encountering these issues. Or they weren't growing up, and I think that's something that has changed. Like me going to college, going off to college in California is different. It's so different, especially for my family. But that's a good thing, that's intergenerational growth. Escaping the cycle is happening. [Jaden]

Both of these students are very aware of how a college education takes them beyond the expectations and experiences of their parents. Being fli is integral to their sense of identity and to their relationship with older family members.

Although our Gen Zer interviewees may not have used the word *class* much, they are certainly not blind to differences in wealth, power, and background. Issues of equity and equal respect are very important to many. But privilege, which might once have been seen as something to be celebrated and flaunted, is now seen as something undeserved and problematic.

Postmillennial attitudes to religion are often complex and ambivalent. Some of those we interviewed had retained the religious affiliation of their upbringing, even if they adapted it somewhat to their own personal belief system so that it remained a part of their identity. A few had converted to one or more different religions, and the very act of conversion—and the choice to convert—made it an important part of their identity. Many were indifferent to religion, and they made no or little mention of it: it was not on their radar screen, so to speak. Others had a generally negative view of religion, understanding religion to be something institutional, potentially oppressive, and externally imposed; they did not even consider making it a part of their identity, though some articulated the view that there are religious individuals who might be good people who get something positive from their faith. Yet others made a distinction between religion and spirituality—like many in the broader population—viewing spirituality as something authentic and worthy of exploring as a part of their identity at some point in their lives, though not necessarily now.

A difference of views about religion between postmillennials and their parents was significant: for some students, there was parental acceptance of institutional religion on one side and a postmillennial orientation of finding values and answers in yourself on the other. Some interviewees spoke of moving away from the religion of their parents. As this interviewee noted of his parents: "They see things very differently. There's the perspective of religion. They believe that God gives them what is right and wrong, whereas I just kind of have to find it for myself, whether it's within me in some kind of human nature or social interaction thing, or if it's just truly nothing and I have to create it from the depths of my own being or something" [Zach]. Some, like this student, rejected any form of religion, while others were open to exploring religion and spirituality at some time in the future, though often starting from a blank canvas. One Gen Zer articulated that her religious identity would, like other elements of identity, be something she would have to discover: "I'm pretty open to all religious beliefs. The only reason why I feel like I don't believe right now in one specifically is because I don't have enough knowledge about any of them. I didn't grow up religious. That makes it infinitely harder because, yeah, you have to definitely explore" [Jenni]. As sociologist Tim Clydesdale found, US students place religious concerns within an "identity lockbox," to be returned to at some later time.[30] As we discuss further in chapter 5, the most common reasons given for rejecting religion are because its rules and frameworks are in conflict with values of diversity and acceptance or were too restrictive of personal freedoms. Even those whose religion is an important part of their identity are often actively negotiating these issues. For example, an African American interviewee explained that the values she holds as an evangelical Christian, particularly regarding premarital sex, put her at odds with the vast majority of her peers. However, she was quick to add that, unlike some others, the church she belongs to stresses the importance of relationships over rules [Malia].

While many Gen Zers have rejected the religion of their parents, they might still retain some sense, within their identity, of that religion as part their heritage, culture or ethnicity, worthy of exploration. As one interviewee said, "I'm technically Hindu, but I don't really practice or know much about it. . . . But I think lately I've been trying to learn more about that, learn more about my culture." When asked, "What kind of things have you been doing to learn more about it?" they replied, "At the moment nothing, but planning on just, like, reading the religious texts" [Lauren]. Some students emphasized the aesthetic and material dimensions of their religious practice, including clothing and food. A Native American student said, "I wear things like this . . . like I'm wearing things from my people, and there's a lot of power in things we make by our hands, and even in our designs, they each have, they all have specific meanings, so I, like, know that when I'm wearing them, I have the pride of my people, and I'm representing them here, especially because there's not many" [Lee].

Gen Zers want to be respectful of all differences and cultural affiliations, including religious ones, but some of our interviewees were clear that they did not want any sort of religion imposed on them: "I'm okay with people who have different worldviews. Yeah, I would be friends with them as well, it's just that if say they have a worldview and then they impose it on me, then we probably can't be friends. I like to think of it as really similar to religion. I have friends in all religions, come from a multiracial society. Singapore has Christian, Buddhist, Muslim, everything. I'm okay with that, but yeah I think it's okay as long as you don't impose it. Believe what you want" [Ping].

This Gen Zer acceptance of different religious views—as part of a broader worldview of accepting difference—can still go hand in hand with a general secularism in campus life.[31] A representative survey of religion on UK campuses carried out in 2016–2017 shows that 46 percent of respondents identified as Christian, 40 percent as "none," 9 percent as Muslim, 2 percent as Buddhist, 1 percent as Hindu, 0.3 percent as Sikh, and 2 percent as "other."[32] In probing the identity of the students who identified as Christian, sociologist Mathew Guest found that about two-thirds never went to church and did not necessarily practice their religion in a public way.[33] He calls these students the "hidden Christians" of university campuses with a "secret religion," and his interpretation of these data is that concealment is driven by a desire not to be publicly associated with an intolerant religion, a tendency to compartmentalize or sideline religion in order to accommodate the demands of the university experience, and a privatization and individualization of religion that conceals it from conventional kinds of study.[34]

For postmillennials in the UK and US, more than for any previous generation, it is common to have had no exposure to religion in their upbringing. The proportion of those saying they have "no religion" has been steadily growing for decades, to the point where just over half of British postmillennials and a quarter of US postmillennials have been raised by parents who identify in this way, and the vast majority of these individuals adopt the same "no religion" identity.[35] Thus, it was no surprise to find that, for many, religious identity was simply not on their radar, though that did not necessarily make them closed to the idea of exploring it. Whether this was out of politeness, respectfulness, or genuine interest was not always clear.

CONCLUSION

In forging their sense of identity, postmillennials focus on gender, sexuality, race, and ethnicity in particular, since these are the inescapable elements that minorities have brought to prominence and that majorities can no longer evade. In doing so, postmillennials are bringing to fruition a revolution in how such identities are handled and—especially in relation to gender and sexuality—bringing greater flexibility and choice. That which until relatively recently was taken for granted as fixed and given has become a site of struggle and opportunity within a broader imperative of self-definition.

But let's not lose sight of the bigger picture. These discussions of particular identity attributes are about the art of molding and assembling various pieces of identity into a coherent whole that gives expression to the inner self. Of course, this general enterprise is not new. It stems from the twentieth-century notion of identity as a social concept, and we may even say it extends back to the project of "expressive selfhood" whose origins Charles Taylor traces back to the Romantics of the late eighteenth and early nineteenth centuries.[36] What is new, however, is the *articulation* of identity in terms of a set of attributes that is, paradoxically, both complex and clear. It is complex in the sense that each individual assemblage is unique, self-chosen, and creative but clear in that it is readily communicable both to self and others. It is an aide-mémoire and advertisement of "who I am" as I embark on my journey through life. Thus, identity itself becomes a kind of public-private representation well suited to a digital age. Self-labeling has become an imperative that is impossible to escape. Why this should be, and why it is so central to the art of living in a digital age, is the subject of the next chapter.

3

Being Authentic

Our interviews began with a question about what these Gen Zers would put in a starter pack to describe themselves: a *starter pack* is an internet meme made up of a collage of images that introduces someone. Their answers were lively, immediate, and insightful, offering a limited number of objects and images that conveyed key things about who they were and what they cared about. Here are a few examples: "pictures of friends, pasta or some other carbs, phone, Twitter, dogs, Netflix or other TV bingeing source, podcasts" [Jordan]; "musical instruments, something related to my major, noodles, a bad pun, something that indicates that I am asleep at 3 a.m. and also have three 30-minute segments of sleep in the afternoon to evening" [Henry]; "several forms of alcohol, laptop stickers, Boba Tea, which I am addicted to, Star Wars, left wing stickers, something about the importance of LA to me" [Andy]; and "waffles, Stanford community, books (I love reading)" [Yun]. Most of all, the starter pack had to be completely authentic; this is what is important to postmillennials in expressing who they are.

THE COMMUNICABLE SELF

Because postmillennials' finely grained identities are so important to them, they care deeply about communicating these identities to others authentically and honestly. As with so many aspects of Gen Z life, the digital shapes identity formation. The starter-pack exercise, and the easy readiness with which our interviewees answered the question, shows how important the internet is in the articulation of identity markers that are clearly communicable in words and images. This raises a variety of issues about such communication. Many of the cues that can be relied on in offline encounters disappear in online ones; so do the contexts in which we used to meet people and work out who they are. Long-term engagements in which we can slowly reveal who we are to a select number of people are still possible online, but there is also more need to advertise immediately who you are so that people will know whether they want to "friend" or "follow" you or not. With scale and speed comes the possibility of vastly more encounters of incredibly short duration: a quick scroll past your post, a glance at a tagged post, or a "swipe left" on a dating app.

The digital also lends itself to simple sorting and classification tools, like online quizzes and multiple-choice exercises. By answering some questions or skimming a few sites, you can find out what sort of personality you have, what sort of partner is compatible with you, or what health issue you may be suffering from. However, the downside is that the quest for distinctive, true-to-self identity in the digital world means that it is taking place with both constant surveillance and constant display. Bullying and policing take place online as well as off. Identity is forged in a consumption-driven, digital environment in which algorithms push products, looks, and lifestyles that claim to be "personalized" but are offered to as many as possible. The pressures to conform are massively enhanced by the use of digital media.

Digital technology also shapes the public curation of identity. Gen Zers curate their image publicly on social media, and they do so with care, evoking the Latin origins of the word *curate*: *curare* means "to take care of." Because they have grown up in an era in which they could decide which pieces of their lives to post on Facebook, which thoughts to tweet, and which pictures to post on Instagram, postmillennials are reflective and careful about the public nature of their identity — or identities. They have the freedom to curate what others see of them — their own "aesthetic" — just as a museum curator chooses which items to include in an exhibition and therefore how they are seen. The teenage children of a professor from one of our three campuses will not leave the house, even for a quick grocery run, without carefully coordinating their clothing, lest they are photographed and subsequently tagged online. Apple Paltrow, the 15-year-old daughter of the actress Gwyneth Paltrow, made headlines in March 2019 when she criticized her mother for posting a picture of her on Instagram without her consent: "Mom we have discussed this. You may not post anything without my consent," the teenager commented on her mother's Instagram post. "You can't even see your face," her mother replied in front of her 6 million followers.[1] Similarly, the daughter of another colleague insists on pre-approving any family photos that her mother keeps on her phone, lest she show them to others. Out of respect for a desire to gain some control over digital identity, it has now become a matter of common courtesy to ask permission from friends before posting a picture in which they appear.

How postmillennials curate their online identities is a complex dance that involves implicit and explicit codes of usage and consideration of the expected audiences associated with different platforms and apps. The use of social media is always changing, but for our interviewees at the time of our research, it was, broadly speaking, as follows:

- **Facebook** is for postings that will be seen by extended family and a wide peer network that includes people from your past and present, including people from your school community and various others whom you may or may not have actually met, though some of our interviewees only used it for the direct messaging app (**Messenger**), mentioned later.
- A regular **Instagram** account (also called *rinsta*, or real Instagram) is used to share images with a broad group of friends and

acquaintances as well as "followers," while a second account, the *finsta* (fake or friend Instagram) is reserved for a close circle of friends and confidantes, with perhaps a third account like a *ginsta* (gay Instagram) for your gay identity.

- **Snapchat** is used to show a circle of friends ephemeral moments in your day—a person's *story*, as it is called—or to send direct snaps back and forth for consecutive days (these messages are set to disappear after a certain amount of time). Sometimes *streaks* of chat will last for long periods, often in real time. There are also, of course, self-created chat groups on messaging apps like **WhatsApp**, **GroupMe**, and **Messenger**, which gather people for many purposes, from family get-togethers, to club and society organization purposes, to intimate chats between two or more people.
- **Tumblr** is used by some (not many) interviewees for blogging and following and engaging with others who share your common interests, especially in writing, memes, fan communities, and art.
- **Reddit** is used for discussion and debate around topics as varied as news, gaming, memes, and sex, as well as niche interests. The culture of Reddit varies substantially depending on the subreddits engaged with.
- **Twitch** is the main platform for streaming and gaming among our interviewees.
- **Tinder** is, of course, for dating, along with other apps such as **Bumble**, **Grindr**, **CoffeeMeetsBagel**, and **OKCupid**.
- The short-video app **TikTok** was just coming into prominence at the beginning of our research (then called **musical.ly**), and at that time most of our interviewees were dubious about it, relegating it to the interests of their younger siblings (toward the end of our research it was more popular).

Almost all the students we talked to belonged to a wide variety of different online communities, some of great importance to the individual's identity and others, such as a group that coalesces around funny cat memes, requiring a "low level of [personal] investment" [Andy]. Decisions about which communities to follow or join are,

TABLE 4. Sample of the platforms and apps most often mentioned in our interviews and the iGen Corpus

Amino	Gab	Melon	Twitter
Ask.fm	Giphy	Minecraft	Vigo
Bitmoji	Grindr	Monkey	VSCO
Boo	GroupMe	Periscope	Wattpad
Bumble	Hooked	Polly	WhatsApp
CoffeeMeetsBagel	Houseparty	Profoundly	Whisper
Discord	Instagram	Snapchat	Wishbone
DOWN	Jott	Slingshot	Yarn
Episode	Kik	Steam	YouTube
Facebook	Lipsi	TikTok	Zello
Facebook	LiveMe	Tinder	Zepeto
Messenger	MarcoPolo	Tumblr	
Fortnite	MeetMe	Twitch	

of course, unique to each individual. As an example, one white queer male interviewee cited the following list of platforms when asked about his online communities: GroupMe, Hangouts, Skype, Slack, LinkedIn, WhatsApp, Sarahah (now defunct), Houseparty, Snap-Chat, Facebook, Instagram, Messenger, Twitter, Tumblr, Tinder, and Grindr. He added that while he "used to play Pokemon Go when it was a big thing, I also play Words with Friends with my mom and dad a lot" [Gabe].

Our interviews and the iGen Corpus disclosed a plethora of choice when it came to social media platforms that are variously frequented by postmillennials, a sampling of which are shown in table 4. Paradoxically, it is on their finsta (fake insta) that many Gen Zers feel they can be most truthful and real because it is restricted to a smaller group of close friends. As one interviewee said: "I like my fake insta a lot more 'cause I feel like I can be real to the people who are following, and it is also private." She noted that she had only twenty followers on her finsta but would let anyone follow her on insta, and at the time of the interview, she had 250 followers [Jenni]. Another student commented on the types of material they would post on finsta: "If I get an internship or something, I'll post about it on rinsta and be like, 'yay, I'm so excited for this internship, blah, blah, blah, blah,' and then on finsta maybe I'll post a drunk selfie and be like, 'haha, yeet.'" They added, "I got into finstas by follow-ing a number of other people's finstas and I would say mine are a lot more, I don't know, milder than theirs. A lot of people don't have problems posting nudity on their finstas." The same student, identifying as nonbinary and gay, explained how they formed a relationship over their finsta:

> This last girl I dated, we got into a relationship over Instagram. I'd say the concept of sliding into one's DMs [direct messages] on Instagram is very powerful, especially because finstas allow people to be more open about things. When this girl requested me on finsta, we'd known each other in high school, but I didn't know if she was queer or not. I was like, how interesting. And so I requested her and then I let her request me and then I just posted a bunch of gay content so that she'd know I was gay. So I'd say that while yeah, technically, finstas aren't really catered to anyone but I think having such a small audience allows you to really think about who is in it, and kind of be a little more targeted than usual. [Ashton]

Another student explained his own curating decisions like this: "My Instagram is public-facing and I like to look professional, semiprofessional—like, good photos. Finsta is just really messy and would be stuff that I'm comfortable sharing with close friends, like me lip synching" [Jonah]. The nonbinary, queer student, quoted previously, explained that even Twitter—a platform that was not frequently used by many of the students we interviewed—sometimes had its uses: "Last year I was in a shitty relationship, and any time the person in question would do something to make me sad, I'd just tweet about it, 'cause I maybe have three followers at most. One of them was a bot. So it was kind of nice to tweet into the void" [Ashton].

This kind of thoughtful presentation and communication of identity is in addition to the various expressions of identity that occur in multiple online affinity groups and, of course, in offline life. Choosing how and where to present the various fine-grained pieces of identity can appear quite complicated, given that there are so many possibilities, but for postmillennials it is done with relative ease, given their shared understanding of the relevant social codes and expectations, and a lifetime of daily practice at communicating who they are in the right way to the right audiences. This brings us to flexibility and authenticity.

FLEXIBILITY AND AUTHENTICITY

I think our generation really highly value flexibility. Flexibility of identity, the flexibility of movement, the flexibility of transaction, the flexibility of time ... in a lot of ways, most of them are very technologically enabled. So flexibility of identity—I think about gender, for instance.... Big picture, there exist many more forms of gender identity and relationship identity.... I think it's a pattern of expanded and more flexible options for sexual identity, family relationships, career paths, and, with Uber, even methods of transportation. [Emma]

So said one interviewee, who went on to articulate the widely held view among our interviewees that individuals are now freer to self-assign aspects of identity than was, until recently, the case: "for me, the value is preserving the understanding that you can step out of most constructs that you've made for yourself or that people have made for you" [Emma]. This bears out ter Kuile's idea of unbundling and remixing. Context may mean that different ingredients are re-mixed at different times. One interviewee reported that she maintains two online identities, one for her friends in South Korea and one for her friends in the United States, because they know her as two very different people [Yun]. Showing separate sides of yourself in varying social or cultural contexts is not new, but it is more complex when affiliations span online and offline settings and identities have become more fine-grained.

Authenticity is absolutely central to the process of identity formation for postmillennials, who are searching for authenticity in the face of many traditional categories breaking down.[2] The values of authenticity and honesty were repeatedly emphasized in our interviews: "I think most people I know value real friendship and true information" [Alisha]; "what I generally look for in a relationship is a sense of authenticity and a sense of sincerity" [Santiago]; and "honesty—a lot of things in my life revolve around that" [Aarna].

One interviewee, asked about what she meant in describing someone else as "inauthentic," responded: "if what they say and what they
do don't align" [Yun].

Flexibility is a part of discovering and articulating your authentic self. It does not entail the fragmentation of the self, or the idea
of plural selves, or even a "liquid" self—all ideas that have been re-
hearsed in the literature on modern identity.[3] A telling incident occurred at Lancaster University when a diverse group of students and
faculty engaged with a theater company that helped them experiment with more embodied forms of social research. In one exercise, participants were asked if they thought of themselves as a
unitary self or many different selves, and to walk to opposite sides
of the room—or somewhere in between—to indicate where they
stood. All but one clustered on the side representing unitary self.
The lone exception, a Chinese student, said she considered herself
one self when she is with her family in China, another self when
she is in her classes in Lancaster, and yet another when she is with
her friends [Jasmine]. This explanation surprised and caused con-
sternation among the other Gen Zer students, who asked her how
they could then know who she really was. Her notion of multiple
selves was challenging precisely because it was so contrary to the
group's shared imperative of discovering and communicating your
true self—a whole self that comprises various attributes.

To discover, express, and live out "who you are" is a moral imperative for postmillennials, not just a pragmatic one: this requires
both flexibility and authenticity, though the two can sometimes be
in tension with each other. Gen Zers want and expect freedom to
make their own decisions and choices, especially in discovering
and expressing their identities. Whether the perception is true or
not, many of our interviewees felt that this is a point of distinction between their generation and older ones. It is widely understood among Gen Zers that parents and grandparents were more
constrained in their choices and more hemmed in by social and
familial expectations. As one interviewee put it, "I sense that our
generation is going more towards a tendency of self-realization or
self-actualization on a personal level, than necessarily from a col-

lective family level" [Santiago]. This mark of generational difference may also be partly ascribed to the exploration that has been possible online for postmillennials for the whole of their lives, whereas the postmillennials' parents, when they were young, were not able to explore their identities through such online immersion. As one Gen Zer said in a BBC radio program, "Our parents are starting to get social media now, but when we just started high school, when we were trying to work out who we were, we had to navigate that ourselves."[4]

While most of our interviewees found freedom in unashamedly articulating their authentic identities to all, including their parents, it sometimes highlighted a clash of cultures. One student who found this difficult to negotiate said, "[My] family dynamic is really complex. They're Catholic and really conservative, like socially and politically. So I'm not out to them at all about being queer.... I would say that the one thing that's keeping me from being fully open and authentic with them is that fact" [Gabe]. Of course, there is nothing new about tensions between parents and children, and difficulties in coming out, but what stands out here is that those tensions are explicitly articulated in terms of authenticity and genuineness, as opposed to shame or embarrassment (although those feelings may exist as well). This tension is solved by careful curation of social media. "I'm not out as queer on Facebook at all or to my family," but he is authentically himself on other platforms. "Twitter, I use excessively, and it's my main platform. I share everything about myself. I have quite a big Twitter following I guess; I have 12,000 followers. So I would say that it's one community that I'm super into. Tumblr is similar. I have a ton of followers on Tumblr, 86,000 of them. And I use that mostly now for monetary purposes. So I have Google AdSense on my blog. And so every time someone looks at my blog, I get money." He made a distinction between the personal and the authentic: "I wouldn't say necessarily that it's more personal, but I feel more authentic in those spaces because I can just be. I can make a joke about something that's going on in my life, and there's a community of people that readily will resonate with that, even though I don't necessarily know them." But the lack of authenticity with his parents still troubles him:

I probably will never be able to tell them I'm bisexual. So what I told my last boyfriend actually was, well it's never going to work out that we get married or anything because I'm going to have to marry a woman in order to keep up the assumption that I'm straight to my parents and never have to come out to them as being bi. So yeah, I don't know. I'm sifting through that. It's super complicated and emotionally so taxing. It's not like one of those decisions where it's like you make it and then you act on it. It's like one of those ones where I'm constantly putting off thinking about it. [Gabe]

We were struck by how significant the word *free* is to this generation in our iGen Corpus.[5] The freedom to discover who you really are is essential if you are to live life authentically and make the most of your own potential. For Gen Zers, this is bound up with "being real" and communicating honestly who you are. Along with *true* and *honest*, the words *real* and *fake* occur with unusual frequency in our data bank of Gen Z language when compared with collections of broader language use.[6]

The postmillennials' emphasis on authenticity can be understood within the context of their having grown up with the internet, which provides so many opportunities to curate and tailor your identity, to take on different personae, and even to deceive. Authenticity therefore connotes believability. One student who had been a YouTuber in her teenage years—posting several videos a week for two and a half years—described being called out for hypocrisy: "I tried to be serious and honest with my followers but I think this may have been a bad decision as it was used against me by my followers if I ever changed my opinion about an issue." She said that she changed her opinion as she "grew older and learnt more about things" but her followers were unforgiving. She experienced firsthand the tension between flexibility and authenticity that can sometimes occur when both qualities are highly prized. Despite having felt that she had previously had an honest presence on YouTube, she felt confusion as to whether she could be honest about the emotions she was experiencing. In the end, she could not deal with the hateful comments any longer and stopped posting videos [Lena].

Postmillennials have a deep sense of what counts as an authentic image on social media. They are aware of the plethora of apps such as RetouchMe and Facetune, which enable you to modify everything about your appearance, from your skin color to the size of your physical features. A posed or edited photo posted on a platform where curated pictures are the expected norm is considered acceptable, as is a posed photo that is displayed as natural—a "plandid" version of a candid—when the editing is not glaring. However, if the poster passes off a doctored photo as natural and lies about it, the action is considered deceptive, inauthentic, and a breach of trust. Researchers at Columbia University have found that the consequences are felt not only by the viewers, but also by the posters themselves. Inauthentic posts on social media (i.e., those that presented the poster in an idealized rather than a real way) negatively affected the well-being of the person who posted. Analyzing data of over 10,000 Facebook users, it was the individuals who were more authentic in their self-expression who also reported greater life satisfaction.[7]

The need to be honest and not hypocritical is considered especially important in relation to the ethnic and gendered communities with which someone identifies, and to which they therefore claim belonging. Body modifications and tattoos were generally viewed as authentic expressions of personal choice and identity, but the rule of thumb for any identity claim is not to pretend to be something you are not. As one student told us, "Nicki Minaj likely has just as many—or more—body modifications than Kylie Jenner, and we all know it. We also don't care, because she isn't being particularly hurtful to any demographic in having these modifications. Moreover, a huge part of her persona is being 'fake,' so these modifications index an identity that she does in fact hold—we thus don't question the authenticity" [Ashton].

Revealing a weakness is honest, authentic, and appreciated— thus the popularity of the Canadian model Winnie Harlow, who celebrates rather than hides her vitiligo skin condition. By contrast, when fans of Kylie Jenner discovered that she had undergone plastic surgery and repeatedly lied about it, they were greatly dismayed.

She had created an image of natural beauty while secretly benefiting from body modifications, causing harm to others who were encouraged to hold themselves up to a standard that was false. It was common for individuals to share stories about the struggles they had had, and were sometimes still having, to be true to self. This struggle was often treated as a marker of authenticity, honesty, and hard-won integrity. Lili Reinhart, the twenty-four-year-old star of the teen soap *Riverdale*, has been lauded for talking openly about her depression. In a poem in her 2020 collection, *Swimming Lessons*, she articulates the postmillennial compulsion to honesty: "I've only told the world / what I feel, / not how to overcome. / It feels fraudulent to be given / a pat on the back / for simply telling the truth."[8]

Remaining authentic to self is a personal challenge, especially given the prevalence of online pressures toward self-improvement and even perfectionism. When so much of your identity is on display to a public audience, the dividing line between being true to yourself and responding to the expectations of others can get fuzzy. As a high school student put it, "Your online reputation is like a trailer to your movie—am I living for me or my audience?"[9]

Other callouts of hypocrisy focus on parents who restrict children's cellphone use at dinner but bring their own phones to the table for work calls. Two of the articles in our *Pacific Standard* Gen Z series note the problem of parents who do not or cannot put their phone down.[10] It was also common for our interviewees to report disillusionment with institutional religion, not just because of rules and hierarchical structures that constrain personal autonomy but also because of perceived hypocrisies.

As children exploring the online world, postmillennials became adept at recognizing empty promises, hype, and other falsehoods as they encountered a slew of advertising slogans, clickbait, and political jargon. Many of the interviewees expressed a clear-eyed awareness that the internet was controlled by mega-corporations that certainly did not have their best interests at heart, as we explored in chapter 1. Experiencing online dishonesty, manipulation, and hypocrisy has influenced their need and desire for honesty, authenticity, and sincerity in their own lives. Positive values are regarded as necessary for grounding and stability in an otherwise uncertain and untrustworthy world.

APPROPRIATION

Appropriation is related to the question of authenticity: it entails the use of cultural products that belong to another identity and/or community for your own purposes and advantage. This is regarded as especially problematic when privileged majorities appropriate the cultural products of minorities, as when celebrity white men and women wear cornrows and gelled-down baby curls. Such appropriation was deeply frowned upon by the students we spoke with from many ethnic backgrounds, not just because those hairstyles "belong" to Black female culture but because celebrities are trying to take credit for repackaging something that Black women have been doing for years. One Black student explained:

> I think the best way to think of cultural appropriation is like this. You have a bowl of water, and in an ideal world it's filled up with all of the great things about your culture, food, family, music, whatever. But depending on who you are, sometimes other people have been taking water from your bowl for literally centuries. Slavery, redlining, police bias, it's just sucking the water dry, taking away your safety and your money and even your family, so you're left with so little in your cup. ... And then, there's all these [white] people coming in and taking what little you have left and trying to call it like it's their own ... and make it yours and not give us credit, and then when they do it's cool and when we do it's trashy or ghetto or whatever. [Travis]

An Asian American student adds: "It's like if you turned in a school paper and you get a D because your writing is 'unprofessional' or 'clunky,' and then a white student comes, copies it word for word, calls their essay by a new name, and then gets an A+ for being 'innovative' or 'forward-thinking.' It's so frustrating" [Eve].

The appropriation of Native American cultures was also cited as an example of desirable pieces of a culture being picked out and re-

hun
@wwhyhun

a kardashian exploiting other people's culture? so shocking
#KimOhNo

GIF

♡ 3,193   3:44 PM · Jun 26, 2019   ⓘ

💬 548 people are talking about this   ›

FIGURE 1. A meme mocking Kim Kardashian's Kimono shapewear brand; after protests, she renamed the brand Skims

packaged for more privileged audiences without credit or recognition. This is because the right to wear certain items of Native American clothing is associated with belonging to a specific tribe. As a Native American interviewee said, "I'm two tribes and so I am the only one who has the right to claim the culture and what I'm wearing right now" [Lee].

The charge of cultural misappropriation can also be leveled at borrowing from majority cultures. In June 2019, Kim Kardashian was forced to rename a lingerie line called "Kimono" when followers on Twitter started a #KimOhNo campaign to protest her appropriation of traditional Japanese culture. She renamed her shapewear "Skims."

A more complex example concerns language, where there is considerable appropriation and borrowing from African American culture. Popular slang used by our interviewees, such as *bae, boujee, fam, shade,* and *woke,* originated in African American English and entered general English slang via rap, hip-hop, and social media. The development of language always depends on borrowing from different languages (i.e., loanwords), and innovation in language frequently comes from specific subcultures. In the past, it may have taken years or decades for the language of those subcultures to enter the mainstream because subcultures remained separate and contained, and the innovative language may initially have been only spoken, and then written down, published, and circulated later. But the internet has speeded up the process of transmission, with Gen Zers being the first age cohort to have grown up with immediate access to the language of a diverse range of speech communities whose words are now being written down sooner and shared on platforms such as Black Twitter (a community on Twitter that bonds over issues related to their Black identity), Reddit, 4chan, and in memes, thereby diminishing the time that it takes for slang, for example, to be adopted more widely.

This can be seen in the adoption of words such as *finna* (going to), *crunk* (lit, excited), *swag* (promotional merchandise), *dank* (usually used in reference to a meme that is unique, weird, or passé), and, most famously, the expression *on fleek* (on point, aesthetically perfect, originally to describe eyebrows) made popular by Kayla Newman, aka "Peaches Monroee," whose six-second Vine "we in dis bitch, finna get crunk, eyebrows on fleek, da fuq" went viral in 2014. Some three years later in 2017, Newman, initially thrilled that celebrities like the rappers Nicki Minaj and Christina Milian had taken up her phrase, was disappointed that it had been used by companies such as Forever 21, an online shopping site that sold an On Fleek crop top, and even fast-food restaurants such as IHOP, which was selling "pancakes on fleek" (meaning perfect pancakes). Newman was the only person who had not benefited financially from it. She has now tried to trademark the phrase and turned to readers of *Teen Vogue* and others online to crowdfund a new beauty line to be called "On Fleek" while she is in college, training to be a nurse.[11]

This is the age of monetizing your identity and personal brands. Although the "selfmark" trend can be traced back to Madonna in the 1980s, who protected her name and likeness, it is the younger influencers and celebrities who have taken it to the next level, seeking trademark registrations for "advertising services" and "endorsement services" for not only their personal names but also their associated words and catch phrases. For example, Hailey Baldwin filed for the trademark Hailey Bieber shortly after marrying Justin; Kylie Jenner's attempt to trademark Kylie was legally challenged by Kylie Minogue, but the postmillennial (Jenner) won; and the Kardashian sisters blocked Blac Chyna, who was engaged to their brother at the time, from trademarking her planned married name of Angela Kardashian. Taylor Swift succeeded in trademarking her associated words: *red*, *1989*, *speak now*, and *reputation* (album titles); *Meredith Grey*, *Olivia Benson*, and *Benjamin Swift* (her cat names); and the phrase "the old Taylor can't come to the phone right now" (song lyric).

EQUITY, INCLUSION, AND "CANCEL CULTURE"

If being authentic is a central value for postmillennials, expressed through their concern to be as accurate as possible in creating their fine-grained identities, the other side of this is a commitment to allowing others to find out and express who they are and, if possible, to offer them support—or at least, remove unnecessary barriers. In other words, identity must be respected in both self and others; what you want for yourself, you should support for others also. Thus, we observed widespread concern with values pertaining to equity, inclusion, and respect for diversity. As one interviewee put it: "Our generation—generally we want to see people of all different backgrounds be accepted" [Lily].

Respect and acceptance are important values. As one interviewee said: "I value the ability of being able to learn and respect and be in the presence of a variety of different ideas, and backgrounds, and stories," and "We're less likely to demand conformity to a group, and have more of a 'do what makes you happy' kind of mindset'" [Andy]. A Pew Research Center report on postmillennials highlights a specific concern about racial inequities: in the US, two-thirds of survey respondents felt that Black people in the US are treated less fairly than white people.[12] In its article about the report, the *New York Times* emphasized the role played by personal experience and access to current information in developing these views when it featured a twenty-year-old white man from Tennessee who said "his feelings on the subject were shaped by an early brush with racism in high school, where a black girl he knew was menaced by a white football player who threatened to lynch her. And ... were solidified last summer ... after a police officer in Nashville killed an unarmed black man."[13] The Pew Research Center report notes that "Gen Z is the most racially and ethnically diverse generation we have seen," and that majorities of both Gen Z and millennials (Gen Y) not only say that "increasing racial and ethnic diversity in the US is a good thing for society" but also are "more likely to have a positive view of interracial and same-sex marriage than their older counterparts."[14] In the UK, social scientists Nicola Madge, Peter Hemming, and Kevin Stenson's extensive surveys and interviews with postmillennials in a number of different schools and colleges across England yield very similar findings, though they add the caveat that although respect for differences is a defining value for this generation, that does not mean that it is necessarily evident in everyday practice.[15]

Coming to grips with inequities of identity is often a personal matter for many postmillennials. Often, they are talking about their own fine-grained identities and those of their diverse friends, and about injustices that have become more personally (even if indirectly) familiar to them through their exposure, online and offline, to events that seem very real. For some, this results in activism around issues of identity, including racial disparities. As one interviewee put it, "When who you are or who your friends are is on the line, you of course need to get active" [Eve].

Gen Zers can be quick to react when they find someone has not been truthful or authentic, that is, when there is a tension between self-idealization on social media and authentic self-expression, as we saw earlier in the case of Kylie Jenner. The audience for whom a poster may be idealizing themselves is the same audience who keeps the poster in check, providing a degree of accountability that prevents individuals from being inauthentic and misrepresenting their identities. When this happens to celebrities, it is their own "stans" (obsessive super fans) or the stans of other competing celebrities who turn on them. "Canceling," originally a form of shunning in which fans dump a celebrity, is a common response to an individual or product that abuses trust, sometimes with significant emotional and financial impact on the target. When the beauty YouTuber James Charles was accused by a fellow YouTuber of dishonest behavior in May 2019, he set a new record by losing over one million subscribers (or "sisters," as he calls his fans) in 24 hours. One by one, thousands of his sisters left messages of one word: *canceled*.

Cancel culture, or callout culture, is a new way for online communities to call out hypocrisy and to hold individuals and groups accountable for their behavior. It allows individuals to exercise personal agency in the online world, where so much power is in the hands of the platform providers. Gen Zers are well aware that depriving a celebrity of their following on social media is equivalent to denying them a livelihood. The expression "you're canceled!" is now being used against anyone online or offline as a strategy to express disagreement with someone's opinions or actions.[16]

Several students described to us the devastation they felt if they were canceled, blocked, or *ghosted* (when a person cuts off all communication without warning) on social media. The effects of such rejection on mental health can be costly. One student explained, "unfollowing on Facebook is okay, but blocking is very hostile." She had slept with a woman for the first time when she was eighteen years old, and afterward, the woman blocked her. "I had not even kissed a woman prior to this. Blocking meant there were no answers, no resolution, no communication. Everything about that person disappears" [Nat].

New language has emerged in relation to this notion of cancel culture. New expressions include *calling out* (someone), meaning to point out someone's error in an aggressive way and *calling in* (someone), meaning to do so in a gentle way. Other popular expressions such as *spill the tea* (tell the truth/gossip) and *throw shade* (insult or shoot a dirty look) are also frequently used as subtle and not-so-subtle retaliations within cancel culture. Although popularized by the internet, these expressions have their provenance in 1960s drag culture and African American English, especially the speech of young Black women. When compared with the general population, the words *cancel*, *ghost*, and *block* occur with unusual frequency in the language of postmillennials in our iGen Corpus.[17]

Postmillennials who defend cancel culture and *deplatforming* view it not as a personal weapon but as a cultural and political tool. As Aja Romano—whom we encountered in the last chapter in a discussion on J. K. Rowling and trans culture—argues, "cancel culture is best treated like a collective decision to minimize the cultural influence a person and their work have moving forward."[18] This is about the power of collective voice to challenge and drown out what they perceive as prejudice in favor of showing empathy and support for vulnerable communities. This is of a piece with the concern for equity. Whereas *equality* involved trying to get everyone to the same level, *equity* has more to do with supporting the vulnerable and different to be who they really are.[19]

A LONG HISTORY

Distinctive though it is in many ways, it is only in relation to a longer history of change around identity that we can fully understand the nature and intensity of the postmillennial concern with being true to self.

In the early 1970s, the American actress Marlo Thomas and some other celebrities introduced the popular record and television program *Free to Be You and Me*. They stressed the importance of being true to yourself and respectful and tolerant of others who were being true to themselves. Thomas, a white woman, was one of the founders of the Ms. Foundation with Gloria Steinem and others. The Free to Be Movement, as it became known, challenged gender stereotypes and introduced notions of racial and ethnic equality. While the movement was controversial in some quarters, it had a big impact on many Gen X children in the US (and to some extent Britain) who subsequently became parents and teachers of postmillennial children. The message about freedom resonated on both the right and the left of the political spectrum. Parenting and schooling became more child-centered, and some families adopted democracy in their households, with every family member now having a "vote," not just the elders.[20] On both sides of the Atlantic, postmillennials have absorbed the "free to be me" lesson and its companion, the "free to be you" message, from birth. The values of personal autonomy and authenticity, as well as equity and inclusion expressed by our interviewees as they spoke about identity, can be traced in part to these early lessons about freedom of choice.

An ethos of individual responsibility has been reinforced by changes in the workplace and wider economic system since the 1970s. Policies of economic liberalization involving the deregulation of banking and markets, privatization of public assets to increase the role of the private sector, and support for entrepreneurial capitalism have often been justified in terms of curtailing the power of the "nanny state" and the paternalistic employer. The idea that either employers or the state had a duty of care for workers and citizens from cradle to grave gave way to social models in which responsibility and risk were more widely shared. Thus, postmillennials have come of age in societies in which each individual, whatever their background, is inescapably responsible for managing their own life and shaping their own destiny and identity. As confidence in endless economic growth and social progress has foundered, the imperative to manage your own life has turned into a source of anxiety and resentment as well as hope and opportunity. The risks and insecurity that postmillennials face—with well-paid jobs and affordable housing increasingly out of reach—were often mentioned by those we interviewed: "We have a pessimistic outlook. Just because economic circumstances are pretty damn dire for our generation," said one [Andy], while another said, "politically, in the news, in the press system, technologically, socially, . . . literally everything is changing" [Eve].

CONCLUSION

Identity is intimately tied to the notion of authenticity. In this postmillennial world, identity is central, and inauthenticity in identity formation is regarded with profound suspicion, which helps explain why battles relating to identity—over everything from what should be included in college curricula to debates about transgender—can be so heated. The distinction between the symbolic and the real falls away when cultural identities are at stake, and the battles are felt as deeply personal, not just political.

For postmillennials, being clear and authentic as you speak your truth involves having fine-grained identity markers that signal to yourself and others who you really are. If you cannot say who you are, you are not really free to be, and if others do not know who you are, they are inhibited from expressing their identities, too. The internet has opened up huge choices that facilitate identity formation on a scale and scope previously unimaginable. However, that does not mean you can be anything you want to be; there has to be a fit between what you feel and say and do, and the communities to which you claim an affiliation. But no one can tell you who you are.

We have suggested here a dynamic linkage between personal discovery and public expression of identity. As the next chapter reveals, the formation of a person's fine-grained identity is connected to online and offline belonging, because the process of discovering an authentic identity is tightly bound with the art of finding others with whom to share the journey.

4

Finding My Fam

When we asked a linguistics class at Stanford in 2016 to select a "word of the year" that summed up their college life, many of the students chose the word *fam*. One of them gave a very moving presentation on the word, explaining to the class that he came from a small town in the Midwest, was gay, and had found friends at Stanford who were his new fam. All of his *squad*—another postmillennial word for community—refer to each other as fam.

Fam refers not to parents or relatives but to a close friend or friends (singular or plural) in whom you confide and trust, and around whom you can be your most authentic self. The word occurs with unusual frequency in our iGen Corpus compared with more general corpora of spoken language in the UK and US. It has spawned a plethora of expressions, like *thanks fam*, *sup fam* (what's happening), *nah fam* (no), *gotchu fam* (I support you), *lit fam* (fun and cool), *yo fam* (hi), and *chill fam* (relax). Similarly, in relation to the memes that are so important for postmillennials, and about which we say more in this chapter, certain fam categories have developed, such as the I-gotchu-fam memes, barber memes, and say-no-more-fam memes. As the example reproduced in figure 2 shows, such memes reinforce fam solidarity through shared humor and in-group references and cues.

The practice of referring to friends with whom you feel a close

Barber: What you want bro?
Him: You ever ate a panini?
Barber: Say no more fam

I gotchu

FIGURE 2. Example of an
"I-gotchu-fam" meme

affinity in terms that used to be reserved for nuclear and extended family members can be traced back to LGBT subcultures in the 1950s and 1960s and beyond. When gay people were shunned or rejected by homophobic societies, they could turn to their families of choice for the kind of solace, support, and solidarity traditionally associated with the biological family. This was a community united by strong emotional bonds—similar to kinship—but formed on the basis of social, rather than biological, connection. Additionally, friendship between women was upgraded in the 1960s and 1970s by the second-wave feminist movement that launched the slogan "the personal is political" and stressed the importance of female solidarity and sharing by the use of the terms *sister* and *sisterhood*. These terms had actually been used centuries earlier by the British white feminist Mary Wollstonecraft (*sister* [1792]), in African American English in the late nineteenth century (*sistah* [1879]), and in the early twentieth century by the suffragettes (*sisterhood* [1914]), but they entered more general parlance via second-wave feminism. Post-millennials' use of *fam* for close friends can more recently be traced to African American English and a line from the song "Renee" by the hip-hop group Lost Boyz in 1996: "A yo, Fam, I got a tender-roni girl, we're sitting on the couch chattin'."[1]

Given that *fam* was word of the year for that linguistics class in

2016 and language changes quickly, the word of the year might be different now, especially since *fam* has come into broader usage, but its choice among a portion of our Gen Zer population nevertheless points to the ways in which postmillennials' emphasis on identity is intensely social. In nearly every element of our research—interviews, focus groups, the iGen Corpus, and the Stanford Dictionary of distinctive words created by students—we came across new words for affinity groups: *squad, tribe, crew, peoples, sibs,* as well as *fam,* to name but a few. One interviewee, when asked about the different parts of identity, put at the top of her list the people she spends time with both offline and online, followed by her sense of adventure and mental health issues [Zoe]. Another interviewee said that "who I surround myself with" was a key indicator of her identity, along with her tattoos and music taste [Jordan]. To find out who you are also means finding out where you fit. One student reflected on the ways in which her identity was an important part of the selection of her primary community:

> I think my communities tend to be mostly other people of color. That's one thing that I've noticed just over the course of my very short life. So that's one big unifying identity. . . . I just feel like people who support you, those are the people who are your community. Sometimes having identity-based groups is great because you share the same struggle. That's why I think that most of my friends are people of color, right? Because we have, in some way or another, experienced some type of prejudice. We've overcome some of that type of obstacle, right? And so that commonality, I feel like that brings people together, but I don't think it always has to be based on their identity. But your group of friends, you're not necessarily all like, "Oh, because we are X, we are friends, right?" [Alyssa]

Finding your fam is intimately connected with finding your identity. As actress and model Cara Delevingne explained: "You need to honour yourself in being confident to speak out about who you are. That's the only way you will ever be able to find your family. We all have our family who we are born with but we all find our family, our tribe, where we belong. So the only way to do that is to be honest." And finding your fam is an ongoing project that need not be set in stone: "Even if you don't get it right—you find out your identity one way and you switch to another. It does not matter. It is not something that is meant to be fixed. It's fluid."[2]

With social media—and the internet more broadly—at their constant and immediate disposal, postmillennials have the opportunity to fine-tune the communities to which they belong in step with their fine-grained identity. The work of anthropologist Mizuko Ito and her colleagues has shown that the choice of online affinity networks with those who share identity and interests "can result in a strong sense of affiliation and social bonding."[3] While the LGBT groups and feminists of the 1960s and 1970s forged alternative families, they necessarily did so in real time and mostly through physical gatherings. LGBT people in the mid-twentieth century usually had to move to a friendly city to find their fam. Now, of course, this quest for affinity groups that match personal identity occurs both online and offline, as we explore in this chapter.

Postmillennials try to balance flexibility with stability, and freedom with security, in this quest for belonging that matches their identity. Just as there is an element of fluidity and flexibility to many aspects of their personal identities, so too with the groups to which they belong. Their art of digital living involves joining and leaving groups as identities become clearer and habits of being change, but with the integrity of the person maintained through the process. Where Gen Zers feel an affinity, they find out who they are; when they know who they are, they can navigate social life and relationships with greater confidence. As one interviewee put it, "You join the group for a reason, you know" [Andy]. Furthermore, there is a continuous refinement in a group's identity, driven by the energy of individuals who find a part of their identity to be elided, excluded, or rendered invisible within a group as it stands. To name and honor who they really are, they have to persuade the community to refine its identity or, if there is resistance to such change, they leave altogether to establish a new community of their own.

FINE-GRAINED CONNECTIONS AND COMMUNITIES

The Facebook group "subtle asian traits" (usually written in lower case) furnishes a good example of this dynamic of differentiation. It was created in September 2018 by four teenagers in Melbourne to share experiences of growing up as the children of first-generation immigrants to Australia.[4] It began as a simple group chat online among friends in real life, who then found that Facebook offered a no-cost platform on which to open the discussion to others. Within three months, subtle asian traits had snowballed into over a million followers (in 2021, it is nearly double that number at 1.9 million members). It grew so quickly, without any commercial backing, because it provided a social space where vast numbers of individuals could share their "relatable" experiences of the trials and tribulations of growing up as a child of Asian immigrants. Here they could poke gentle fun at themselves and others and discuss everything from childhood meals to parental pressures and mental health issues. Participants could explore and express personal identity by belonging to a community of similarly situated individuals. One student told us that one day, out of the blue, she received twenty Facebook notifications saying that friends had tagged her in a post on subtle asian traits: "They just kept on coming," she said, "it wouldn't stop. Before I even understood what page I had just been added to, I was already swamped with posts, comments, and tags from my college friends, high school friends, and even middle school friends that I had not connected with in years." At first, she was unsure if she wanted to be a part of the group but as she scrolled through, she was

> intensely struck by how many long-buried memories of my second-generation childhood came bubbling to the surface. It was stunning to see how many people related to fixtures of my life, ranging from the plastic bag filled with other plastic bags that my mom kept stashed away in the kitchen to watching your relatives aggressively fight over the check when they take family out to dinner. There was heavier content too, including memes about strict tiger parenting,

struggling to explain mental illness to relatives, and being bullied for being Asian. [Eve]

Soon she was hooked. She added all her friends who identified as Asian or Asian American and became an active member of the group.

Checking into Facebook throughout the day, followers of subtle asian traits see content that names and claims things as Asian, plus accompanying commentary from members. Memes consisting of humorous images, videos, and pieces of text with an emphasis on shared experience are popular on the site. For example, one meme is made up of three panels. The first shows a giggling Pikachu (a cute, furry Pokémon) captioned "Me laughing at all your relatable subtle asian memes." The second, with a tearful but smiling Pikachu, says, "Me realizing I'm not alone in the world." The last panel shows a surprised Pikachu with the caption: "Me, realizing there was nothing unique about my experience."[5]

Three other examples of relatable memes demonstrate how the site supports shared identity and belonging. Figure 3 pokes fun at white Americans who, while intensely concerned with the particulars of their own European heritages, remain oblivious to the differences in Asian heritages. Figure 4 contrasts the Asian experience of having to do chores without payment with the experience of white friends who receive an allowance for the chores. Figure 5 depicts frustration with strict Asian parents that the author presumes is shared with others. Creating or sharing a meme and getting lots of likes and further shares can turn private frustrations or embarrassment into a positive plank of identity and build solidarity. "We labeled the group as 'family,'" says one of the founders of subtle asian traits, "so that's what the group's purpose is, to allow people to feel like they all belong to something."[6]

Before long, however, subtle asian traits branched into a multitude of even more finely grained websites—well over a hundred at the last count. Jocular references to English slang in Mandarin, Korean, Cantonese, Vietnamese, or Japanese are frequent on the site, and a bias toward East Asia began to grate on some South Asian followers, who then decided to start their own group, called "Subtle

White people: "I'm %38 German, %35 Swedish %25 Danish, %2 Milk

Me: "I'm Korean not Chinese"

White people:

😀😮😆 Malaya Neri, Glory Jain and 16K others   1K Comments

White friend : "I hate my life, my parents give me just $10 for doing chores"

Me:

You guys are getting paid?

Mark Angelo Serrano-Crutchley
January 18 at 8:15 AM

That feel when you can't go to your friends house.

MARVEL
CANT-MAN
MY **Mom** SAID NO

😀😮😆 Dustin Lang, Heejoo Ko and 11K others   1.7K Comments

FIGURES 3-5. Examples of relatable memes

Curry Traits." Other subgroups that spun off from the original site or one of its derivatives include Subtle Asian Dating, Subtle Asian Pets, Subtle Asian Gaming, Subtle Asian Eats, Subtle Asian Women, Subtle Asian Makeup/Beauty Squad, Subtle Asian Ravers, Subtle Asian Cars, Subtle Asian Mental Health Support, Subtle Halfie Traits (for individuals who identify as mixed race or multiracial), Subtle Asian Adoptee Traits, Anti-imperialist Subtle Asian Traits (self-described as a more "woke" version of subtle asian traits), Subtle Asian Activists, and Subtle Queer Asian Christian Traits. This branching is emblematic of many new online communities. "I think one of the beautiful parts of this is that one of the promises of the internet did come true," said an interviewee. "Marginalized communities can group together and constitute a large enough group that even they can split into smaller groups" [Eve]. The growth of subtle asian traits and its derivative groups illustrates many of the distinctive features of Gen Zer belonging—for example, the role of the internet, the connection to finding and communicating identity, pluralism, and diversification.

The unprecedented scope and scale of the internet makes it possible to quickly find communities of shared identity and interest. As Simone Dawes, a postmillennial, explained in a radio broadcast, "Online it's like you can find people who think exactly the same, so I found this community [Helena Bonham Carter fandom via the Harry Potter fandoms]. . . . Joining Instagram was like entering a universe of fandoms. It was like tumbling down the rabbit hole. It was like a global experience. There was no one who knew you, apart from how you wanted to portray yourself, which in some ways can be quite dangerous but also exciting. You have the power to mold how you want to be."[7]

MODULAR BELONGING

Gen Zers find stability and social anchoring without subsuming their whole identity in one group or tying themselves to it forever. We have come to think of this as "modular belonging," as analogous to modular furniture or fashion systems: at any one time various modules of identity and belonging fit together, but it is possible to move them around and replace modules one at a time as the need and inclination arises, without destroying the whole array. Post-millennials rarely belong to just one community or invest all their identity in one or two relationships. A unique individual identity is composed of multiple social commitments. As was the case for prior generations, family members may constitute one modular belonging, and friends from school and university another, but now an array of additional groups, many of them online (e.g., subtle asian traits), offers a variety of modules that can be added to support and define the whole person.

Gen Zers easily combine online and offline belonging, with some online platforms being chiefly used to support offline relationships when it is not possible to be physically co-present. Responses to our national surveys confirmed the variation in how postmillennials use social media and how important it is to them: in both the US and the UK, just over a quarter said that social media were very important to their social lives, just under a quarter said that social media were not important, and the remaining half took a moderate view, saying that social media were moderately important in their lives.

The dynamic of ever more fine-grained belonging fits the established idea that in-groups need out-groups to define themselves. This is a recurring pattern for the development of any new social movement, group, or language variety. For example, the standardization of a regional variety of a language (e.g., Australian English) requires differentiation and self-determination from the dominant language variety (e.g., British English). Likewise, the counter-language of slang reacts against the standard language (out-group) to become a sign of belonging to a subculture (in-group). As we discuss further later, the humor and irony of memes has a similar social function of including and excluding, creating in-groups and out-groups.

Different online platforms support this dynamic of differentiation and belonging in varying degrees. A Facebook group such as subtle asian traits, in which differentiation and belonging are cemented by humor as well as hostility, exemplifies how this dynamic can work.

Twitter is something of an outlier, more useful for communicating information and building a personal brand than forming communities, and more specialized in its hit-and-run hostility. Platforms like Facebook, Reddit, 4chan, and Tumblr lend themselves to the continuing refinement of fine-grained belonging through humorous expression and mutual recognition within communities. Reddit, for example, which was popular with many of our interviewees, is structured so that users can navigate to "subreddits," subtopics that cater to a plethora of more niche interests. A Reddit group like "Advice" or "Games" will have a wide membership, but subreddits that appeal to smaller groups, like those who want to discuss a particular plot device in Game of Thrones or specific strategies for the game of Fortnite, are also prevalent on the platform. 4chan, a platform associated with the alt-right alongside Gab and Telegram, was originally set up for discussion about manga and anime, though over time parts of it became increasingly misogynous, racist, and a haven for trolls and hackers (it was the birthplace of the hacktivist group Anonymous). Often referred to as "the asshole of the internet" and notorious for pranks, illegal content, and threats of violence, it is an extreme example of in-group bonding through overt hostility to other social groups that are viewed as weak and inferior.[8] Trolling, mobbing, and bullying on this and other platforms serve the same purpose, especially when such activities are carried out in order to win the admiration of others in your tribe(s).[9]

One interviewee knew firsthand the experience of bonding within such groups. He had spent his teenage years on 4chan and 8chan (pronounced "infinite chan" or "infinity chan," 8chan was created in 2013 as a reaction against a tightening of protocols on 4chan).[10] He described shitposting (posting absurd or offensive comments online), shitlording (posting provocative and bigoted content online in order to provoke social justice warriors), trolling female gamers and camgirls (young women who engage in pornography on image boards), and lurking on 8chan's extremist forums, which offered him anonymity and minimal moderation [Liam].

From a young age, postmillennials have been exposed to online hate speech and abusive language that targets people who are systemically marginalized, especially on the basis of their race, sexual orientation, or religion. In this way, our interviewees were impressive in their ability to recognize and protect themselves from such abuse and harassment. They all spoke of differing norms for what is appropriate according to various social media platforms and were expert in their agility in switching from one platform to another and "cracking the code" of a platform.

The Twitch data for our iGen Corpus includes chat logs taken from February 2016, which was an important date for the live-streaming gaming platform: it was just before Twitch introduced "auto mod," an algorithm that suspends potentially harmful and inappropriate comments from appearing in the chat box until they are reviewed by a human channel moderator, who then allows or denies the message. Hence, the data in our corpus are unmoderated and uncensored, and they contain the full gamut of hate speech, harassment, and sexual content from this age group. Perhaps unsurprisingly, analysis of these data reveal that the abusive speech relates to four main categories: words for sex and body parts; bullying speech; swearing and cussing; and taboo terms for race, religion, gender, sexual orientation, and disability. Recent class action lawsuits have revealed the current inadequacy of artificial intelligence systems to detect sensitive content and the negative consequences of large tech companies farming out moderation tasks to low-paid national and offshore workers, whose mental health often suffers from having to dredge through trauma-inducing content with no psychological support.[11]

Postmillennials are adept at inventing creative workarounds to the barriers imposed by a platform's rules or algorithms, some more successful than others. Users in countries where TikTok is banned simply change the region (usually to Canada) in their settings or remove their SIM cards and activate a VPN. Users who want to spread political information that might be censored or blocked on TikTok might try wrapping that information in more innocuous content. For example, seventeen-year-old Feroza Aziz (@getmefamouspart three) used a makeup tutorial to hide information about the plight of the Uighur population in Xinjiang: ". . . Curl your lashes obviously, then you're gonna put them [the lash curlers] down and use the phone that you're using right now to search up what's happening in China, how they're getting concentration camps, torturing innocent Muslims, separating their families from each other, kidnapping them, murdering them, raping them, forcing them to eat pork. . . . Be aware, please spread awareness. So you can grab your lash curler again!" But TikTok's smart algorithms still found the video and blocked the user, whose account was eventually reinstated after the company was publicly shamed into doing so.

Subcultures can quickly and easily be created online around any issue, any topic, any identity, and even an aesthetic, such as *egirls* and *eboys*, who are emo-styled anime and gaming fans, or *VSCO girls*, who use TikTok to create a distinctive aesthetic through use of the editing app VSCO, which became especially popular in late 2018 as a platform for sharing photos without the pressure of likes and comments. In mid-2019, a campaign started on YouTube to ridicule the VSCO girl as a type of "basic" girl whose typical aesthetic included a shell necklace, hair scrunchies, friendship bracelets, an oversized t-shirt, Mario Badescu spray, Birkenstocks, lip gloss, metal straws, and a sticker-covered Hydro Flask water bottle ("to save the turtles"). Like many online communities, the subculture built around the aesthetic even developed its own catchphrases ("And I oop I dropped my hydroflask sksksksksksk") and expressions (e.g., *VSCO food*, pictures of food taken using the VSCO filter C1 to make it look fun and edible; *VSCO words*, screenshots of relatable quotations; *VSCO friends*, pictures of friends having "so much fun"; *VSCO save the environment* posts). Like all fashions and trends, many of these online subcultures are ephemeral and will (or have) run their course. In 2019, each of these aesthetics (eboys, egirls, and VSCO girls) became the subject of mocking memes, parody videos, and hashtagged insta posts, all of which usually signals that an online trend or subculture will soon drop in popularity.

In the early days of digital networks, online communities were constrained by the limited functionality of the platforms available to them (e.g., Usenet, IRC, listservs), but today's robust platforms, home to Facebook groups, subreddits, and Tumblr niche blogs, encourage and facilitate modular belonging through their site structures and interfaces. These platforms make it easy for like-minded people to cluster and spin off new groups, as was the case with subtle asian traits. An interviewee made this point when telling us about a "Numtots" subgroup that split away over a disagreement about whether it was right for the police to have removed a woman on a Los Angeles train for putting her feet on the seat: "It still kind of amazes me how many niche groups have been created," he said, "but the sheer size of Facebook allows these spaces to be created because with a billion followers you can find someone who likes anything" [Andy].

The internet vastly expands the pool of groups with which you can make a connection and, if you cannot find exactly what you are looking for, it allows you to engage in social DIY. "You can essentially create a community for anything that you want," commented one student. He went on to explain that although some online communities (e.g., Reddit) are characterized by anonymous postings, it is still easier to find like-minded people—what he called "internet pen pals"—online than offline: "someone that you happen to encounter on the internet who seems to have similar interests, or they have a similar personality. I guess it's essentially like meeting friends in real life except the scope of places where you can meet these people is much wider, because it's not limited to the activities you participate in, or the place where you live, or places that you go" [Henry].

In addition to social media, our interviewees described how group chats on messaging platforms have become a highly modular, customizable way of encouraging fine-grained belonging. To create a group chat, the originator decides whom to include and why. Some groups respond to an immediate need or opportunity, like planning a party or working on a joint project, but others become long lasting and very important for exchanging information and sustaining solidarity. At any given time, our interviewees had anywhere from two to ten group chats active as well as many more defunct or dormant ones. For example, a student at Lancaster told us that she has a group chat with her two closest friends from home and another for her two closest course mates. Then she has various other groups that she uses less often "just to keep in contact, that kind of thing"; "bigger course chats," where people only really message about "generic kinds of questions about work"; and "one that's about ten of us that's closer, more social conversation. . . . I also have various messages with the girl I live with . . . and other conversations with various people" [Jo]. A student from Foothill told us about two group chats he has an eye on a lot of the time. One is with a close friend, and they "just send memes to each other all day," and the rest are with people with whom he goes to music festivals. The group chat is essential as it is "where we try to plan everything out" [Nathan].

Gaming also forms important platforms of belonging, as Mizuko Ito and her collaborators have documented in their work. "Gamers . . . will often become involved in more structured kinds of social arrangements, such as guilds, teams, clans, clubs, and organized social groups that revolve specifically around gaming."[12] Gaming is often thought of as a white, male world, but we were struck by the ways in which gaming engaged our interviewees across lines of gender and ethnicity, and among students from all three campuses. Among our interviewees, the Steam platform was popular not just for games but also for chat with other gamers. An African American and Native American woman explained to us how she uses the Steam platform not only for games but to chat with other gamers as well [Malia]. A male student of Indian heritage studying at Foothill explained, "I use Steam. I have lots of friends on League of Legends. I use that to chat with them as well" [Ravi]. An Asian American student at Foothill saw the platform as "super game-related. It creates a community that wants you to play games, which is good if you want to spend time on games because they'll support you on how to get better at games" [Ping]. For one Asian American woman, whose favorite games were League of Legends and Pokémon, it was the global dimension of playing with thousands of people around the world that excited her most about games — "there are, like, thousands of people playing right now, so it's awesome" [Mei]. The strong sense of "community" forged on gaming platforms kept one of these students playing for "three to four hours every day" because, as he explained, "I have a community on League of Legends—a group of five people, and we usually do five-man queues. The friends that I have on League are not necessarily people who I know in real life. They're more people who I meet playing the game, and I interact with those people in a different way from people who I know on Facebook" [Ravi]. There were, however, students such as a Chinese American woman at Stanford who said they used to play games in high school but came to experience the gaming community as toxic, with "people feeling they can say whatever they want on the gaming platform," including trash talk and racial slurs [Jenni].

Fine-grained, modular belonging makes it possible to move in and out of groups over time without total disruption to social life. It is flexible. You can leave home and move to a new place without having to give up your old ties. Alternatively, old ties can be replaced or downgraded as changing identity and circumstances demand. If a group or relationship turns out not to be a good fit, it is possible to edit and exchange it for a better match, like those who left subtle asian traits for Subtle Curry Traits or other spinoffs. When faced with major life transitions like leaving home for college, or leaving campus life for paid employment, it is relatively easy to shed some modules of belonging without losing others. To use a different image: the deck can be reshuffled. Kin groups may become more important again, campus solidarities may fade, a new relationship may flourish, new friends and interests may gradually eclipse some old ones, while other belongings persist. "I joined this group to see content I want to see and I don't see it," one student explained. "I'll just quit. There's a lot of fluidity," and "there's very low barriers to entry, I guess" [Andy].

CONVERSATIONAL BELONGING

The kind of belonging that the internet has helped make normal is not just modular; it is also conversational. In online communities, you can listen in before you decide whether to take the plunge and contribute. You belong by expressing yourself and by sharing things you like. You learn the rules and norms that govern the ongoing conversations through active participation. If your contributions are well received, your status grows, and your connections deepen. In the process, your identification with the group deepens.

Conversations often spill across offline and online contexts, though some students told us that they found conversation online easier than IRL due to shyness or English not being their first language or for other reasons. Many, across lines of gender and ethnicity, said that there is more flexibility of participation and more time to get it right on social media. Online in "a big group chat," one Vietnamese American student at Foothill explained, she would just type out her reaction then and there, whereas in person, "I would be like, 'Oh no! Like the conversation's moving and flowing,' so by the time I finish formulating my thoughts the topic is gone . . . [so] I'll just keep quiet" [Becca]. A white female American student identifies the ease with which she speaks out online because she can hide behind the computer [Jordan]. Such online anonymity provided one young Black British woman with respite from curiosity about her appearance: "Everyone wants to touch my hair [offline] because it's an afro. It was funny online because with nationality, race, and ethnicity, it all kind of disappeared. Obviously, no one could see my hair; no one could reach out and ask me why it's oily, or something like that. I don't think I even got much interest about me being mixed race. It's almost like you're just you."[13]

An appeal of online conversation for many is the easy capacity to lurk and surf silently, just reading and listening, before taking the plunge and joining in a conversation. As with any conversation, interesting contributions made online will be tagged, appreciated, and engaged with, while others will simply be ignored as the conversation moves on. As such, conversational belonging online is generally less demanding and less coercive than membership in offline communities, and it is far more easily tailored to individual needs and identity. Individuals can participate on their own terms or not at all and exit when they want (unless they are caught in a drama or with friends in need). There is more room for voice, choice, and participation by all. In online conversational belonging, you do not have to speak out or make a contribution, but it is important to know that you can if you want to. In that sense, conversational belonging is resolutely nonhierarchical. The ability to exchange experience, ideas, and humor in structures in which authority is generally distributed among all is valued and expected.

Style is an important element of conversational belonging online. Pictures, symbols, and emoticons take the place of sensory and bodily cues in offline interaction. Abstract reflection and "objectivity" are less compelling than the ability to give voice to feelings and experience in a way that is felt to be authentic. The most potent combination, one student said, is when "people with personal experience and expertise discuss a topic they are knowledgeable on with authenticity" [Ashton]. While most groups are supportive, some flare up into "flame wars" and heated debate in which people end up "just yelling at each other" [Andy]. But shared expression of anger and hatred can build solidarity by communal venting and the feeling that others are validating your anger.

Each social media platform has its own character, personality, protocols, and even language, and this means, as an interviewee put it, "each group is like its own little bubble" [Andy]. These bubbles are especially dangerous when the style and language are extreme and hate-filled, as they are on 4chan, and this was widely recognized by our interviewees. One cis white male student at Stanford, whom we discussed earlier in this chapter, joined 4chan at the age of eleven; he said that looking back at his activity on 4chan, he could "chronologically trace myself being-a-terrible-person to not-being-a-terrible-person." He explained, "I could see points at which certain conceptions that I had—that I am now diametrically opposed to—were just being shed off slowly over time as my engagement extended." It was actually through arguing about issues and being challenged by feminists on other platforms and IRL that he started to change. He credited the importance of "the whole collective community as a mentor thing—there are definitely strong motifs of, like, self-criticism and the community interventions. I have definitely seen that a lot and experienced that a lot" [Liam].

The language used on different platforms offers insight into their

TABLE 5. Keywords used by postmillennials on social media platforms 4chan, Reddit, Twitter, Twitch, and YouTube

4CHAN	REDDIT	TWITTER	TWITCH	YOUTUBE
it's	it	emoji: crying	lappa ("bad or frustrating")	like
don't	switch	laughing	lol	I'm
you're	they	checked	pogchamp ("surprise or	screen
anon	not	me	excitement" emote)	y'all
her	but	followed	stream	don't
doesn't	it's	YouTube	4head ("laughing" emote)	gonna
fucking	games	unfollowed	Kreygasm ("intense	I
they're	Nintendo	automatically	emotion" emote)	yeah
she's	questions	emoji: smiley	xo1action	you're
shit	post	heart eyes	biblethump ("grief" emote)	finna ("going
		person	wutface ("shock" emote)	to")
		video	u	

respective personalities. By analyzing data from our iGen Corpus, we can see the top 10 most salient words, or keywords, on 4chan, Reddit, Twitter, Twitch, and YouTube (see table 5).[14]

Part of conversational belonging involves learning the language of the particular communities, which becomes an important element of belonging. This can be seen in keywords on 4chan that are neologisms not as salient on other platforms (e.g., tfw [that feel when], pol [passed out laughing], kek [laughter on World of Warcraft], mfw [my face when], cuck [a weak or inadequate man], bait [blatantly obvious]), and in the occurrence of other keywords that give insight into the topics and the negative attitudes and hatred of others of the 4chan community (e.g., fucking, retarded, trans, trannies, faggots, tits). In contrast, the keywords of Twitch reveal a community more focused on sex, gaming, and policing (e.g., switch [Nintendo console], halo [a game for Xbox], pokemon, removed, wii, concerns, moderators, sex, console, cp [combat power]). Each social media platform supports a particular community bubble and creates its own subculture and language, facilitating modular and multiple types of belonging. The words or images used on a particular site might never be understood by people who are outside that bubble.

The language of one domain sometimes seeps into another, with words that have their origins in one digital platform taking on new generic meanings outside them. There are examples in our interviews and iGen Corpus of the exclamation "RT!" being used in conversations as a general term of agreement (from Twitter, on which users will retweet [RT] a tweet with which they agree). Similarly, approval is often expressed with "swipe right!" (from dating apps such as Tinder or Grindr on which users swipe right on the screen to indicate that they find someone attractive) or "swipe left!" to express approval or disapproval, respectively. Other examples include saying "hashtag" to emphasize or categorize something (sometimes with a mental or actual roll of the eyes, indicating sarcasm), and "subtweet" to describe talking about someone behind their back (to subtweet on Twitter is to talk about someone without typing their handle so they do not see it in their feed).

While Gen Zer slang now spreads quickly on social media, many of the terms have much older histories that might surprise its speakers. Indeed, many of their words taken from African American English predate not just them and the internet but also their parents and grandparents: *woke* (1962), *stay woke* (1972), *dope* (1981), *fam* (1996), *fresh* (1972), *gangsta* (1988), *hoochie* (1989), *props* (1990), *throw shade* (1990), *hip* (1904), *hood* (1969), and *ho* (1964). Several of our British interviewees were also using language that may have appeared new but in fact was as old as they are (e.g., the word *bare* [many] dates back to Caribbean English in 1996). Some is even as old as their grandparents and great grandparents (e.g., the word *lit* [drunk] dates back to 1914, *lush* [cool] was first recorded in 1928).[15] Other general terms that might seem new, for example, *ship* and *shipping*, meaning "to advocate for romance between two fictional characters or celebrities, especially in fanfiction," such as *Drarry* (Draco and Harry in *Harry Potter*), can be traced to 1990s discussions of pairing Mulder and Scully from *The X-Files* and the earlier desired pairing of Kirk and Spock (K/S) in *Star Trek*. The same is the case for the popular variants *slash shipping* and *femslash shipping* between two male and two female characters, respectively.

Online group conversations, or threads, are often continuous and have an unstoppable momentum of their own, which differentiates them from offline conversations. The online conversation is larger than those who take part. By posting even a small comment that is appreciated, you become part of something bigger. As one of our interviewees remarked about the Numtots Facebook group, "It's shockingly active and it's shockingly engaging" [Andy]. With thousands of members across the globe, the posting never stops. Contributions take many forms. Some are funny, others "get really deep or really technical." He recalled a recent magazine article in which someone explained that they joined Numtots just for the funny memes and after a few months "feel like they deserve a bachelor's degree in urban planning because of how much they've been exposed to." Our interviewee particularly values the way the conversation brings together amateurs with an interest in cities and professional experts: "It's this really interesting dynamic where the less educated are being educated and the professionals are—okay, sometimes they're arrogant, but other times they're actually seeing people who may be less educated in formal academic vernacular, but still have intuitive understanding for these issues, and seeing their perspective" [Andy]. As this example shows, the line between learning, socializing, and entertainment can be blurred—an element of what some commentators refer to as "connected learning."[16]

This informal online social engagement, in which many can participate, flows over into ways of being together offline. It means that postmillennials can therefore sometimes find more formal social spaces and institutions, such as universities, governmental agencies, and places of worship, somewhat alien. For Gen Zers, shaped by the online and offline groups to which they belong, where everyone can participate and express themselves in equal ways, an institution's formal modes of communicating can seem off-putting, oppressive, and too focused on hierarchy. They perceive a mismatch between what the institution might say and what it actually does—and how. They feel disillusioned when large institutions fail to deliver on what they promise: inclusion, equality, and high ethical standards. We talk more about such disillusionment with institutions in the following chapters.

CONNECTING THROUGH EMOTIONAL SHARING AND MEMES

What in earlier generations might have remained wholly private or buried, like a sexuality that was once labeled deviant, can now become the basis for joining in conversation with others who may "like" and identify with it. Shame and self-doubt can be turned into something positive through such conversation. Private experience becomes shared experience, and vice versa. Even anonymous sharing online about experiences and traits that might have made people feel odd or embarrassed can transform into the basis of a clearer sense of self and a more comfortable stance in the world.

Gen Zers especially value talking about their emotions in their online places of belonging. Our interviewees described, for example, the benefits of being able to share personal comments like "having a really shitty day today" in a group chat or Facebook community and knowing that others there would pile in with supportive comments. One student spoke about how important it was to him to be part of a "depression meals meme group" (a *depression meal* is a meal you eat when you're feeling down, lonely, or depressed, which can range from a messy pile of whatever food you can find to fast food or takeout). People post pictures of the meals they are eating as a way of signaling if they are feeling OK, or lonely and depressed. This student loved the fact that group members will wade in with supportive comments even though "this is like a very public group filled with strangers, right. But people are sharing things on this group that I imagine some of them wouldn't share even with their friends." He reflected that such intimacy of sharing is possible precisely because participants are strangers to one another. For him, that is freeing: it means that he can post without "worrying that you're adding some emotional toll to them" because they can leave at any time, "whereas your friends are sort of obligated to help you" [Andy].[17]

Memes have become a primary and highly effective vehicle for postmillennials to communicate how they feel. Memes are relatable or humorous images, videos, or pieces of text that are copied and circulated rapidly by social media users. They can succinctly express

FIGURE 6. Zoomer Wojak meme

not just individual feelings but shared perceptions, understandings, or experiences, typically in a witty or funny manner as *in-jokes*. Memes and in-jokes have become so emblematic of postmillennial life that many Gen Zers view them as defining attributes of their generation. As one student explained it, "Because we have grown up with it [the internet and smart phones], we have developed our own ways to have jokes, ways to pass on different types of information, and growing up with that has shaped us as people and how we learn."[18] As further evidence of this generational ethos, if a meme is incorporated into mainstream advertising or is adopted by older people, it generally falls out of favor.

The popularity of the word *Zoomer*, now sometimes used to describe Gen Zers, itself came out of a meme character called "Zoomer Wojak," created on the 4chan website in June 2018. Based on a version of the popular internet meme Wojak—also known as "the feels guy," who generally expresses melancholy and loneliness—this version appeared with glasses and an *undercut* (a haircut with long hair on top and buzzed back and sides) and was depicted as loving mumble rap (emo rap) and battle royale video games such as Fortnite. The term grew in popularity from there and has taken on new meaning since the COVID-19 pandemic, influenced by the widespread use of Zoom videoconferencing.

Memes are central to the majority of postmillennials' online lives. In our survey of representative samples of US and UK postmillennials, we asked the following: "How often, if ever, do you currently interact with memes, for example by liking, sharing or tagging?" At least 85 percent in each country said they interacted with memes, over half in each country saying they did so frequently or all the time. Moreover, over a third in Britain and 39 percent in the US reported that they had personally created one or more meme(s). There was not much difference by gender, or between college-educated and not. Meme groups now run the gamut of postmillennial interest. If you like scientifically based memes, you can check out Dopamemes for Reward-Seeking Teens. If you are part of a particular college or organization, you can follow its meme page. Whether you want edgy or wholesome or dog-themed or Minecraft or *Harry Potter* memes, you can find them all online—in addition to a community of individuals who have a similar sense of humor. Many of our interviewees mentioned memes in passing, sometimes when talking about a meme group they were following, like Stanford Memes for Edgy Trees (a pun on the Stanford tree mascot) or Grindr Aesthetic Memes (screenshots of weird things happening on the gay hookup app Grindr), and sometimes when describing how they tagged a friend with a meme they thought the friend would find funny or personally meaningful. Various interviewees said they would put memes in their starter packs, some describing a meme or two that they especially liked, so important were they to their identity and daily life. One interviewee who described all memes as "shitty" was an exception [Jenni].

Memes are frequently puzzling to those outside the particular group that generated them and often very confusing to those of other generations. A Facebook user who creates obscure physics memes does not expect people outside physics and physics-adjacent communities to understand them. Memes made in queer Facebook groups do not cater to the understanding and experience of cis-hetero people but rather aim to undermine them. Even inside a small friendship group, memes will be created solely to reflect their own in-group experiences that foster a greater sense of closeness. Meme groups often innovate their own unique language codes, including, for example, deliberate misspellings or uses of symbols around words.

White person: racism...is bad

Y'all: OMG YASSSSSS. YOU INVITED TO THE COOKOUT. YOU SO WOKE

FIGURE 7. Example of a meme from Black Twitter

While some memes express deep meaning, others exist just to be funny, and still others combine both qualities. Depending on the meme, the humor may contain an ironic, sarcastic, satirical, or cynical bite that can be impenetrable to an outsider. Like the subtle asian traits memes in figures 3–5, the meme in figure 7, which originated with the Black Twitter group, demonstrates the humor that characterizes many memes, which — as in this example — often makes a political point.

Memes are the new slang. Just as slang is a counterlanguage that reacts against the standard and is used to create in-groups and out-groups, so it is with memes. Memes and slang have their origins on the margins of the mainstream. The first internet memes started on message boards in the late 1990s as image macros with Impact font; today they are image posts that often originate with groups such as Black Twitter, weird Twitter, trans Twitter, or leftbook (left-leaning Facebook groups), intended for their own communities. If they are not impenetrable to external communities, they can spread more broadly beyond the initial platform (e.g., from Twitter or Facebook to Tumblr, Reddit, and Instagram). As one student explained, "Instagram users do share memes, but memes rarely originate there, and spread slower, because it is harder to directly repost content" on that platform [Ashton].

A single meme generally lasts for no more than a few months, but

FIGURE 8. Example of a Drake Yes/No meme

FIGURE 9. Example of a Kermit vs. Evil Kermit meme

there are some meme formats, such as those that lend themselves to personalization, that can be longer lasting. An example is the Drake Yes/No meme, consisting of two images of the rap artist Drake holding his hand up to the side of his face, looking disgusted in one photo and satisfied in the other. As this meme circulates, people can change the photos paired with the two images of Drake as a shorthand way to communicate their own specific likes and dislikes.

Kermit vs. Evil Kermit is another example of an easily personalized meme; it uses Kermit the Frog as a vehicle for expressing socially unacceptable thoughts. In the meme, Kermit looks at a hooded version of himself with the caption formula "Me: [observation of some event]. Me to me: [unethical or perverse response to that event]."

Sarcasm and irony can also underlie other forms of shared Gen

FIGURE 10. The Kappa emote (i.e., the image of Josh DeSeno) used at the end of a sentence to indicate sarcasm

Zer communication, including emoticons and copypastas. For instance, a popular emoji called *Kappa* (an image of a man's face) is often used at the end of a sentence to signify sarcasm. The Kappa started on Justin.tv (now called Twitch) when developer Josh De-Seno was creating new emoticons (or *emotes* as they are called on the platform) and jokingly included one of his own face, calling it "Kappa." Once it was discovered by users, the faux emoticon went viral; it is now one of the most frequently occurring words in collections of social media text, and the Kappa emoji of DeSeno's face is Twitch's unofficial brand mascot (coffee machines in the Twitch offices in San Francisco serve Kappuccinos).

Similarly, the *copypasta*—a piece of text rewritten (copy and pasted) with the addition of slews of emojis for emphasis—uses irony and sarcasm to make fun of the earnestness of the original author. Like memes, copypastas often go viral (see figure 11 for some examples). As a student explained: "They usually originate in large Facebook groups; someone will unironically write a long, usually ranty, post in the group and then to make fun of that person, many people in the group will repost the text ironically" [Ashton].

In addition to helping consolidate communities of identity and interest, memes and copypastas serve to express shared disillusionment, frustration, skepticism, and disappointment. They serve as a bonding mechanism not just for particular groups but for the generation as a whole. The ironic, satirical, or cynical humor in memes

FIGURE 11. A selection of copypastas

is, as one student said, so "relatable" [Cyrus]. Another student elaborated: "There's just a lot to satirize because satire is the only way you could make sense of the fact that the economic future is highly uncertain" [Andy].

ETHICAL VALUES AND MODULAR, CONVERSATIONAL BELONGING

The modular, conversational communities so central to postmillennial existence are saturated with ethical values, forged and expressed in how people speak and treat one another, with the rules worked out discursively. Although there are often common themes, these rules become distinctive to each different group, undermining the weight of more universal commands, laws, and rights and increasing the internal, pluralistic nature of ethics.

Values are integral both to the choice of where to belong and how to behave in those social settings. One of the students we interviewed speaks about how she and her friends "align" around values: "I kind of group myself with people who share my same views," she says, "since we are exposed to the same things or we at least share common interests, so we are really alike in terms of our values" [Becca]. Many explain how they find their "people" (i.e., select their modules of belonging) on the basis of shared "aesthetic" and shared values. As one said, after the 2016 truck massacre in Nice, France, she looked out for people who posted with the French tricolor symbol because it signaled to her that these were people with shared values. That was important because "it tells me if I want to interact with this person or not" [Malia]. Generally, this leads to considerable ethical alignment within groups—including groups, like 4chan, that take delight in attacking their opponents. "I feel like the majority of things that people post publicly are aligned with the popular, socially acceptable opinions, but there is always the occasional few that don't. . . . I feel like for me, since I'm normally on the opposing side of most people, I just have to kind of go in with humility and knowing that I'm probably not going to persuade the person" [Malia].

Belonging and identity are intimately connected for Gen Zers, and both are infused with their values. We have already noted how, when identities are claimed and forged in purposeful ways, values are closely invested in them—and that is true of the groups with which a person identifies. Now, disrespecting someone or their identity feels like it is also disrespecting their community and the others who are part of it. #MeToo and #BlackLivesMatter are good examples of people finding strength and solidarity through the intersection of value-laden identity and belonging.

The close ties between individuals and their communities also mean that, in the case of some groups, belonging carries the responsibility of representation. When the member of a minority group speaks, they will often do so with the sense of representing not only personal opinion but also the wider group. Once they have committed to a group and made it integral to their identity, they take on the responsibility and privileges of speaking in the name of the collective as well as the individual—or being very clear if they are only speaking for themselves. This sense of collective responsibility is then attached to majorities as well, whether they like it or not. Even if a person does not try to promote the interests of white middle-class *Anglos*, for example, that may be how they are received—as a representative of entrenched privilege. This relates to the high value placed on authenticity and helps explain the widespread taboo about cultural appropriation among Gen Zers, as discussed in the previous chapter.

The concern for ethical behavior in contemporary belonging finds its most formal expression through the ethical statements and guide-

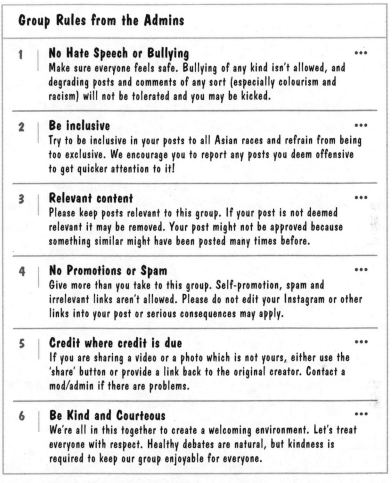

Group Rules from the Admins

1 | **No Hate Speech or Bullying** ...
Make sure everyone feels safe. Bullying of any kind isn't allowed, and degrading posts and comments of any sort (especially colourism and racism) will not be tolerated and you may be kicked.

2 | **Be inclusive** ...
Try to be inclusive in your posts to all Asian races and refrain from being too exclusive. We encourage you to report any posts you deem offensive to get quicker attention to it!

3 | **Relevant content** ...
Please keep posts relevant to this group. If your post is not deemed relevant it may be removed. Your post might not be approved because something similar might have been posted many times before.

4 | **No Promotions or Spam** ...
Give more than you take to this group. Self-promotion, spam and irrelevant links aren't allowed. Please do not edit your Instagram or other links into your post or serious consequences may apply.

5 | **Credit where credit is due** ...
If you are sharing a video or a photo which is not yours, either use the 'share' button or provide a link back to the original creator. Contact a mod/admin if there are problems.

6 | **Be Kind and Courteous** ...
We're all in this together to create a welcoming environment. Let's treat everyone with respect. Healthy debates are natural, but kindness is required to keep our group enjoyable for everyone.

FIGURE 12. Rules of the "subtle asian traits" Facebook group

lines that attend many online community sites, as well as through the moderators (*mods* and *admins*), who are responsible for monitoring conversations and posts to ensure that the rules are being respected. While a set of rules may be posted on every page of the site, they remain subject to constant interpretation by the moderators and may be amended in response to challenges, arguments, or issues that emerge. In that sense, group morality is never finished, never closed, never a fixed set of commandments, but is an active and constant negotiation. As an example, figure 12 shows the posted rules for the subtle asian traits site in 2019.

Because online communities have diverse characters and personalities, the site rules vary accordingly. Some are nonexistent or lax, and others are restrictive, including a process for screening entry to the community. Numtots, for instance, has what one member described as a "hyper formalized team of mods" in different time zones across the world who vet every post not only to make sure content is appropriate and follows the community guidelines, but also to ensure that it is relevant and of "quality." The depression meals group has stringent rules because "it is a vulnerable space so you don't want people to feel harmed or threatened in any way" [Andy]. Very leftbook groups were mentioned as having a great deal of heavy ethical screening; as our interviewee explained, they might ask a prospective member "how many genders are there, with the correct answer being something along the lines of, like, 'gender is a spectrum.' If you just answer 'two,'" he said, "you won't get approved, right!" That, he explains, is a good example of "when mods are very intentional about the spaces they want to create, and it's, like, self-segregating in a way, but it's also . . . creating the atmosphere they want to create" [Andy].

Moderators are often peers who are selected for their willingness to serve, commitment to a group, experience, and length of time active within it. Generally, their work is done in the background; it consists of removing or blocking posts and preventing conflicts from escalating, but sometimes they will intervene to reinforce the group's ethics and remind the community that their moderating authority derives from those values. If the moderator seems to be too heavy-handed, members of the group may push back, resulting in a peer-to-peer conversation about the community's wants and needs, as can be seen in the dialogue from subtle asian traits shown in figure 13. In extreme cases, members who are unhappy with a moderator may leave a group to start another with a different moderator.

One of our interviewees explained that in a large online community, several mods may work as a team, and "a good mod team tries to represent a number of demographics." The mods can also "participate in the group and post fun things and stuff." If they make a good contribution and share personal things, respect for them

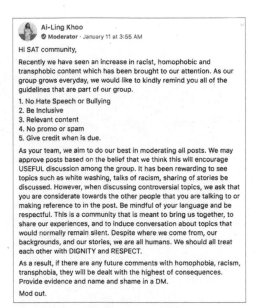

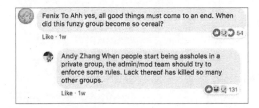

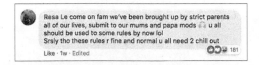

FIGURE 13. Moderator dialogue on the "subtle asian traits" Facebook group

grows. What really counts, however, is the judicious use of their power to ban people from the group. Mods who are able to handle a conflict well gain respect, but those who are too lenient or too harsh become a problem. This interviewee noted that "because [the mods] are in power . . . it kind of seems they're above criticism, and that it's just really hard to criticize a mod without getting banned, and so a number of groups are starting to have anonymous feedback systems." As the interviewee went on to say about social media in general, "the rules . . . are fairly fluid and ultimately just dependent on its users entirely" [Ashton].

CONCLUSION

Contrary to a stereotype that views every recent generation as more individualistic than the prior one, postmillennials are finding and forging new modes of community that lessen the contradiction between being a *me* and a *we*. Far from "bowling alone"[19] or "Generation Me"[20] gazing narcissistically into their screens, many young people are as concerned about belonging as they are about finding who they really are, and they do not necessarily see the two as distinct.

With modular belonging, postmillennials are involved in a new experiment in sociality. Each person's unique combination of identities, expressed through belonging to a variety of communities, gives them multiple social supports (without becoming entirely dependent on any one), while also enshrining their uniqueness. As the social theorist Michel Maffesoli puts it, "Participating in a multitude of tribes, which are themselves interrelated, allows each person to live his or her intrinsic plurality."[21] Such belonging is inherently flexible, informal, and conversational. It prioritizes forms of community in which everyone who wants to can have a say, governed by peer-based values, consensus, and a system of rules that are the product of such values and consensus.

5

OK Boomer

Yazz . . .

two members of her uni squad, the Unfuckwithables, are seated either side of her, Warris and Courtney, hard workers like her because they're all determined to get good degrees because without it they're

stuffed

they're all stuffed anyway, they agree

when they leave it's gonna be with a huge debt and crazy competition for jobs and the outrageous rental prices out there mean her generation will have to move back home forever, which will lead to even more of them despairing at the future and what with the planet about to go to shit and the United Kingdom soon to be disunited from Europe which itself is hurtling down the reactionary road and making fascism fashionable again and it's so crazy that the disgusting perma-tanned billionaire has set a new intellectual and moral low by being president of America and basically it all means that the older generation has RUINED EVERYTHING and her generation is dooooomed

unless they wrest intellectual control from their elders

sooner rather than later.

BERNADINE EVARISTO, *GIRL, WOMAN, OTHER*[1]

The Gen Zer character Yazz in Bernadine Evaristo's 2019 Booker Prize–winning novel, *Girl, Woman, Other*, embodies many of the attitudes of postmillennials, who tend to be skeptical about institutions, are largely disillusioned with what they have inherited from their elders, and feel the burden to sort out the messed-up world they have inherited. They have grown up in an atmosphere of constant innovation and increasing complexity and uncertainty caused by a range of factors, including massive global connectivity, overloads of information, a slew of disintermediating technologies, the unknowns of where artificial intelligence may take humankind, and threats to the planet—and human existence on it—from a warming climate. They have found it difficult to look to parents for guidance precisely because their elders were themselves trying to understand this fast-changing world.

For many postmillennials, this has grown into wariness about, and even a distrust of, parents and elders, so-called experts, didactic truths, and other traditional forms of hierarchical authority. They have often rejected or adapted many of their inherited values and practices—such as those in religion—with an unerring capacity for sniffing out hypocrisy and a commitment to keeping their eye on the authentic. Many therefore have minimal loyalty to traditional institutions that appear to them to operate on outdated values and principles. They prefer instead to place their trust in allies whose values seem closer to their own and whose actions can be more immediately tried and tested. Exploring platforms and modes of belonging that were unfamiliar to their elders, Gen Zers have come to rely more heavily on themselves and their peers for information and advice. Why ask their elders when those elders are the ones who have handed Gen Zers a broken world?

Postmillennials have also grown up with rapidly changing family models; their skepticism about institutions has led to changing attitudes to, and shifting values about, marriage and relationships. And, undoubtedly, technology and the internet have significantly shaped modes and patterns of dating and ways of perceiving romance.

In this chapter, we look at postmillennial attitudes toward their relationships with parents and friends, and in their intimate relationships. We also look at how they view institutions and inherited values in religion and through their ideals of leadership.

DISTRUST AND DISILLUSIONMENT

In 2019, the expression *OK Boomer* went viral among postmillennials to describe an older person (of the baby boomer generation) whom they considered out of touch and closed-minded. The satirical and cynical expression, said or written with something of a mental eye roll, also expressed postmillennial discontent with their inheritance from older generations, as well as their frustration that boomers don't seem to "get it" — that the huge responsibility of fixing boomer mistakes and building a better world now rests heavily on Gen Zer shoulders.

Postmillennials barely remember a world before 9/11, though the 2008 financial downturn was a lived reality for many who were old enough to understand and share in their parents' sense of insecurity during that time. A perpetual atmosphere of crisis, whether local, regional, or global, has been brought right into their bedrooms through their internet feeds. Terrorist bombings; mass shootings in movie theaters, classrooms, and places of worship; wars in Iraq, Afghanistan, and elsewhere; pandemics; and typhoons, earthquakes, floods, wildfires, and hurricanes of unprecedented size have been their felt realities, even if their experience of them was indirect.

At the same time, postmillennials grew up experiencing change in various long-standing social institutions: understandings and experiences of the family and marriage shifted; institutional religions were losing members and entangled in scandals; public facilities, including schools, were increasingly stretched to meet the needs of growing populations; and workplaces were becoming ever less reliable sources of job or income security in the face of mergers, downsizing, and the use of contract or temporary labor in the gig economy. Even government was looking less stable, as awareness of inequities, illegalities, and hypocrisies became more widely known. This interviewee poignantly discusses what to do about deep-seated, systemic problems and the place of traditional institutions in trying to solve them:

I don't know. Dismantle them [traditional institutions]? Easier said than done. I don't really know. I always have this question. Whenever you go to hear someone speak, like an activist or someone on campus, and they're talking about all these problems, and you're like, "Oh, but what is the solution?" and really they don't have very many. It's a very daunting problem when you can't explain it by "one person did this thing and let's get rid of that person and the problem will be resolved forever," right? Like, "Oh, a police officer shot an innocent Black teenager; let's arrest him and therefore the problem is nonexistent." Unfortunately, that's not true. And so I don't know. [Alyssa]

Postmillennial disillusionment with the existing institutions and political systems goes beyond the Gen Zer student population. In our survey of representative samples of postmillennials in the US and UK, we asked whether the political systems in their respective countries needed reform. Only 3 percent of the respondents in Britain and 6 percent in the US said the system did not need any reform, and, on the other end of the spectrum, around 15 percent in each country thought that the system was completely broken and needed to be replaced. But the majority in each country believed that their political system needed to be reformed — either to "some" extent (35 percent in Britain and 27 percent in the US) or "a lot" (40 percent in each country).

Postmillennials understand that they will have to deal with the ramifications of climate change, police violence, racial and gender injustice, and frightening new technologies (like drones carrying lethal weapons), as well as the prospect of potent viral epidemics; they accept that they cannot shirk their responsibilities. As one eighteen-year-old British man from Huddersfield put it in a 2018 BBC radio program, "I think as a generation, we are quite resilient. We've grown up with the recession and so many things that could have hindered us. I think we're ready to just move forward and just take anything on, to be honest, and that's exciting and nerve-wracking."[2] Nonetheless, many are feeling some resentment about this inheritance.

In early 2018, the American journalist and commentator David

Brooks reported on his conversations with college students across the US, describing a spirit much like that which we saw in our interviews and surveys. He spoke of the students' "diminished expectations" and distrust of large organizations. "It's not that the students are hopeless," he wrote. "They are dedicating their lives to social change. It's just that they have trouble naming institutions that work." Instead, the students he talked with were looking to "local, decentralized, and on the ground" agents of change—people, said one student, "that look like us."[3]

The view that they cannot rely on historical institutions to address contemporary problems often makes postmillennials more skeptical of "experts" who purport to have the answers. They also understand the problem of fake news bots, or "deepfakes for text," which use artificial intelligence systems to generate biased content in their feeds. It reinforces their expectation that they must garner their own resources to find those answers. This leads to attitudes of self-sufficiency, self-reliance, and self-direction, which permeated the interviews. This interviewee's comment captures the essence of this orientation: "There is a sense of 'I want autonomy.' In making a choice, I want to have your advice, certainly. I want your opinion, and I want to hear what you have to say. But I want to be able to make my own choice at the end of the day. And take what you have to say into consideration. I'm going to ultimately do all of the calculations, but I want to know how what you say factors into that, if that makes sense" [Gabe].

Our US and UK surveys similarly revealed a strong orientation toward self-reliance. When we asked respondents about whom or what they rely on for guidance in living life and making decisions, in both the US and UK "own reasoning and judgment" and "own feelings and intuition" were very highly valued. "Parents," "trusted friends," and "past experience" were also cited as reliable sources of guidance, while strikingly few said they would rely on science, religion, or history and tradition. (Respondents were allowed to select up to three among fourteen possible answers; see figure 14.)

Our iGen Corpus provides potential complementary evidence of how much postmillennials rely on their own views and determina-

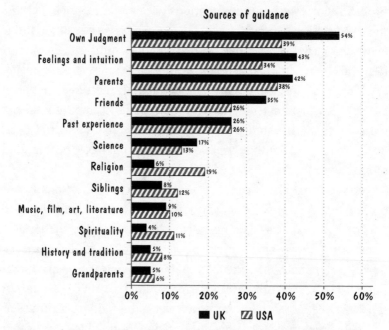

FIGURE 14. Gen Z Survey, UK and US responses to the question "Which, if any, of the following do you rely on most for guidance as you live your life and make decisions? Select up to three."

tions. The first-person pronoun I occurs three times more frequently in the corpus when compared with general corpora, most frequently occurring in the expressions "I have," "I think," and "I don't."[4]

LEADERS AS GROUP MEMBERS, NOT BOSSES

Postmillennials' attitudes about institutions and self-reliance, as well as their comfort with collaborative work and their experience with online moderators, shape their attitudes to how leadership should be exercised. The vast majority of the Gen Zers we interviewed, when asked what kind of leadership they favored, said that they prefer leaders to be respectful, caring, and willing to take on responsibility for the good of the group, and some cited skillful moderators of online sites as models. As one explained, "A leader would not be better than the others but just would have maybe a stronger willingness to try to help out the group" [Mei]. Another interviewee underscored the role of equality among all in the group:

"So it's like coming to a consensus together and just going in there together. Because leadership is not just one person, leadership only comes if you talk to other people and you decide that whatever feels right is among the majority" [Priya]. Above all, they were clear that leaders should not be authoritarian: "I don't get along well with people who just tell me what to do mindlessly. . . . A leader, they're willing to work with you one-on-one and actually have a conversation and not be so demeaning towards you" [Amber]. Rather than being directive, leaders should lead through influence and guidance: "Guidance—I like this term the best because I so value individual autonomy, but I like someone who can maybe guide me but not restrict me" [Jonah]. One interviewee expressed a sense of everyone getting along easily in groups without distinct leaders: "I think the most comfortable groups to be a part of are where there aren't distinct leaders, where everyone is kind of comfortable with everyone. . . . I was on a debating team in high school . . . and that worked so well because we all had different roles" [Nicole]. Relatability, a priority for Gen Zers as we have discussed, comes into play here, too: "I definitely like when leaders are vulnerable. So it makes it like, 'Oh, you've been through this too.' Or even—'You can relate to me in a way and I can relate to you,' instead of being like, 'Oh, my leader is someone who has no idea what I'm going through'" [Vedika].

For members of older generations, who grew up experiencing hierarchical power structures and more individualized effort, an orientation to collaborative work can be bewildering, especially if there is no leader directing the work, as we saw in chapter 1, with the encounter between university administrators and WTU student activists. Boomers often cannot understand how an organization can function without an elected set of officers, while postmillennials cannot understand why officers are needed if the organization can get its work done without such formality. However, one of our interviewees did take a markedly different view from her peers, commenting that leaders should be identified when they are needed to take responsibility, "otherwise, things are just utter chaos"—for example, organizing things in her sorority—but she also noted that in other instances, "everyone has their own clear individual part that they play or want to play," suggesting a more collaborative framework [Nicole].

Across the broader population of postmillennials in the US and UK, group leadership and collaboration are also favored, as the results of our survey demonstrated. Nearly 60 percent said that they preferred either a group that "works things out with the help of a leader" (32 percent) or that the "group and leader share the power" (27 percent). Only 14 percent preferred one designated leader, while 19 percent liked rotating leadership among group members "as and when needed." Approximately 8 percent of the respondents said they preferred no leader at all.

The preferences for collaboration and light-touch leadership go hand in glove with certain orientations and values we discussed previously—most notably, respect for individual identity and diversity, and a desire for equity and community consensus. Finding social structures that support personal autonomy in the context of collaborative work is one of the big challenges postmillennials will continue to wrestle with, especially as they observe weaknesses in the more hierarchical social structures that are a legacy of the industrial age. Factories thrived on top-down leadership that coordinated the disparate functions and parts needed for the finished product, but work in the digital age requires new techniques for harnessing the combined power of workers sitting in front of their individual screens in scattered locations. Indeed, several scholars have recently begun to debate the questions of whether or how digital "peer production" might replace more hierarchical social structures in the future.[5]

PARENTS AS FRIENDS

The institution of the family has changed especially rapidly over the past few decades.[6] This means that postmillennials' experience of family is different than that of boomers. Many postmillennials treat their parents as friends: calling a parent to talk about the day or to share gossip about celebrities is not very different from calling a peer to talk about such topics. This contrasts sharply with previous generations, who tended to see their parents as authority figures rather than peers (even after they had themselves become adults). This aspect of the parent–child relationship came through strongly in the interviews, with the vast majority of our interviewees saying that their relationships with their parents remain close. It was not unusual for our interviewees to report that they send pictures, for example, of their meals, to their parents throughout the day. Many said they talk or text with a parent—usually a mother—daily, sometimes multiple times daily (and they also talk regularly with siblings). In Laura Hamilton's *Parenting to a Degree*, one college student talked to her mother every single day during college but it was not until graduation that her parents learned what her major was.[7] While the communications may be "check ins" initiated by the parent, the students will call to ask for favors or to chat. As one interviewee described: "I call my parents every day . . . [and] text them but not as much. . . . It's mostly all texting if I need something, and then I'll call them if I just want to talk. . . . I normally talk more about my day with my mom, . . . and then I'll talk to my dad about physics all the time because I'm really bad at it, and he needs to help me. Also, for some reason, he's really up on the celebrity goings-on, so I'll talk to him about that" [Malia].

This relates to another feature of the parenting of postmillennials: what we came to think of as "parental project managing." Modern parents with the means to do so become something akin to project managers when their children are quite young, sorting out playdates, doctor appointments, after-school activities, and summer plans, and that role becomes a habit that is difficult to break.[8] Parents are often very ready to help their children solve practical problems; if the car breaks down or physics is hard, a knowledgeable parent will be on hand to help. This modern trend was caricatured in a recent *New Yorker* cartoon that shows a young boy explaining to his friend that the adult sitting nearby reading a newspaper is "less of a parent and more of a fixer."[9] It has also led to labels such as *snowplow parents* (who go ahead and prepare the path for the child), *helicopter parents* (who hover over their children), and the *curling generation* (alluding to the sport of curling, in which team members dash ahead of a moving stone to sweep away obstacles in its path). Some psychologists have expressed concern about this parenting model.[10] It can lead to a push/pull experience for some Gen Zers: on the one hand, they are self-reliant and effective at juggling the abundance and complexity of their lives, but on the other, they welcome the familiar assistance of a friendly parent for some of the details—and may come to depend on it.

There is one area, however, in which the Gen Zers help parents: a role reversal has occurred, with parents looking to their children for help with new technologies and social codes, and this is also an expression of the change in parent–child relationships for postmillennials. Digital technologies have made a significant impact on these changing family dynamics, and vice versa. Postmillennials' frequently expressed exasperation at what they see as their parents' digital illiteracy is sometimes real, but it is also a symbol of wide generational tensions.[11] This was a common trope in the interviews. One person, for example, related what happened when her mother's phone died: "It was just really difficult, I think, and frustrating, and sometimes funny . . . to be like, seriously, mom, like, yes it's dead, like, you haven't charged it in four weeks. . . . And I think that kind of education for my parents is a weird thing to do, as like a teenager to teach them how to use stuff when it's usually the other way around" [Emma]. Another student similarly commented that when children have to teach parents how to use a culture's tools, there is a reversal of the expected passing of knowledge from parent to child, which can lead to subtle or overt resentments in both generations. This student went on to say that it is also painful when today's children realize that they cannot necessarily turn to their parents for advice about the future; given all the changes that are afoot, the parents are often as unsure about the future as their kids. As Simone Dawes, a Gen Zer from Yorkshire, explained on BBC radio: "When we became teenagers, the online world was growing so fast the adults couldn't keep up. We had no choice but to teach ourselves." The difficulties of such a knowledge gap in the online world are illustrated sharply by the case of cyberbullying. As Dawes goes on to say in the same interview, "It was tricky to talk to your parents. If there was a problem in the playground then mum knew how to deal with it but online it was new for both of you."[12]

The redefining of the relationship between parents and children can be confusing for the parents, too. In the past, parents could at least overhear phone calls or music blaring from bedrooms. Today parents feel increasingly removed as their children work in front of their computers or listen to streamed music and podcasts, earbuds in place. One mother of postmillennials, writing in our *Pacific Standard* series, described these feelings of exclusion: "Music has always contributed to, and helped to delineate, the generation gaps between parents and children. But in decades past, those gaps mainly involved disagreements over changing musical styles, social mores, and nostalgic attachment. For Gen Z, the vast digital music universe and the ability to live in it secretly and silently is all they've ever known. My kids were born into a changed world. I'm still struggling through the transition."[13]

The result of this redefinition of relationships can be a confusing mix, with children as parents' teachers, equals, dependents, and charges all at the same time. From this perspective, it is easier to see why the family-as-friends model works. As parents help their children manage the day-to-day complexities of their lives, they become the kind of collaborative "guides" that our interviewees and survey respondents equate with good leaders. That, in turn, offers their children more room to explore and find for themselves who they are and with whom they want to be close. It is another aspect of the move from ascribed identity and belonging to self-direction and collaboration, with sometimes considerable help received from others on an as-needed basis.

These more democratic aspects of the parent–child relationship are taking place against the backdrop of many new understandings and experiences of what is meant by *family*; growing up, many postmillennials experienced changing family forms. Single-parent families, blended families, and families headed by same-sex couples are increasingly common, while the postwar family unit of "married man and wife with kids" has become more unusual. Whereas what demographers refer to as the first demographic transition, which took place somewhere around 1870–1945 in Britain and America, had strengthened heterosexual marriage and the nuclear family unit, the second demographic transition—which is still ongoing—has expanded what we mean and experience by marriage and family. The 1960s, especially, witnessed a sexual and gender revolution, in part enabled by a contraceptive revolution; as a result of this, women and children have often gained higher status and a more independent say within the family.[14] As the sociologist Elisabeth Beck-Gernsheim observed in 1998, "The character of everyday family life is gradually changing: people used to be able to rely upon well-functioning rules and models, but now . . . more and more things must be negotiated, planned, personally brought about."[15] This means that Gen Zers were increasingly likely to experience, growing up, what Sonia Livingstone and Alicia Blum-Ross refer to as "democratic families," in which parents feel "the responsibility to involve [their children] in key decisions, even becoming accountable to their children in a relationship founded ever less on asserting authority and ever more on building mutual respect."[16]

Because family structures have changed rapidly in the past few decades, the family structures that were familiar to boomers are no longer necessarily the norm for Gen Zers. Medical and technological changes have helped make different forms of family possible: 1978 saw the birth of the first test tube baby. This led the way to children conceived by egg and embryo donation, children born through sperm donation, and children born through surrogacy. This has enabled same-sex couples to have children, single women to become mothers by choice, and older women to become mothers (through egg-freezing technology). In her 2020 book We Are Family, based on research among a variety of new forms of family, Susan Golombok concludes that the children of such families are just as psychologically healthy and well-adjusted as the children from traditional nuclear families.[17] In a 2019 article in the New York Times titled "What's a Normal Family, Anyway?" Claire Haug talks about her family, composed of her birth mother, her mother's female partner, the partner's children, and the gay man who was the sperm donor for all of the family's children, and notes that it is hardly unique today.[18] Many of our interviewees commented that they or their good friends were children of divorced parents, and one even called his family "weird in a way" because his parents were not divorced [Jun]. According to the Pew Research Center, as of 2015,

> There is no longer one dominant family form in the U.S. Parents today are raising their children against a backdrop of increasingly diverse and, for many, constantly evolving family forms. By contrast, in 1960, the height of the post-World War II baby boom, there was one dominant family form. At that time 73 percent of all children were living in a family with two married parents in their first marriage. By 1980, 61 percent of children were living in this type of family, and today less than half (46 percent) are.[19]

Moreover, Pew reported, many children today experience fluidity and change in their living situations as parents separate or change partners. Furthermore, growing numbers of people are continuing to live as singles. Euromonitor International predicts that "over 2016–2030, single-person households will see faster growth than any other household type globally . . . with around 120 million new single person homes to be added over the period."[20] For postmillennials, the family is therefore increasingly fluid, varied, and chosen.

FRIENDS AS FAM

While family may be more like friends, close friends can be more like family. As we discussed in the previous chapter, many Gen Zers now use familial words like *fam* and *sib* to describe their closest circle of friends. These are friendships characterized by deep bonds of care—someone who truly cares about you and for whom you truly care. As one interviewee said, close friends are important because they "will always be there in a way, kind of as your family" [Kayla]. A recent article in the *Atlantic* that describes the growing use of geolocation apps among friends as "gesture[s] of trust and intimacy" contains this rather similar statement from a twenty-four-year-old woman: "I have been trying to frame a lot of my friendships in terms of family.... I don't really plan to have kids or get married. I'm thinking about social structures and the kinds of things that you're supposed to get from nuclear family, and evolving other relationships to fill that gap.... I feel safer knowing they [friends] know where I am."[21]

These kinds of close friendships offer trust, authenticity, and safety, a point underscored by the Lancaster student who said that she would text a friend when she was awakened by a nightmare because the knowledge that her friend would see the text in the morning was comforting enough to get her back to sleep [Liz]. As another interviewee put it, "I've come to the conclusion that my friends, my true friends, like me for who I am" [Amir]. The importance of friendship to postmillennials is also very evident in their language: in addition to the popularity of new words like *fam*, *sib*, *tribe*, *squad*, and *crew* described in chapter 4, the word *friend* itself appears with unusual frequency in our iGen Corpus relative to its usage by all age groups.[22]

Gen Zers are careful to differentiate their close friendships from friendships that are temporal or more limited in scope, including those often developed in online communications. One interviewee explained that "we are so oversaturated by interacting with social media and dealing with people who we only know through Instagram, ... I think it's just generated this craving to have those deeper connections with people ... to actually understand who they are" [Madison]. This is not to say that significant relationships cannot develop from online interactions. One of the students who talked to us about Numtots gave an example: "So it's, like, a real interesting community that came out of nothing, and I feel ... weird calling it a community, because I generally hold the belief that online virtual communities are not as real as real life communities, but this really changed my perspective a lot because this enabled a community that could never form in real life, like actually form. And they have these real-life gatherings now. I saw this picture: there's a bunch that got together in Boston" [Andy].

Similarly, in September 2018, six gamers, who had known each other for five years but had never met in person before, gathered around the hospital bedside of their online friend, Joe, 23, who was dying of Ewing's sarcoma. They had traveled to New Jersey from different parts of the US and Canada. "We always had an idea we would eventually meet up, but after finding out that our time was limited we knew we had to do it sooner rather than later," explained one of the group. "We all knew we had to do it."[23]

ROMANCE AND SEX

Always complex, categorizing romantic and sexual relationships seems to be harder than ever now. Two of the Gen Zers we talked to had a poignant dialogue about how difficult it is for them to know what constitutes a friendship or a romantic partnership today. They talked about the confusion that comes from sharing nude photos or having intense conversations online with people they might not even recognize on the street, the "weirdness" of being invited to weddings of people they had not seen in many years, and whether an intimate hookup with a stranger or a *friends with [sexual] benefits* arrangement could be considered a relationship. What, they asked, are the boundaries between what constitutes a romantic, sexual, and platonic relationship? "I think, speaking on behalf of our generation," one concluded, "something I've heard from a lot of my friends at least, is a desire for clearly demarcated boundaries but not really finding them.... People don't know how to do that" [focus group]. One interviewee succinctly summed up the complicated nature of romantic relationships relative to platonic friendships: "If you're friends, you're friends—there. But if you're more than friends or you're trying to date or whatever, it's just there's so many steps inbetween.... I know a lot of my friends have kind of deviated from having a relationship to just doing whatever they want because they just don't understand the process" [Priya].

This confusion leads to a variety of strategies for managing relationships, dating, and feelings. Some postmillennials have decided to stick to friendship, such as this Chinese gay male student: "If I invest too much in a romantic relationship, it's more risky in a way.

I really want to invest my time and energy to build long-term relationships, so friendship is my choice. I value it more." In this student's case, the prospect of his return to China and his gay identity have in part determined his decision: "Because I don't know what will happen in terms of romantic relationships, especially because I will return to China one day after graduation" [Jun]. For others, their approach entails compartmentalization "because people have feelings, and these feelings get mixed in with friendships, or they might contribute to conflict, and I think I learned how to do this more in high school, where I found that feelings interfere with my natural and genuine interaction with others, and I wanted a way to preserve the more natural, genuine interaction. Being able to set aside romantic feelings has been helpful" [Victor]. As another interviewee put it, the confusion of friendship and romance "doesn't end up well.... I'm like, 'That's too much for me.' I'll try to keep to myself and my friends until I'm ready to move on to the next step, which I have no idea when it will be, though" [Becca].

One key response to the category confusion is a questioning of serious or long-term relationships, at least in this stage of their lives. While many of the interviewees mentioned having a boyfriend, girlfriend, or enbyfriend (nonbinary significant other), we heard over and over again that romantic relationships had to be approached with caution, given their potential to interfere with life and work. One interviewee said, "Right now because I'm trying to go to a new school, I am trying to apply to all these things, I'd prefer a more structured one [relationship]. I don't want to overcommit. Personally, I don't think I'm ready for a long-term relationship. I'd take it if, say, the partner is okay with accepting some preset boundaries, say if I have an exam we're not going to text so much." This student had clearly tried this tactic but without much success in the past: "If I'm, say, in the future studying for the LSAT [law school standardized tests], you're not going to get a reply within one hour. That has not worked really well in the past, but yeah, somebody might be OK with that" [Jian]. As this comment reveals, the always-on nature of smartphones is a factor; as the sociologist C. J. Pascoe puts it, this "increases expectations of availability and reciprocity," with "intensified contact as a way to differentiate romantic relationships from other relationships."[24] Another interviewee articulated the constant nature of relationships as being off-putting: "I think we want to do things on our own and progress on our own for ourselves rather than with someone else.... I think friendships are valued a little bit more than romantic relationships just because they are not as serious and you're not constantly with someone" [Amber]. One nineteen-year-old interviewee, who was in a long-term heterosexual relationship, explained, "There's an assumption that people either hook up because they're too busy for an actual relationship or, if they're in a relationship, it's super serious because [at this university] students are serious people" [Lucy].

Some Gen Zers also question the model of long-term, exclusive relationships—including marriage. Even those interviewees who were in such relationships made comments to the effect that "we are together now, but we know we'll break up when...." The "when" could be the end of the school term, graduation, or some other defining moment when the partners anticipate that the relationship will become inconvenient. While many still harbor a dream of true love in their future, the more common expectation is that romantic relationships are transitory. As one interviewee said, "I don't believe in marriage anymore in the way my parents do. They believe in marrying really young, and I just don't believe at all in marriage. I feel like you could just have partners and not be just tied up to just one person. I think that has an effect because of the environment I live in, the people I hang out with." When asked if they thought this was a shared view among postmillennials, the interviewee replied, "Yeah, I think so" [Aaron]. This expectation of sequential romantic relationships may also reflect an early exposure to divorce and single-parent families, as well as longer life expectancies for postmillennials. One interviewee poignantly articulated this:

Growing up with romantic and relationship role models that I had in my life, why would I believe that happily ever after actually exists?

I very much believe it's a privilege to actually believe and think you can have that for yourself. If you did, you had a good-ass childhood. ... Most families in the United States have been through a divorce or have lost a parent, some kind of thing or another. If you had a happy family, you can believe in, like, oh, perfect marriage forever. Like, I'm really happy for you. That's wonderful, but that's not the majority, and that's a privilege that you get. [Eve]

It is not surprising, then, that romantic relationships were variously described as "time consuming," "energy draining," "complicated," and, thanks to online dating apps—on which more shortly—"more a hobby" or "almost like fast food" in that they could begin and end quickly. As one interviewee responded to a question about romance: "Romantic? . . . I think my generation thinks it's something almost like fast food. You know? Like, you date someone one day and then you date somebody else. It's, like, really easy" [James]. Another said that relationships are "seen as a burden or a step down from where you're at. . . . Not so much as being part of a team and having someone on your side to help you move forward. It's more, you're being with someone who could potentially hold you back, even if that's not really the case" [Amber]. For some Gen Zers, *catching feelings* in a dating or sexual relationship is something to guard against. In our iGen Corpus, these sentiments were most salient on Twitter: "Catching feelings hella fast. This is so dangerous" [@Sydney_godfrey]; "When I start catching feelings, I get sad" [@111amandali]; "Do you ever just feel yourself catching feelings for someone and you're like, no! Stop! What're you doing!" [@aam berrleigh]; "Fucked around, caught feelings & got hurt" [@Yo_Girl _Chiina]. The ambivalence was well expressed by one of the students we interviewed, who said, "If I was a boy, I would be a fuckboi [a man who is interested only in casual sex] probably. I would love to just have a very chill thing, but, at the same time, part of me wants to be loved and have a romantic relationship" [Hiba].

The prevalence of hookup culture is integral to so many of these shifts in behavior and attitudes for postmillennials. Lisa Wade's book *American Hookup* investigates student attitudes about romance and sex at twenty-one colleges and universities across the US and suggests that, although hookup culture is central to student lives, it frequently makes them unhappy and confused about relationships.[25] The Gen Zers we talked to expressed a range of opinions about hookups. One said, "I think that a lot of people judge other people for engaging in the hookup culture, but I also think that a lot of people also think that being in hookup culture is almost like a rite of passage or like a coming-of-age thing" [Bella]. However, for a heterosexual woman who came to study in America from the Middle East, the sexual mores of the society in which she is now living are freeing: "Growing up in a conservative community where sex was a big taboo . . . coming here and letting go of all those restraints that held me back for so long back home, first I wanted a platonic relationship. Then with time and after accepting myself more, especially this summer, I've had very casual hookups and one-night hookups and I didn't feel bad about them" [Hiba].

The internet has transformed how we meet each other, and this has added to the category confusion about what a relationship, friendship, or hookup might be and mean.[26] Dating, which in the past was generally a private activity, is now semiprivate, sometimes anonymous, and hugely facilitated by technology and apps such as Tinder (a dating app popular among our interviewees for casual hookups), Bumble (similar to Tinder but where only women can message first), CoffeeMeetsBagel (for both dating and relationships), or Grindr (for hookups between gay men). While sex "is easier to get" because of dating apps, some students described using them for personal affirmation and validation from others, regardless of whether they led to dates or sex. "When first using these apps," one heterosexual student explained, "it just seemed a little—well, not even a little—very superficial. Like I'm going to base my entire assumption on whether or not I want to meet you off of four pictures and five words. I don't know how I feel about that. And then, lo and behold, my roommate one day manages to find his girlfriend off of Bumble. And she's great, a great person, and I'm just, 'Well, I guess it is possible.'"

He also noted that in his experience, as an African American, some dating apps were racist, "Bumble racially profiles people. It is like Tinder but everyone is white for some reason" [Alex].

Tinder is used by a lot of postmillennials in a public and social way by sitting around in groups and swiping left and right together, and a set of vocabulary has developed around this culture: *hookup* (sexual encounter), *side chick* (someone with whom you regularly hook up), *rave bae* (someone who acts as your significant other for one night or one weekend; *bae* = before anyone else, or adaptation from *babe*). Students use many words to imply that group sex is not unusual (usually between two men and one woman). Examples include expressions such as *to get dicked* (to be penetrated by a penis (either man or woman), *hitting it from the back* (to penetrate someone from behind), and *unicorn* (a bisexual person who joins a straight couple—not to be confused with another sense of *unicorn*, used to refer to someone with a unique combination of attributes). One queer cis male interviewee, who uses both Tinder and Grindr, says, "Romantically, Tinder and Grindr are basically the same. Tinder is, like, at least the social etiquette is that it's more where you have conversations first, and then you meet up and go on dates with people or hookups with people. Grindr is, like, an explicitly gay platform and so it can be kind of dicey in terms of the men that are on there only looking for sex. A lot of times you'll just get an unsolicited, very graphic photo—that is kind of characteristic of Grindr interactions" [Gabe].

Many Gen Zers speak of dating apps as a fun game that they do not take too seriously. "I'll definitely have my friends with me when I'm scrolling," explained a nonbinary student, "and we'll just, like, make snap judgments. It's definitely entertainment" [Ashton]. "My roommate is kind of the same way, she more goes on it for entertainment purposes and, like, seeing who's on there," explained one heterosexual cis female, "and you can get some really funny profiles—it's great" [Jenni]. Most interviewees acknowledged that dating apps were based on shallow assumptions but they still used them. "The interface for Tinder," explained a young heterosexual cis female, "is conducive to just really basic surface level, 'you're hot or you're not,' and then that's it" [Madison]. As a heterosexual cis male explained,

> At some point, you realize they're not taking you seriously and you're not taking it seriously, and it's just bad jokes, weird flirting, and then you move on to the next person. At some point you just swipe right on everyone and you see how many matches you get. It's like, "Do I really feel like talking to these people?" No. And then at some point I realized, "Oh my God, I have become who I hate." It's just a weird experience. Three out of ten do not recommend, unless if you're extremely bored on a Thursday night. It's like, ugh, okay. [Alex]

Technology has contributed to this significant shift in behavior and attitudes; one of the interviewees articulated that change like this:

> So "romantic relationship," it kind of lost its meaning I think. Courting used to be something very important. Now it's just match, match, no match. It used to take time. You'd have to court a woman. . . . Now it's like, "So, I have a boyfriend. How did that happen? Oh, just matched on Tinder and went on a date, and we're together now." . . . So now, that aspect of relationships being super quick, I see it as kind of being meaningless, and now it's very respectable and impressive when you're with someone for more than four months. . . . So I guess time became the new relationship. Before it used to be if you were in a relationship, it's something serious, meaningful. You took your time, and you like the person. Now, if you're with a person it kind of means nothing unless you're with them for a while. [Benoit]

Technology has not only profoundly affected how Gen Zers meet people and the logistics of sexual encounters, it has also introduced the possibility of romantic relationships that are born on the internet and never go beyond the digital, which can include talking, sexting, and "sleeping together" via, for instance, FaceTime or Zoom. Eighteen-year-old Simone from Huddersfield, UK, speaking in a BBC radio program, recalled her first romance with a woman in Germany whom she knew online through a fandom but never physically met:

> I was cautious about the whole internet relationship status, because there's a stigma around it, a very big stigma that it's not real. And I was kind of scared about judgment from my friends and family. . . . After we both established we had feelings for each other, I asked if we could be "talking." Sometimes you just have to go for it. . . . When you're first in love, you get swept up in it all. Sometimes the intensity got too much. We used to sleep on the phone, like on Face-Time, or just on a call, or whatever. And I remember at first feeling really romantic, because it's like, "You're here, almost a presence." And then as time went on, it used to really annoy me because I got all those wires around me, all these earphones, and I just wanna sleep, and also it's harder to argue through a phone, and text arguments are so much worse. We were arguing a lot and, I don't know, growing apart, I guess. . . . It fell apart because of who we were but also because the online thing was too much for me. Not because I'm condemning internet relationships, just personally for me I felt like I got too sucked up into my phone. I felt like I could never turn my phone off. I don't really talk to people like I used to.[27]

Looking back on the whole romance, Simone reflected that if she had to give her younger self some advice, it would be this: "Don't let anyone tell you it's not real. Love is love, and that applies online as well. But also don't let yourself get carried away so that you're not living in the moment as well. Your life is still your own."[28]

Notwithstanding the array of feelings about romance and dating, the prevalence of hookup culture, and their ambivalence about committed relationships at this time in their lives, many interviewees said they want to be in a committed relationship in the future. When we asked representative samples of postmillennials in our surveys in the UK and in the US, "How important do you feel it is to find a life partner?" nearly 80 percent in both countries thought it was important or very important. There was not much variation by gender or for college-educated and not. One gay male student we interviewed commented that, although marriage could impinge on the personal freedom highly valued by his generation, many of his age peers want to marry and have kids because "a hypothetical future family is really the only stable, comfortable, safe place they could know." He added:

I just don't have a lot of negative thoughts toward marriage. It's like, the old ball and chain argument, I just can't understand it, and maybe that is a product of my own upbringing, or my generation's upbringing, because safety and security and being settled down, what's not to like about that? ... I'm not saying that freedom is overrated, but I want marriage and I want kids and I feel like that's very different from the picture painted of my generation by people, but mostly it's what I believe in, and frankly, among my peers is not that uncommon, even ones who are politically liberal in every other respect. [Andy]

This desire for marriage and, in some cases, children came through clearly when we asked our interviewees about their fears and hopes for the future. Some expressed a fear of not finding a marriage partner, like a male student who said anxiously, "I don't know if I'm going to find a person that's right for me or that's into me" [Cody]. Many expressed a fear of not being able to find a job that would support a family. As one female student said: "I'm totally terrified that I will not end up in a career that can financially support a family," but then went on to say that "the thing that gets me really hopeful is just trusting that it'll work out and that I will be able to live in a place that makes me feel happy, and then have this incredible family life too" [Madison]. This alternation between hope and anxiety was very common among the interviewees.

Other students were ambivalent about marriage per se, but not about the desire to have a stable romantic partner. A female interviewee said, "I want a partner, but I don't know if I want a marriage. ... I don't necessarily feel like marriage is something that's important, like actually legally binding yourself" [Kylie]. A male student focused on all he would have to do, including finding a stable job and home, before he could think about building a family but concluded that he did want a relationship because "it's nice to come home to someone who's a break from work, [with whom] you can share everything that you've been through and make you feel better about yourself" [Nigel]. Finding that special trustworthy person was the essence of a romantic relationship, said one student: "Being able to have an account of life experiences, learn from one another, being there when you need them ... it goes a long way when you have someone who is willing to help you out with something throughout the days, someone that you can trust" [Santiago].

RELIGION AND SPIRITUALITY: SKEPTICISM ABOUT INSTITUTIONS

We know Gen Zers are skeptical about formal institutions, especially hierarchical ones, so religion is an especially tricky area for postmillennials. Our interviewees covered a wide range of religious backgrounds, affiliations, and beliefs: some have rejected outright all organized religion, some have continued to identify with the religion of their parents but adapted its beliefs and practices in significant ways, some are still exploring, and some are indifferent to or uninterested in the whole topic. We found that terms relating to religion and spirituality appeared relatively infrequently in our iGen Corpus, suggesting that neither topic raises widespread generational passion,[29] and disaffiliation from any religious group or identity is higher among postmillennials than any previous generation, as we noted earlier in the book. In the UK, around two-thirds of postmillennials identify as having "no religion,"[30] and in the US, over a third do,[31] indicating that although this shift to an increasingly nonreligious society is deeper in the UK than in the US, it is a marked feature of both countries, and more marked still among younger generations.[32] Gen Zers are not responsible for the rise of nonreligion, a change that represents the continuation of an existing trend, but the trend has deepened as they have come of age and made their choices. In the UK, being nonreligious is now the norm among this age group, and even in the more-religious US, it is more common than ever before, with less stigma attached.[33] Although Christianity remains the dominant religion in both countries, Gen

Zers are more likely than any previous generation to have encountered people of other faiths and no faith, and to have been schooled in the affirmation of religious diversity and religious freedom as a legal as well as moral norm.

For many postmillennials, organized religions, at least in their traditional forms, can seem too "old-style," formal, dogmatic, hierarchical, male-dominated, paternalistic, and authoritarian; in other words, too much in conflict with their values relating to autonomy, diversity, tolerance, and acceptance to be credible or meaningful. Even in more liberal and experimental churches, formal worship and hierarchical authority structures can be a stumbling block. As one interviewee said about such authority in general, "I think it can be done well, but often times it tends just to lead to abuse." He went on to compare organized religion to organized crime because it "creates more suffering than benefit" [Ethan]. Another offered this explanation on behalf of postmillennials as a whole:

> Religion is, like, really looked down on in this generation because I think people are just kind of, like, realizing that—well, all our values conflict with a lot of religious values. I mean, as a generation, I'd say most people believe in accepting gay people. That goes against most religions. Our generation believes in sex without relationships. That goes against most religions. One thing, we just swear a lot, you know. . . . I feel like our values conflict too much with religions for people to be able to like it. Plus, I don't know, we just grew up with technology and a lot of science and stuff and it's hard to believe in made-up things, when it's all presented to you. [Noah]

These negative generational stereotypes about religion may cause some postmillennials to hide or downplay their religious identities when speaking with peers, as we discussed in chapter 2.[34] In several subreddits devoted to the subject, for example, there are fierce debates, pro and con, about religion as "absolutist," strict, authoritarian, patriarchal, dogmatic, and antiscience. One of our interviewees who grew up Mormon mentioned this absolutism as the reason he decided to leave his religion and "retake [his] authenticity." As he explained, "There's the perspective of religion. They believe that God gives them what is right and wrong, whereas I just kind of have to find it for myself, whether it's within me in some kind of human nature or social interaction thing, or if it's just truly nothing and I have to create it from the depths of my own being or something" [Zach].

Those who self-identify as nonreligious are not necessarily atheists or hostile to "authentic" religious commitment. Some hold the view that organized religions are at the core good and tolerant, even if their essential nature has been corrupted by power-hungry authoritarians. A self-identified queer student, for instance, noted that although she had stopped believing in the Hindu religion of her parents at the age of twelve, she appreciated that her parents' values of being kind and helping others were connected to their devotion. She went on to say that she did not think she would ever be religious in her life but that "just talking to people who are religious and noticing that a lot of religions do have similarities in what I believe in . . . I think I swing between thinking religion is really dumb or thinking it's neutral. . . . It's probably one of the easiest ways to give people a set of values and a foundation that is built on kindness and love and giving back" [Alisha].

Gen Zers who remain engaged in organized religion often articulated that it is necessary to select what they believe and how they practice that religion, in order to reflect their own deeper values. A Roman Catholic Mexican American student explained that within his church there are "many different ideas and beliefs that I don't follow. . . . Because everyone is entitled to their own beliefs." He went on to say that in particular he disagrees with the Roman Catholic Church's views "on gay marriage, or someone being queer" and so concludes: "I guess I am Catholic, but I think some of the ideas or beliefs I don't agree with" [Nathan]. Similarly, rule-based religions are unappealing. A Black evangelical student explained, "I feel like I don't like a lot of religions. My personal experience with it has been very positive, but that's because the churches I grew up in emphasized the relationship with God, not just random rules to follow." Pointing out that "it literally goes against most of what's in the Bible to be this terrible towards gay people," she affirmed the possibility of doing things differently, and went on to say that "I don't like religion as an institution per se when it doesn't emphasize what the Bible is actually saying . . . or it just takes little nitpicky sections of it and tries to make them this whole big issue" [Malia]. A related comment came from a Jewish student at Stanford who attends synagogue sometimes and calls herself "religious," as distinct from "super religious":

> I think people that are super religious subscribe to pretty much all of the hard and set values of their religion. And I think most religions now are kind of outdated in their strict views, but if you're willing to be more loose with them, then I would say—I would call it religious, not super religious. I also think people that are super religious are very observant, . . . but if you're a subscriber to the general values of the religion and enjoy the rituals on occasion or, like, on a frequent occasion and are involved in the community on a frequent occasion and have friends and a support system from the community then that would be—that's what I am and I would call that religious. [Jess]

Some students, especially from Christian homes, downplayed claims of religious distinctiveness, and suggested an approach to religion and the divine that could bypass specific forms of organized religion. One said, "I stopped going to a church when I was younger, but my grandparents are Protestant and my mom was raised free Methodist. I was raised nondenominational, and I identify spiritually as Christian now, nondenominational" [Lee]. Another said, "I don't believe that Christianity is the only religion. I believe that the Creator—which is what I prefer [to "God"], I use both terms—are all like the same person, just manifested through different lenses, but I identify as a Christian by convenience and just to appease my family, but just because I have gotten stuff out of it" [Maya].

Given this skepticism about institutional religion, it is not surprising that some interviewees talked about turning from religion to spirituality and of how this had allowed them to tailor a personal spiritual practice outside the boundaries of organized religion. A Middle Eastern interviewee, raised Muslim, said:

I think religion is spirituality but with the addition of a few tasks that you're expected to do as part of that faith. For me, I feel spiritual is a more elastic concept than religion. Because no matter how much you try to interpret religion . . . it's a very structured and restricted social frame . . . or topic or thing, that to feel connected to it, to feel religious, you just have to go by certain things. . . . If spirituality for me means being connected with God, then that's what it is. If it's being a good person, then that's what it is. Like, you can define it however you want. And it's more, I feel like it's more about yourself and your inner peace and your relationship with people than it is about, like, praying five times a day or going to church. [Hiba]

When asked to describe where she was on that spectrum of religion and spirituality, she replied: "I started off as being religious or semi-religious. But then it slowly shifted away towards spiritual. Now, I would say it's more spiritual than religious just because I decided to take the spiritual part of religion and go by that. . . . I'm still somewhat religious in some aspects, in some regards. But for the most part, I would say I'm spiritual-ish" [Hiba].

Spirituality, as something personal, is easier to claim than institutional religion, because it allows your own and your peers' values to be your guide, rather than the rules and regulations at the core of religion, which are often regarded as outdated and possibly hypocritical. As one put it, "I see spirituality as more of an individual thing. And of course, religion is a group. So I see that there are similarities because it shapes a person. But there's definitely differences on how much free thinking it'll give you, because with religion there's not really much room for interpretation or how you see it. It's just this is what has happened, this is the rules" [Kayla]. They deemed a range of personally significant, special things "spiritual," including talismans like treasured items of jewelry or clothing, time spent in nature, meditation, certain tattoos, and an appreciation of beauty in the world. One said, "If spirituality can be defined by seeking awe and wonder and appreciating beauty and looking for connection, then I would certainly call myself spiritual. . . . I would say my spirituality is not at all about faith. It's not about believing things I can't see or making explanations for inexplicable things. It's about appreciation and care" [Emma]. Another said, "Spiritual. I connect that term [with] what you feel for yourself and what you do for yourself. Kind of your understanding of how you fit in the world and what you do." They then made a contrast with religion, understood as "something you are believing in, but that's something that doesn't exist. For spirituality you believe in the world as something you could touch and feel, versus religion you have this kind of blind faith in something" [Becca].

The personal nature of these decisions about religion and spirituality has been noted by Christel Manning, who found in her study of how nonreligious parents raise their children that there is no escape from "the imperative of personal worldview choice."[35] Even interviewees who adopted the religion in which they were raised were keen to stress that it was a personal decision. A Korean American graduate student explained, "At some time in undergrad, I went to church just for the sake of going to church, and I hated that so I stopped going. And life was great, I was like, okay, I feel free now. ... But then ... I started going back and learning more about it, and I think now [my faith] has become more of an important part of my identity" [Lina]. As noted earlier in the chapter, when asked in our survey about their sources of guidance for living life and making decisions, respondents in both the US and Britain selected "religion" relatively infrequently. Much more commonly, respondents indicated that, more than religion, their sources of guidance were their own judgment, feelings and intuition, parents, friends, and past experience.

Rejecting religion did not necessarily mean rejecting belief in a deity or spiritual power. Several interviewees mentioned that they were personally wrestling with the existence of God (or gods), even if they wanted little or nothing to do with established religion. As one student put it, "I don't exactly believe in a God and I don't exactly not believe in a God. Like, sure there might be something but, like, possibly, like 99 percent, I think there isn't, so I don't identify as an atheist but I don't not identify as an atheist" [Irina]. Another student spelled out his belief in a larger force, explaining that it was not God but something that he struggled to name:

> Yeah, I believe that, um, not God, the term that we've made for it, but definitely something else out there that helped create and affect the way we live, but not the God that we say it is. So not like a holy God, so not like Jesus or Buddha, not like an eternal being, like all-powerful, but definitely something. . . . This, all these definitions of what God is, so people made it out to be a human being or another being, but to me it could be like, I don't know, like a term or a phrase. So God to me is a creator, so creator could be evolution, it could be the Big Bang. . . . I'm open to the idea of some deist creator, who isn't a person, who is just, or not even he — he's the wrong pronoun . . . I don't know what it would actually be, but some kind of creator force possibly, but not a God or any religion I've heard of. [Nigel]

And a self-identified nonreligious student said, "I don't know if God is a guy, you know, because if you think about it, like, these religions were based — were created in a patriarchal time, so of course they would think of God as a guy. A lot of the gods in a lot of countries are guys, like Buddha or Jesus Christ or God or things like that. So I don't know how God looks, it can be he or she or yeah, it doesn't have to be white or Black. I just think it's something out there" [Sara].

Gen Zers are also finding a sense of spiritual connection through their work in community. The Nones and Nuns movement, for example, brings young, generally nonreligious adults who care about social justice together with nuns, not to learn about Roman Catholicism per se but rather to learn about how to express community and live a whole life of caring about and giving to others.[36] Moreover, as Angie Thurston and Casper ter Kuile have reported, the desire for spiritual community has fueled the popularity of seemingly secular entities like SoulCycle and CrossFit and led traditional religious groups to engage in totally new practices that highlight interfaith and community service elements.[37] Christel Manning, writing in our *Pacific Standard* series about Gen Z, notes the postmillennial "culture of choice, self-actualization, and freedom of expression" and suggests "when young people respond to a survey about religion by saying they have 'none,' it can be a way of opting out of existing religious categories." Just as there is now gender fluidity, she says, religion too can take many forms.[38] David Brooks, writing in the New York Times, similarly says, "We're living in the middle of a religious revival; it's just that the movements that are rising are not what we normally call religion."[39] Brooks goes on to cite as examples astrology, witchcraft, mindfulness, and wokeness in the social justice movement. Other observers would also include fandoms, with their worshipful devotees, and the widespread interest in fantasy and other worlds, in the list of modern alternatives to traditional religions.[40]

RELYING ON SELF AND PEERS TO MAKE A BETTER WORLD

Although postmillennials express exasperation at boomers for messing up the world (while claiming to be woke), this has not extinguished their hope; rather, it has shifted it. Gen Zers' hope largely lies in trust in their peers. As one interviewee put it, the fact that young people are starting to take charge gives her hope and makes her realize that you do not have to have a parent or an older person to make a difference [Sunita]. One said that what gave her hope was her generation's attitude and her peers using their voices to speak out, [Zoe] while another said, "People give me hope. . . . Although I feel more aware of the shit that goes on in the world, I also am more aware of all the people in all the communities that are fighting so hard to do something about it, and that's very inspiring" [Eve]. Defending against a popular perception of Gen Zers as "offended" complainers, one interviewee made clear that this generation is neither passive nor ineffective and will address the problems it has inherited:

I think the college generation right now—I have hope in people. My hope is in people, which may be a stupid thing to do, but I can't help it. I think there is a sort of backlash [against] my generation . . . as "offended people," [but] the previous generation fucked the planet for us. Climate change is real. The housing market is done. There's no jobs. The previous generation didn't care about that. We did. . . . Those things that previous generations didn't care about, that could be very, very irreversibly dangerous, I think we're going to take care of it. If anything, we may fuck a lot of shit up, but at least when I'm 70 or 80 I'll tell my grandkids, "you're breathing air because of my generation." [Benoit]

One fear among the postmillennials is that there will be no further progress in fixing serious problems. The steady belief in progress that was the backdrop to boomer life, and especially boomer activism, has withered. Our iGen Corpus shows that the words *stuck* and *stagnant* are more salient than in the data banks of language use in the broader population.[41] Sophia Pink took a road trip across America in summer 2016 while she was still a Stanford undergraduate and conducted her own study of postmillennials, uncovering something she calls "stagnaphobia." Writing for our *Pacific Standard* series on Gen Z, she explained that when she asked twenty-one-year-olds to express their "greatest fear," she assumed they would talk about a fear of change. "But over and over," she remarked, "twenty-one-year-olds told me just the opposite. They said things like, 'My biggest fear is that things just keep going on as they are.'"[42] Given their concern for both global and local issues, and anxiety about the incapacity of their elders or traditional institutions to bring about necessary change, it is no surprise that our interviewees repeatedly noted the imperative of tackling the challenges and inequalities they saw all around them. "I know what 'progress' is supposed to look like," said one interviewee, "and knowing how much progress has been made in history, I feel like I can almost taste it, yet it's so, so, so far away, and current events can feel like you're being dragged further and further away from that goal" [Eve]. Some students were very ambitious in their aspirations for changing the world, such as this one, living in the midst of Silicon Valley's ethos of "disrupt and change the world": "I want to make a huge change, especially in the visually impaired field. I want to be able to create technology that increases literacy to 100 percent ... big impact, and you can't really do high impact just working a normal desk job" [Ryan].

Intergenerational misunderstanding, or "disconnect," as one interviewee put it [Alisha], is exacerbated for Gen Zers—not only by their values, which differ from those of their parents, but also by a sense that they will need to do something different than their parents expect, in order to stick authentically to their values and take on the challenges they see in the world. For example, a Chinese American interviewee, whose parents had migrated to the US, remarked that her parents were "typical Asian immigrants" who wanted their children to do well and save money: "It's like, 'Oh, I want my children to do well. I want them to be successful.' Sometimes they can be so focused on that, that they can forget other things" [Jenni]. Parents and their children also hold different "fundamental beliefs" about the more equitable world postmillennials want to build. That interviewee's parents are "not very accepting of gay people" and "they only know the existence of male and female." Another student, who regards the major challenges of the world as climate change and discrimination against minorities, feels that she has grown up with a pessimism that her parents did not have. "So I think it's harder for me to have hope for the future than it is for my parents who have not seen that their whole lives," not least because "they've actually seen great progress" [Zoe].

This trust in their peers also means that many postmillennials are committed to trying to make a difference themselves. Nearly every person we interviewed, across our three campuses, made some kind of direct or indirect reference to having an impact or otherwise doing something to make a difference in the lives of others, whether in their immediate sphere or farther away. A Foothill student said, "Giving back to society, that's something big, I would say, like, leaving your legacy here. That's something I always wonder: what am I here for?" [Chao]. And a Lancaster student explained the significance of making others happy: "that can be, like, the tiniest little thing ... if you can make someone else happy, then you've made a difference to someone else's life at least ... something that'd mean someone would remember you, that sort of thing" [Tessa]. A Stanford student said, "I definitely want to do something that has to do with people and helping them in terms of on a day-to-day level where you interact, and so maybe that's why I'm kind of drawn to [being a] doctor" [Nicole]. Another, speaking of her good fortune in being at a top-rated school, said, "It feels like the stakes are so much higher because I've come all the way here, so I need to do something that's actually helpful for humanity or something" [Lina]. These comments accorded with our survey of the US and UK postmillennial population; when we asked whether they thought caring for self or caring for others should come first, the largest proportion of respondents in both countries said "both equally."[43]

Making a difference to and for others rates highly when Gen Zers assess what would make their own lives meaningful, not because they are looking for personal glory but because they want to add their personal efforts to a greater cause. This is not to say that they are not worried about making an adequate living: they are concerned about job security; it is rather that acquiring personal wealth and material goods is not nearly as high a priority as being able to contribute to making the world a better place. Pink's study of twenty-one year-olds also indicated this value: when she asked what would make a meaningful life, she "expect[ed] to hear about aspirations toward wealth, comfort, or happiness." Instead, she found that "most members of Gen Z desperately want to make a mark— they are just trying to figure out the right scale."[44] Our survey of a representative sample of American Gen Zers complements Pink's findings. One question asked the respondents what they personally felt was most important in their life and gave a list of options. They chose the following as their top six, in this order:

1. Having a happy marriage or life partnership
2. Having a positive impact on the world
3. Having career success
4. Having fun
5. Realizing your potential
6. Having a good education

The other options—How I look/my image, having lots of money, and owning a home—were much less popular choices.[45]

CONCLUSION

Gen Zers express a strong sense of inheriting institutional forms that are broken or incapable of solving the enormous problems the world is facing without significant change. They are therefore interested in reinventing the ways and means of effecting change, and living their daily lives.

As the next chapter explores further, rather than hoping for slow, incremental improvement to come from those currently in charge, many look for more fundamental change and either try to bring it about right now in their own lives or join with others who are campaigning to make the world better, putting pressure on institutions to change. As chapter 6 elaborates, in the US and UK some Gen Zers are pragmatic, working with what there is but remaining aloof from institutions and being careful not to be "sucked in." Others are activists working for change, though they are not necessarily averse to demanding it from existing institutions and their leaders. Yet others are just trying to make the best of what feels to them like a difficult situation, living a worthwhile life, building stable relationships, and helping others as much as they can along the way. Underlying it all are widely shared generational hopes, values, and aspirations, which often clash sharply with existing hierarchies and institutions. We will now address the tensions and paradoxes that arise from those clashes.

6

The Difficulty of Being a Gen Zer

At the click of a button, we can start a movement. . . . The weight of the world is heavy. And there's a lot going on, and there's a lot of change that we need to make and a lot more justice that we need to achieve. I would say that my peers are passionate, and I would say that my peers are frustrated, but also I think my peers are optimists. . . . We're looking at a world where there is so much injustice and brutality and unfairness and bias, and we're saying, damn it, we can't just let this keep going.

ZIAD AHMED, TWENTY-ONE-YEAR-OLD YALE STUDENT
WITH 17,000 FOLLOWERS ON TIKTOK[1]

This chapter delves into how Gen Zers are wrestling with the difficulties, paradoxes, and contradictions of the world they live in. Some of these are amplified by clashes and contradictions generated by their own value system, and others are generated when their high ideals and hopes for a better future clash with the grim realities they encounter. As their own words reveal, in the midst of ground-shaking technological and social change that has created what scholars John Seely Brown and Ann Pendleton-Jullian call "a white water world,"[2] they are struggling anew with issues that have also long engaged philosophers, political scientists, and others, including how to find an acceptable balance between the needs of the individual and the needs of the community—as well as how to preserve human values in a digital age.

We begin by looking at questions about the mental and emotional health of postmillennials; during the time when we have been doing the research for this book and writing it, hardly a week has gone by without some article in the media questioning whether post-millennials are especially prone to mental health problems. We discuss Gen Zers' openness to discussing their emotions and why they place such great value on that open expression and on self-care. We then broaden our lens to look at how Gen Zers are communally responding to the broader issues and challenges they are most worried about, including climate change, racial justice, socioeconomic inequities and uncertainties, and global violence. We describe how they perceive activism and activists differently from their elders and how they are organizing themselves for political action in new ways.

Customs, beliefs, values, and institutions that seemed entirely reasonable not long ago are being challenged, creating pressures and paradoxes that this generation feels with a particular intensity. Perhaps most significantly, this chapter offers a glimpse into how Gen Zers are wrestling with a postmillennial value system that emphasizes honoring the dignity and authenticity of every unique individual—that is, every "unicorn"—and yet, at the same time, recognizes the need for consensus and compromise among competing views and beliefs.

SNOWFLAKES WITH EXISTENTIAL CONCERNS?

Some critics of postmillennials have proposed that Gen Z is less willing than previous generations to take risks or assume adult responsibilities like driving and after-school jobs,[3] or that it is a fragile, coddled, or *snowflake* generation.[4] This was not what we found among the Gen Zers in our study, and it is certainly not how they see themselves. Several of our interviewees talked about their parents' need to stay involved in their lives, more than vice versa. As one put it, "I think my parents are just having difficulty coming to the realization that I'm more of an adult than they give me credit for" [Lauren]. Another interviewee talked about the contrast with his parents' generation, when a college degree was a guarantee of a job; as he explained, "I value hard work, even though it's like a cliché that our generation is lazy. I think it's the opposite. . . . It's so competitive [today]" [James]. Other sources underscore this point. A 2019 *New York Times* article cited stagnating wages; increased costs of college, homes, health care, and child care; and enormous student-loan debt as reasons "it has become harder to be an adult,"[5] and a 2018 *Wall Street Journal* article calls postmillennials "parsimonious" and "a scarred generation, cautious and hardened by economic and social turbulence," much like the children of the 1930s who endured the Great Depression and World War II.[6]

For the most part, Gen Zers are serious minded, even if they are not yet in the workforce or raising children, and their attitudes about what it means to be an adult, which many refer to as "adulting," are influenced by their disappointment and disillusionment with what they believe previous generations of adults have wrought. As one British student noted, "My generation feels bitter about all the things we won't be able to do because of what the older generation chose."[7]

Postmillennials believe that those judging them as snowflakes have an outdated perspective and are making unfair comparisons with the context in which they grew up. For example, in an era of Uber, Lyft, and bike sharing, having a driver's license or a car seems far less necessary to urban dwellers than in the past. Similarly, "after-school jobs" can look quite different today; some of our interviewees reported that they earned their spending money in high school and college by creating apps or adding "product placements" to their blog postings. Many have to work to support their college careers. And with the average life expectancy for their age group now moving into a person's late eighties or beyond,[8] many Gen Zers simply do not feel the same need as their elders did to get such an early start on their careers and childrearing. They are, as writers on longevity put it, already rethinking their life maps.[9] They may not be doing the same things as their parents did at their age, but this does not mean they are unprepared for adult responsibilities. On the contrary, they expect to have to work hard if they are to accomplish a widely shared goal: achieving financial security in an uncertain future.

MENTAL HEALTH: ON THE STRUGGLE BUS

For postmillennials, mental health challenges are normal. They talk openly about them all the time: it is a mark of authenticity to talk about what is going on in your life. Many of our interviewees talked honestly about experiencing periods of anxiety and depression and feeling burnout, compassion fatigue, and, at times, hopelessness. One interviewee encapsulated it: "I think that, just in general, when I'm dealing with feelings of sadness or loneliness, . . . it's best just to understand where those feelings are coming from, why you're feeling them." This student recognized that not everyone has the capacity to do that but concluded, "for me I'm able to do that pretty easily" [Cody].

Gen Zers also perceive the importance of mental health for overall well-being, and the value of connections and friendships: "I really value friendship. I think we're getting more and more lonely in a way. So friendship is important, and social interaction is important. It really matters in terms of life expectancy and things like that, you know, your psychological well-being" [Jun]. Being able to talk openly is also an important part of a generational survival strategy. As one student said, "Sometimes it feels we're just screaming at these institutions to care about us, but at least we're screaming together" [Malia].

The clear articulation of mental health issues raises the question as to whether this generation has greater mental health issues or is simply much better at naming their problems and seeking care. It is noteworthy that the word *stressful* appears in our iGen Corpus with unusually high frequency when compared with broader language use.[10] By some standardized measures, postmillennials have worse mental health than previous generations. The American Psychological Association's 2018 Stress in America (SIA) survey of 3,500 individuals across all age cohorts, for example, found that 91 percent of postmillennials aged 15 to 21 reported experiencing physical and emotional symptoms associated with stress, including depression and anxiety.[11]

What part does social media and the constant sense of being "on" contribute to mental health issues? Although some commentators have put the primary blame for this stress on social media and smartphones, as already noted, studies conducted by Andrew Przybylski and Amy Orben at the University of Oxford and Netta Weinstein at Cardiff University found that the association "between digital technology use and adolescent well-being is negative but small, explaining at most 0.4% of the variation in well-being."[12] Assessing the digital-screen usage and the mental health of 355,358 participants aged twelve to eighteen years across the UK and US, they concluded that, statistically speaking, eating a potato each day was worse for your well-being than using social media. Indeed, some of our interviewees found social media helpful in times of anxiety or loneliness. As one put it, "I would say social media has kind of helped me with a lot of college stress." This student used it "not to check out" but rather as "a reward after a class or after I do an assignment, or something like that. So it's a bit of a motivator, kind of like a good thing to look forward to, I guess, in the sense of there's going to be funny, new information waiting for me on my phone" [Bella]. Another student suggested that the "one reason why so many people in our generation turn to the internet regularly [is] 'cause maybe [when] they were growing up and their parents were both busy or uninterested for a while so they had to find something else." This comment was not the occasion for a criticism of social media so much as a wish that people might go back to "being closer with our neighbors, living with more extended family" [Vedika].

Paradoxically, some of the aspects of digital life that bring more support also bring new pressures. Social media and dating apps and the greater ease of finding relationships and community are a good example. Postmillennials speak of FOMO (fear of missing out), a term that has now come into wide usage, and while we often think about that as being largely about missing out on exciting events, parties, and socializing, there is a more serious angle to the phenomenon. For those who, despite so many possibilities, still do not find meaningful relationships and communities, the pain is particularly sharp. At scale, it feels even more isolating and lonely if you still cannot find your tribe amid the thousands of communities of people and seemingly limitless opportunities for connection. Just as the opportunities are amplified, so is the loneliness, making people think that something must truly be wrong with them if they still cannot fit in. Just as it is frustrating to try to fix a problem hundreds of times and still fail, it is hurtful to try to belong in hundreds of groups and still feel you are failing at making meaningful connection. This is the downside to the explosion of fine-grained communities and opportunities for modular belonging.

Another significant factor for mental health issues is the pressure of young adult life today and the anxiety that can come with that; the Gen Zers' context growing up has been rapid change, violence and conflict, a loss of confidence in economic growth, political uncertainty and flux. As the president of the American Psychological Association, Arthur Evans, commented on the SIA survey results cited earlier: "Current events are clearly stressful for everyone in the country, but young people are really feeling the impact of issues in the news, particularly those issues that may feel beyond their control."[13] A high-schooler in Silicon Valley made the same point: "I don't understand why adults are so worried about social media. I'm much more likely to get killed at school than I am on Instagram."[14] Seventy-five percent of the SIA respondents said that mass shootings are a significant source of stress in their lives, a finding that jibes with what many of our US (but not UK) research participants said. One of our interviewees described the impact of an unprecedented information overload about traumatic and disturbing events, which earlier generations did not face at the same scale:

In this age, we have information overload. You can go look at pictures from the Vietnam War, or the Syrian Crisis, or, like, the Rohingya Crisis and, like, the ungodly amount of other atrocities in the world. And the question isn't "Can you?" It's "Will you?" and "Do you want to?" and "Are you willing to put in that emotional energy and time?" And for most people, it's going to be no, on one of those counts. And I get it because it's like, if I get into—like, if I read the news for too long, like, I get into, like, a news hole, and it feels like, shit, like, oh God, everything is hopeless. So I understand. But I think it's more of a matter of filtering out the excess content that we have been given, via technology, that other generations didn't need to think about. [Eve]

Gen Zers especially are drawing new attention to the significant impact of racism on mental health, pointing to the ways in which constantly struggling against systemic and institutional racism, and experiencing multiple microaggressions every day, is both exhausting and stressful, and can be profoundly traumatic.[15] Our Black interviewees were especially aware of this issue. One, when asked what causes were important to her, said: "Just taking the care that needs to be shown because so many populations, especially women of color, are really, really vulnerable" [Ayotunde]. Young Minds, the leading UK charity fighting for young people's mental health, notes on its website, "Being treated differently or unfairly because of our race, skin colour or ethnicity can negatively affect our mental health," and then offers practical advice and resources for help.[16] A young Black male, Wes, blogging on the Young Minds site, points out that, because racism is damaging to mental health, in the UK "Black British people are more likely to be diagnosed with psychosis, to encounter inpatient mental health services and to be detained under the Mental Health Act than white people — these are things we need to talk about."[17] The link between activism and mental health here is important; while activist postmillennials report that their mental health is affected by racism, they also feel hopeful about the future because of the widespread support that the Black Lives Matter movement has received.[18]

Postmillennials grew up "more aware of and accepting of mental health issues"[19] and in increasingly medicalized societies amid increasingly common diagnoses of ADHD, autism, dyslexia, and more, and with the growing acceptance of personal and family therapy, the use of mood-regulating drugs for children, and what one psychiatrist termed "a cultural shift toward pathologizing everyday levels of stress."[20] It is natural for them to include a mental health diagnosis in the different attributes or markers of their identity, as this interviewee did: "my different identities, I think they make me who I am ... [but] not to say, oh, my only identity is being Black, and a lesbian, and someone with ADHD, or ad nauseum" [Ayotunde]. They also grew up being told to respect their own feelings. Add to this the high value they place on honesty and being aware of how they are and how others feel, plus a deep level of digital connection and sharing among close friends, and it is no surprise that talking about mental health has become both a symptom and a way of dealing with some of the many pressures of the digital age. As one student commented: "I think we're actually under huge pressure—my generation" [Jun].

FINDING SOLACE

So how do the Gen Zers find solace and respond to their own and their peers' mental health issues? When our survey respondents in both the US and Britain were asked "What do you do if you feel overwhelmed in life?" and could choose two out of nine options, including "other" and "don't know," they gave remarkably similar answers: 45 percent selected "fix it myself," around 30 percent selected "retreat into myself," while about 25 percent chose "reach out to friends" and another 25 percent said "reach out to family." Interestingly, there was some national difference (perhaps confirming the British stereotype of "keep calm and carry on") in the two surveys: a quarter of Brits said they would "ignore and carry on" compared with one-fifth in the US. Twice the number of Americans said they would "consult a professional" (10 percent) compared with about 5 percent in the UK. The answer that they "never feel overwhelmed" was selected by less than 5 percent of the respondents in each country.[21]

Gen Zers highlight reliance on self and peers to address emotional concerns. Among the interviewees who talked about using self-help and self-care for their emotional problems was this student, describing how she deals with anxiety: "First, I try to meditate. Secondly, if this anxiety is so intense, really, really intense, I will make an appointment with psychological services. Thirdly, I will talk to my friends and hang out with them. Simply having interactions makes a complete difference" [Liling]. Others said they would try to "get away" from negative emotions, taking time for self-care activities like gardening or working out [Phoebe, Cody, Vedika], while another said her approach is "reflecting a lot on, like, why am I having these feelings in the first place?" [Sara]. A male student described self-care behaviors as a useful "way of asserting control and finding comfort in an unstable world" [Lee].

Owning your vulnerability and inability to cope extends to the classroom, and students increasingly prioritize self-care over their studies, even if that means accepting lower grades because of incomplete or late assignments. As one student put it: "This quarter especially, I'm prioritizing my happiness over anything else, because in the past two quarters I got a 4.0 [a high grade] but at the cost of having fun, and I went out quite a bit but also I was just too stressed and too hard on myself. Like today I have something due that I'm not that stressed about. . . . I'm not holding myself to the standards that I used to because those standards aren't realistic" [Lee]. Teaching and advising undergraduates over the past few years, we, along with many of our colleagues, have encountered students willing to accept a late grade penalty rather than endanger their well-being. Their priority is to balance time for themselves with producing a quality paper, and they respect the associated grade penalties.

Another aspect of self-reliance in mental health for Gen Zers relates to trigger warnings and safe spaces. They think of these things not as signs of snowflake sensitivity but rather as elements of mental self-care and consideration of others, offering opportunities to make choices and exercise personal control over issues that might be emotionally distressing. Triggers are anything that remind someone of a previous trauma, so warnings are a way of enabling people to prepare for what is coming up. As one interviewee explained: "When there are trigger warnings, it's not that we don't want to read the content, it's just we want some sort of warning as to what to expect. . . . I feel like trigger warnings get so excessively politicized when it's really just like a polite 'Heads up—this might get a little dicey!'" [Ashton]. Our interviewees expected trigger warnings and explained the unwritten rules: "I'm in a variety of Facebook groups that are originally meme groups where people share stories and stuff, and so most of them have a rule where you—if there's anything questionable—you put a trigger or content warning and then you add a bunch of dots so that by the time your text is there it shrinks it . . . so I'll be like, 'Oh, content warning, OK, I'll just skip by it'" [Ashton]. This can be seen as kindness and consideration for others' feelings.

For Gen Zers, a safe space allows a person to step away from potentially stressful situations into a place of comfort and support. Many of our interviewees articulated the need to feel safe and secure, especially in light of the kinds of abusive opinions and behaviors that have become so prevalent online. Growing awareness of racial, sexual, and other forms of abuse and harassment is another part of the background. The issue of caution and safety is complex for this age cohort, many of whom were allowed to roam freely around the internet as children but warned about the physical dangers of their neighborhoods. As danah boyd notes of many of the teens in her study, they "believed that danger lurked everywhere."[22] Our interviewees saw the pros and cons to the fact that social media give everyone a voice. One interviewee said that the internet had toughened them up and prepared them for the more difficult aspects of life at an earlier age than had occurred for their parents: "You learn early that there will always be haters." The same student felt "more exposed to and expectant of negativity" but felt that "learning to not care about this is a rite of passage that everyone must go through, especially celebrities" [Eve].

In addition to clearly articulating their strategies for self-care, our interviewees thoughtfully talked about seeking help from others. One student who was diagnosed with depression and anxiety said he preferred talking with his friends over his parents because his parents "don't understand mental health at all." He went on to say that "it's a lot more okay now to say you have depression or anxiety about life in general, it's becoming a very normal thing, whereas . . . to be accused of having one of those things in [my parents' generation] was absolutely the opposite . . . and associated with lunacy." As a result, he "doesn't check in with my parents emotionally because [he] doesn't want them to worry . . . and it would probably make me feel worse." Instead, he "exclusively [goes] to [his] friends," because they can give him the kind of emotional support that he needs [Gabe]. In turn, interviewees expressed the wish to help others, like a student who was diagnosed with major depression when younger but got better with psychotherapy, antidepressants, and meditation, and wants in the future to use his experience and help by offering "some valuable assistance to other people" [Jun].

Even over the three years that our research took place, we observed a growing openness among our interviewees in discussing their mental health issues, as illustrated by a change of language. At the start of our research in 2016, many Stanford students still spoke about themselves as having *duck syndrome*, a term long used on that campus to describe maintaining a composed outward appearance while paddling furiously beneath the surface. When creating a dictionary of iGen [Gen Z] language in a linguistics class, the students chose to demonstrate the meaning of the term with this sentence, "Duck syndrome is so real at Stanford, everyone tries to look like they're not trying."[23] An article in the student newspaper, *Stanford Daily*, noted in 2016: "Whether we're talking about our culture of overwork or obsession with perfection, or even if we're talking about the grim realities of college suicides, duck syndrome is our way of talking about mental health on college campuses."[24] A year or two later, however, students had stopped using the term *duck syndrome*, replacing it with expressions that admit vulnerability, like *struggle bus* or *The Struggle*, which they define as "an ongoing state of insecurity, or stress and anxiety." Openly discussing their emotional issues has become the norm on that campus, and Facebook groups such as The Stanford University Places I've Cried helped facilitate this change in culture. "Initially it started because it was funny, but I also wanted it to be a place where you can combat duck syndrome," said the group's creator, "It's okay to be kind of messed up."[25] Students also became more sensitive to, and respectful of, how their varying experiences could cause different kinds of stress: "The able-bodied, heterosexual cisgender white man who struggles with engineering classes experiences 'stress' or 'mental health' in completely different ways than does the queer woman of color involved in activism and cycling through different medications for her depression or the first-generation international college student scraping through with insufficient financial aid," explained the author of an article in the student newspaper.[26]

In speaking out about their mental health concerns, Gen Zers are both inspired by, and strive to emulate, the public figures they admire who share their own struggles. Influencers, celebrities, and sports personalities of all ages are now using their platforms to share their personal experiences with depression, anxiety, and stress. Pop icons like Selena Gomez, Demi Lovato, Justin Bieber, Halsey, Lili Reinhart, and Ariana Grande have all been candid with their fans about their struggles with mental health, taking to social media to share their stories, talk about how they sought treatment, and encourage others to destigmatize mental health by talking about it. In tweets and emotional Instagram posts, including a photo of her brain scan, Ariana Grande shared how the posttraumatic stress disorder caused by the bomb attack at her concert in Manchester, UK, was later triggered by the death of an ex-boyfriend. In the immediate aftermath, she had the strength and sensitivity to lead a moving tribute event for the victims, which many survivors found very healing. These public statements have helped shape the ongoing movement to end the stigma surrounding mental illness and make people more aware of their own emotional and mental health.

The postmillennial singer Halsey describes the sense of responsibility she feels in relation to discussing publicly her bipolar disorder, treatment for it, and self-care. Her album *Manic* was so named because of her own mental health diagnosis. In a *Time* story about her as a next-generation leader, published in autumn 2020, she said that she started taking medication during the COVID-19 lockdown, admitting that she was deprived of her nightly cocktail of dopamine and applause. Previously she had avoided medication for fear it would dampen her creativity but now says, "It has changed my life." The article goes on to discuss that sense of (public) responsibility:

On social media, she feels a responsibility to document these pieces of her life. She'll reference SSRIs [antidepressants] in an offhand response explaining a vivid dream, post an unedited selfie or go off about her frustration at seeing people in line for nightclubs. She spends time lurking on fan group chats too. "Every couple months, I'm learning about a new orientation I've never heard of that makes a group of people feel valid," she says. "The best thing that I can do with my given platform is to adapt as the world adapts."[27]

Memes are one of the ways in which Gen Zers deal with mental and emotional health issues. "People take their depression or mental health issues and turn [them] into weird memes," said one interviewee. "All the horrible things—not only are we already looking at [them], we're making jokes so it's less scary" [Andy]. Another student, who described herself as someone who "internalizes everything," said it was often difficult to talk to others about feeling "pretty anxious and stressed, like, all of the time" but that humor provided solace: "I'm not great at dealing with emotions of any kind really. Mostly, I just laugh" [Lauren]. One Instagram and Twitter meme group, called "manicpixiememequeen," has over 100,000 followers who make, share, and repost mental illness memes.

While such meme groups have been criticized as minimizing the seriousness of mental health issues, or fueling the problem, they also offer a way to assuage pain and anxiety through a medium that is well suited to offering "relatability" and some sense of personal control and support ("you are not alone" is a reiterated Gen Z message). A study at Sheffield Hallam University investigated the use of depressive memes and found that the emotional valence, humor, relatability, shareability, and mood-improving potential of mental health memes were beneficial for people suffering from consistent symptoms of depression.[28]

Memes provide an arguably "shallower" way of talking about the issues, but it is that shallowness that makes it easier for some people to externalize and talk about their worries, fears, and problems. Not only do the memes provide a humorous take on a negative emotion or experience, but they allow the perception of peer support and a sense of belonging to a community that understands and shares in your pain.

CHANGING THE WORLD: GEN ZERS' BIGGEST CONCERNS

Gen Zers feel a responsibility to "make a difference" and make the world a better place, whether in big ways or small, alone or as a generation. They worry about environmental degradation, inequality, violence, and injustice. Many wish for civil and political institutions that, as one person put it, will "protect the right for [all] individuals to be their authentic, real selves without dictating who they are" [Eve].

Our interviewees revealed that their deepest concerns were related to big, global issues. This was true across the three campuses. Of all the issues discussed, climate change was mentioned with the greatest frequency in relation to their hopes and fears for the future. As one student said, "Climate change. I think that's the only thing that can make people take responsibilities because their own interest is at stake. We are all self-interested. We're not selfish, but we're self-interested, so we know that if this is going to do harm to us we will try to limit [it]" [Jun]. Another student called climate change "a huge existential threat on a level that hasn't really been seen in the world before" [Clare]. Yet another said, "I'm very scared that the earth will die [from climate change] while I'm still alive" [Grace]. The recent extinction of certain species was also highlighted, as was a loss of empathy toward the planet, animals, and nonhuman life in general. This concern with climate change also stretches across the political party spectrum in this generation, and a recent Pew Research Center Survey has confirmed that climate change is not just an issue for liberals among postmillennials. That survey shows that postmillennial and millennial Republicans (eighteen to thirty-nine years old) are more concerned about the climate than their elders are. By a nearly two-to-one margin, they are more likely to agree that "human activity contributes a great deal to climate change," and "the federal government is doing too little to reduce the effects of climate change."[29] Some Gen Zer conservatives are starting environmental groups and becoming climate activists. Benji Backer, for example, a self-described "entrepreneur and political activist," started the American Conservation Coalition (ACC) in 2017, after his first year in college."[30] It is striking that the entire leadership team of the ACC is made up of Gen Zers. In an interview with NPR, he said that his love of nature comes in part from his family. "They were Audubon members, Nature Conservancy members. But they were conservative, and I grew up not thinking that the environment should be political at all."[31]

Inequality, especially in relation to race, gender, and sexuality though also in connection with questions of global resources, is not surprisingly an area of high concern for Gen Zers. A heterosexual East European student said she hoped that in ten years' time, same-sex marriages would be recognized everywhere and that it would no longer be illegal to be gay anywhere, including the Middle East [Irina]. For a Black gender-fluid student, it was the criminal justice system that was their number one concern: "I really care about that just because I know people who have family who were incarcerated, . . . whether that be in jail or prison. Yeah, that's just the reality. It's not, like, anything to be sad about, . . . [but it is] a very, like, huge thing that I care about" [Travis]. On issues of resource distribution, a white student of Danish descent pointed to global population growth and said, "We have to find a way to make sure that everyone is getting a piece of the pie because there's so many more who have to share" [Nicole]. A student from the Middle East listed her big concerns as refugees, Islamophobia, perceptions of Arabs—especially Muslim Arabs—as terrorists, and sexuality and freedom [Hiba]. A queer Black cis man stressed that voting rights were an issue of concern: "I've seen how indifference in communities can lead them to not having the best results. . . . People where I live just don't know that things are happening. Or don't know about the forces that are at work in a general manner, or in a general sense. So for me, political activism is about informing people about those things" [Jaden].

The prevention of violence is also regarded as a high priority. An interviewee in the US named gun control as one of her top priori-

ties, one she felt was widely shared by her age peers: "With everything, the shootings going around now in the States, I feel like you
have kids, even—well, us college students, but high school students
as well, they just want gun reform. They want stricter laws that pre-
vent people from buying guns that are not really—shouldn't be—
that accessible to have" [Maya]. A student at Lancaster also talked
about global violence and global warming and other looming dangers: "I feel like the world in ten years' time, ideally for myself I'd like
it to be politically at ease. Like, the war in Syria will have ended, the
threat of terrorism will be less of a threat, and that kind of thing. The
threat of global warming will have decreased. Just generally looming, I don't know, apocalyptic things will become less of a danger"
[Kylie]. For another student, domestic violence is a priority to be
tackled; as she put it, "relationship violence, intimate partner violence has always been really important to me" [Ayotunde].

Gen Zers across the UK and US—not just college students—
more generally share these concerns. In our representative surveys
of postmillennials in the UK and US, we asked: "Of the following
large-scale issues, what worries you most?" Respondents could
select two from the options we gave them. As figure 15 illustrates,
by far the biggest worry in both the US and UK was the future of the
planet, and the least worrisome issue was technology. The biggest
difference between respondents in the two countries was the higher
level of concern about crime and violence in the US, where the level
of both is indeed higher.

When the lens of ethnicity is added to the survey of biggest concerns, there is an important variation in priorities. While the differences between college-educated or not were insignificant, there
was substantial variation by ethnicity, as table 6 shows. Crime and
violence are more important concerns for Black, Latino, and Asian
postmillennials than they are for white people, whose main priority
is the environment. This should not be surprising, given the ongoing
police violence against African Americans, in particular, in the US.

Some interviewees characterized themselves and their peers as
liberal. As one student said: "I think our generation is a lot more
liberal than previous generations." This came from a deep sense

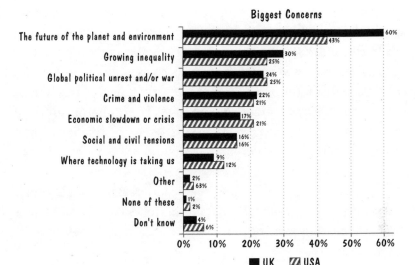

FIGURE 15. Gen Z Survey, UK and US responses to the question "Of the following large-scale issues, which worries you most? Select up to two."

TABLE 6. Gen Z Survey, UK and US combined responses by race to the question "Of the following large-scale issues, which worries you most? Select up to two."

	WHITE	BLACK	LATINO	ASIAN
Fugure of planet and environment	51%	29%	35%	38%
Economic slowdown or crisis	15%	19%	18%	15%
Social and civil tensions	22%	23%	15%	30%
Growing inequality	27%	23%	25%	21%
Crime and violence	21%	33%	27%	28%
Global political unrest and/or war	23%	16%	18%	30%
Where technology is taking us	11%	13%	12%	15%

that her generation shares values and concerns about issues such as "immigration, education, healthcare, racial equality, and police brutality," all concerning respect for others and their well-being. She concluded, "I don't know why we've become a liberal generation ... [except] I feel like over time we become more progressive" [Sara]. We recognize that younger generations—especially those in the eighteen- to twenty-five-year-old range—often identify as more liberal. We also note there were some students in our interview groups across the three campuses who did not fit with this sense of being progressive, whether because of their political position, their religion, or their cultural background. They were quick to articulate how conscious they were of not sharing the prevalent thinking of their generation. We have tried to represent their views throughout this book, and we were struck by those conservative students who articulated their position as that of the outlier, such as this American student: "I'm a bit more conservative. I'm Christian, so I have a different set of values. Freshman year, I was much more open to talking about those. And a lot of people would get pretty mad at me." The hot topics on which she differed with her peers were "gay marriage, or abortion, or I guess welfare programs, things like that. Sometimes it'd be about taxes or gun control. Some of which I have since changed my mind on, but I feel my core beliefs have stayed the same" [Malia].

IDENTIFYING AS AN ACTIVIST

Today, "coming of age" means marching in the streets to protest the deaths of your friends by gun violence, resigning yourself to decades of student debt, and crossing your fingers and hoping you'll one day be able to buy a house. [Postmillennials] know that issues like gun violence, climate change, international conflict, the threat of nuclear warfare, and racism will not end before they come of age. They know that these are the challenges that will face their generation as soon as they are old enough to take charge of the world. But for now, many can only worry, while waiting in the wings. [Eve]

Activism among postmillennials has made a big impact during the period that we researched and wrote this book (2016–2020). The big areas of concern articulated by Gen Zers indicate the range of issues, some local and close to home, some national and some global, that those who are activists choose to embrace. Certain causes close to home—for example, on campus—were viewed as microcosms of bigger issues, like racism and inequality or global warming. As we have seen, students protest about a lack of diversity among faculty and in what they study, calling for a decolonization of the curriculum; others seek divestment of fossil fuel stocks from university endowment funds. Student activists and their supporters regard campaigns to take down campus statues and rename buildings that pay homage to those involved in slave trading or colonialism, like "Rhodes Must Fall" in Oxford or the renaming of Serra Mall in Stanford, as essential—removing symbols of historical wrongs indicates that norms have changed and that such wrongs will no longer be tolerated or perpetuated—while critics regard this as merely symbolic or the dangerous removal of history.

The term *activist* is used as a term of esteem and respect among Gen Zers. We found that many of our interviewees would not call themselves activists precisely because they did not feel their work on social issues was significant enough to merit the label in comparison with those who were investing substantial time and energy in community organizing or political action. As one white cis female student explained, "I think generally activism is more defined just by people who have a really passionate stronghold on something and want to actually see change realized, so I think there is a spectrum of people who are on that" [Madison]. One Black student who self-identifies as queer said this about whether to call herself an activist:

> I wouldn't consider myself an activist mostly because I think I really wanted to be. I wanted to be for a long time, but I think that for me, there's a distinction between doing community work and being an activist, and I wish it was a distinction that more people made. Not to say that people shouldn't be activists because people should be activists, but I think a lot of people don't have the time or the care to really focus in on activism. The time, or the care, or the experience. [Ayotunde]

This interviewee illustrates the careful thought that Gen Zers put into whether to call themselves an activist; there may also be a sense of perfectionism, too. The postmillennial singer, songwriter, and activist Halsey reminds her followers that activism does not need to be perfect: "There is no such thing as a perfect activist. Everyone has said something, done something wrong.... I fall in between two chairs, ... which means sometimes, I end up on the floor."[32]

TABLE 7. Gen Z Survey, UK and US
responses to the question "Are you
involved in any social causes or
activism?"

	UK	US
Yes	19%	26%
No	69%	60%
Don't know	12%	14%

By contrast, in the language of Gen Zers, calling someone a *social justice warrior*, or *SJW*, is not a compliment. The term mocks those who are seen as advocating for progressive causes more out of ego than heartfelt concern or who are overly ideological and too easily offended. Gen Zers also use the terms *snowflake* and *slacktivist* to insult those whose public advocacy feels less than fully authentic, either because it reflects too extreme a sensitivity (e.g., the alt-right often calls liberals "snowflakes") or because the advocacy efforts are too minimal or risk-free to have any real impact.

Activism is not merely the preserve of campus politics or college students. In our survey of UK and US postmillennials, we asked if they were "involved in any social causes or activism." In both the US and the UK, the majority answered "no," but one-fifth in the UK and one-quarter in the US said "yes," and a small but significant percentage responded "don't know" (see table 7).

However, given that postmillennials are reticent about self-identifying as activists, these figures may underestimate what they are actually *doing*, in terms of trying to make change. The "don't know" category may therefore be of particular significance here. Furthermore, initial polling suggests that the number of postmillennials engaging in activism increased in 2020, in the wake of continued police brutality against Black people and the spread and increased influence of the Black Lives Matter movement.[33]

We have seen lots about Gen Z activism recently, and not only in light of the high visibility of the gun-reform campaigns organized by high school students in Texas and the climate change movements inspired by the actions and words of Greta Thunberg.

Some commentators criticize these efforts as naïve and unsophisticated,[34] while other scholars suggest that a new kind of activism is afoot—one that reflects a new "participatory politics," defined as "interactive, peer-based acts through which individuals and groups seek to exert both voice and influence on issues of public concern."[35] Henry Jenkins and Sangita Shresthova, referring to the findings of a study by the Youth and Participatory Politics Research Network, amplify the point: "We can sum up some of the shifts we are describing as a change from thinking of politics in terms of special events, such as elections, toward understanding political participation as part of a larger lifestyle, one closely integrated into other dimensions of young people's social and cultural lives."[36] John Palfrey and Urs Gasser make a similar comment based on their study of those who were "born digital": "This is not an apathetic bunch; it's just a group of young people getting engaged in civic life on their own terms, in their own way."[37] Veronica Terriquez, working with student coauthor May Lin, has studied activism among the teenage and young adult children of immigrants and has pointed to the ways in which that group has mobilized the vote among their peers.[38]

GEN ZERS' MODES AND METHODS OF ACTIVISM

Postmillennial activism takes a variety of forms. Whether calling themselves activists or not, various interviewees expressed their disillusionment with the usual means of political engagement because they feel that political and other institutions are overly hierarchical and distant, and are failing to solve the world's biggest problems. Some students in both Britain and America reported being actively involved in mainstream politics and political parties, but they were relatively unusual. It was more common to target politics as a means of bringing about change over a particular issue. One Black male student described activism as taking two main forms: "informing people about issues" and "working with people like politicians, organizations, that are making decisions" [Jaden].

Social media is central to Gen Zer activism.[39] The same student noted that it is vital in "spreading information" and "helping people to become better and more informed." The two key issues that he posts about are voting rights and the criminal justice system, and its failures. In the second area of activism that he highlights, his main engagements are campus-based, "protecting and defending minorities." It is through campus politics that he has become disillusioned about the capacity to make change through existing institutions: "I feel like I'm someone who is very ambitious about what they want to do, and about how they want to change the world, and change their communities that they're involved in. But I've come to understand, sadly, that there are a lot of institutional limits. And that's the way that systems and institutions are set up" [Jaden].

During the 2020 US election, TikTok, by then one of the most downloaded apps among postmillennials, went from being a platform for teenagers to lip-sync and dance to being a platform for political engagement and campaigning. Virtual collab houses, or *hype houses* (*hype* is slang for exciting), that is, collectives of postmillennial social media creators, discussed in a previous chapter, emerged as important conduits for political engagement. Representing all political persuasions, but overall, more conservative than liberal, these groups of like-minded activists shared TikTok account usernames and passwords in order to collaborate with each other and post political content. In essence, these hype houses became short-form TV networks, which were dubbed "cable news for young people."[40]

Gen Z activists also use platforms such as TikTok to disrupt systems and highlight issues of concern. Postmillennials—especially KPop fans—used TikTok to book seats for Donald Trump's rally in Tulsa, Oklahoma, in June 2020, with no intention of showing up. Ahead of time, Trump's team had reported that they had been overwhelmed by requests for tickets, but on the day of the rally the 19,000-seat venue was only partially filled, with just 6,200 tickets scanned for entry.[41] The postmillennials had used internet ticket booking sites to disrupt a controversial event: it was a political rally—launching Trump's campaign to be reelected as president—in a place that had witnessed a terrible massacre of African Americans in 1921; it was initially scheduled for a date that was meaningful to African Americans, Juneteenth, the anniversary of the emancipation of slaves in the US; and it was a live event scheduled while the COVID-19 pandemic raged, without seeming concern. The idea for the protest came from Mary Jo Laupp, a fifty-one-year-old woman in Iowa (known as "the TikTok Grandma") who then partnered with postmillennials, after the TikTok video, in which she suggested the protest, went viral.[42] She and postmillennials continued their cross-generational collaboration to protest Trump's campaign in other digital ways: excessively clicking on Trump campaign ads on Facebook so that the ads expired after a certain number of clicks and cost money to be relaunched and deliberately reducing the available inventory on Trump's campaign merchandise website by loading up their shopping carts but never actually buying the products.[43]

As we complete this book, the 2020 developments of the global COVID-19 pandemic, the Black Lives Matter demonstrations, and the Presidential election in the US have all had considerable impact on postmillennials (and their elders). Already, the Black Lives Matter movement, and postmillennial championing of it, has had a striking effect, stirring universities in the US and UK to reconsider their curriculum and look at the calls to decolonize it, as well as making greater efforts to increase ethnic diversity among faculty and staff. The toppling of statues, such as the late nineteenth-century statue of the seventeenth-century slave trader Edward Colston in Bristol, UK, resulted in high-profile events. Describing how Black Lives Matter inspired her own activism, the singer Halsey said, "I went to the first protest not knowing what to expect. I came home shot twice with rubber ammunition. . . . That was a real wake up call for me." She later returned with medical supplies, helping injured protesters with skills picked up from her emergency medical technician mother, and then launched the Black Creators Funding Initiative to award $10,000 grants to Black artists.[44]

Gen Zer employees are also increasingly bringing their concerns about justice and respect for others to the workplace: they are asking that companies pay attention to diversity in their workforce, monitor their supply chain and the effects of what they are producing on the environment, and eliminate the gender pay gap. In addition, they are asking that companies make provision for their employees' mental as well as physical health—a key issue, as we have seen.

WHEN VALUES CONFLICT

In this chapter, we have looked at the pressures on Gen Zers, the issues they care most about, the sense of burden that they carry, and how they respond to all of this. These pressures and the postmillennials' responses to them can produce paradoxes and conflicts, in light of the values that so many of them share, as discussed throughout this book. Furthermore, Gen Zers' commitments to dealing with their biggest concerns raise questions about how change might occur in the digital age given their prevalent ways of being.

Controversies about freedom of speech reveal one of the paradoxes with which postmillennials are wrestling: they strongly value autonomy and individual freedom of action, but they equally strongly value diversity, equity, and inclusion, as well as the righting of past wrongs, and those values come into conflict when a speaker is free to say something derogatory or otherwise harmful to certain persons and groups. Respect for authentically forged identity is at stake. This kind of conflict has long been associated with the exercise of free speech, as we saw, for example, with the Salman Rushdie affair in 1988, when Rushdie was subjected to death threats after a Muslim cleric declared a novel he had written to be blasphemy, but the issue is magnified in the digital age, when access to powerful digital "megaphones" is so easy, and a large, potentially global audience is in reach.

Gen Zers are struggling with freedom of speech on their campuses and in their communities, online and off. The majority of the interviewees across the three campuses in our study expressed anxiety about the effects of hate speech, drawing on their own values and influenced by the way moderators of online groups successfully impose some limits on speech within their communities. As one interviewee put it: "You just know that if people aren't held responsible for what they say and think, it's just going to go wrong" [Jess].

A 2018 survey of over 4,000 university students in the US, conducted by College Pulse and commissioned by the Knight Foundation, reported that "students are divided over whether it's more important to promote an inclusive society that welcomes diverse groups or to protect the extremes of free speech, even if those protections come at the expense of inclusivity." In this survey, the students were divided about 50–50, with the balance tipping toward believing that hate speech ought to be protected under the First Amendment overall; a notable exception was seen, however, in the view of students from historically marginalized groups, such as African Americans, and those who are gender nonconforming, gay, or lesbian, for whom hate speech has had, and continues to have, a disproportionately negative effect on their daily lives.[45] A 2020 Gallup study, also supported by the Knight Foundation, looking at the views of 3,000 American college students about the First Amendment and free expression, underscores that this particular tension between values remains unresolved and further confirms that there is a variation of opinion on this matter according to race, ethnicity, and gender.[46]

The conflict between stopping hate speech and allowing freedom of expression online indicates another twist in this dilemma. Increased policing of hate speech on the main social media platforms (e.g., Twitter banned both the rapper Azealia Banks after a racial attack on the pop star Zayn Malik and the alt-right political commentator Milo Yiannopoulos after harassment of the actress Leslie Jones) may be widely regarded as positive, but it has also spawned the growth of new "free speech" platforms such as Parler, created in 2018, and Gab, created in 2017. However, a study of hate speech on Reddit in 2015, before and after its closing of two particularly obnoxious subreddits, one on race and the other relating to appearance/body weight, revealed that banning on social media can work: more abusive accounts than expected stopped using the site, and those that stayed moved as "migrants" to other subreddits and drastically decreased their hate speech by at least 80 percent.[47]

There are contexts in which many Gen Zers are critical of attacks on free speech. As discussed in a previous chapter, the Chinese-owned short-video app TikTok has received criticism for banning and censoring content. Behind the lure of TikTok's carefree branding of "optimizing happiness" lurks a more sinister side, which is not lost on postmillennials, especially those from minority backgrounds who have experienced censorship and silencing on the platform. "Isn't this funny—TikTok doesn't silence Black creators?" asked twenty-three-year-old @bjfromtheburbs ironically. She continued, "Then why did they take my sound down from my video, my pro-Black rap that went viral yesterday? I wonder, huh?" In this case, far from silencing the voice of a postmillennial activist, these censoring tactics inspired her to tag her future posts with hashtags which helped surface her videos in other feeds and searches (e.g., #blackcreatorsfedup, #blackvoicesheard, #blacktiktok), thereby widening her audience.

Resolving the issue of free speech, along with other value conflicts and tensions, is a work in progress for all of us, but it will continue to fall significantly on the shoulders of postmillennials.[48] Henry Jenkins, in talking about the two "core concepts" of "democracy" and "diversity" and the need for "new personal and collective ethics," puts the conflicts in context: "Right now, we are at a moment of transition. For many of us, we are experiencing a significant expansion of our communicative capacities within a networked culture, yet very little in our past has taught us how to use those expanded capacities responsibly or constructively. If that transition takes place, it's bound to be enormously disruptive. It's confusing, there are ethical dilemmas, [and] none of us know how to use that power."[49]

A clash of values also occurs with the related issue of identity and its role in both expressing and resolving larger social problems. Gen Zers prioritize identity as central to their lives, as so much of this book shows. This means that many of them see identity as central to politics, and they understand and support a single-minded approach to righting historical wrongs. As one interviewee said: "A generation that recognizes the 'personal is political' is one that is aware that all political issues will fundamentally affect others' ability to live their life. The political has *always* been personal—but historically, the people who have been harmed by these political decisions have not always had the voice or communities to say something about it" [Eve]. This was the perspective of the vast majority of students we interviewed. However, figuring out how to structure social institutions that honor and respect diversity, equity, and inclusion, on the one hand, but can determine and promote what is in "the common good," on the other, is a huge challenge. As another interviewee said, identity politics can lead to a sense that "truth and facts . . . no longer carry the meaning that they used to," meaning "we're kind of in this era where it doesn't really matter what people say. It's who says it that matters. It's no longer 'what does that person have to say?' It's 'does that person belong to my group?'" [Benoit].

In thinking about how to resolve the tensions between these conflicting values, the political scientist Francis Fukuyama, in his 2018 book on identity, suggests that the current emphasis on identity needs to be brought into public policies and actions. He argues, "We will not escape from thinking about ourselves and our society in identity terms. But we need to remember that the identities dwelling deep inside us are neither fixed nor necessarily given to us by our accidents of birth. Identity can be used to divide, but it can and has also been used to integrate."[50] Veronica Terriquez, working with student coauthors, has shown how postmillennials are developing organizational skills to achieve their political ends of creating more equitable institutions.[51] This takes postmillennial politics beyond simply putting pressure on institutions, important as that is, to developing and enacting strategies for change. Another idea is that of "deliberative democracy," which "involves using scientific sampling methods to recruit a body of average citizens indicative of the public at large to discuss and debate key issues in calm and sober settings."[52] All of these suggestions indicate that cross-generational work will be needed to resolve effectively the tensions between old and new ways of thinking about identity, diversity, equity, and inclusion.

Working out how to balance the values of self-agency and self-care with the value of honoring the identity and agency of peers, while promoting the common good, is another area of tension for Gen Zers. Value conflicts can be felt in uniquely personal ways, as we saw with the student who had been an early member of the 4chan community but left when he found that community's misogyny and racism was conflicting with his growing appreciation of feminism and minority rights. Another of our interviewees described her confusion about what to do about a friend who always was late to meet with her. She explained that while she of course wanted to honor and respect his unique identity, choices, and lifestyle—including his habitual tardiness—she was also frustrated by how that conflicted with her sense that he was then not respecting her identity and preference for timeliness [Lily].

Finally, Gen Zer concerns about self-care, mental health, and achieving a good work/life balance can bump up against a variety of behavioral norms and traditional values. There are indications, however, that the expression of those concerns is already affecting various aspects of daily life and society, including the workplace. A 2019 article in the *New York Times*, titled "Young People Are Going to Save Us All from Office Life," reports that while the trend is just starting, "more companies are offering sabbaticals; free plane tickets for vacations; meditation rooms; exercise or therapy breaks; paid time off to volunteer; and extended paid family leave," all in response to demands from young employees for flexibility and balance. The article concludes with this statement from a young employee: "We are just fed up and fired up about asking for what we need. . . . We're changing the rules. We're the ones tasked with: Let's change the system so that we can all succeed."[53]

The coronavirus lockdowns unexpectedly brought about some of this change more broadly, as our homes became our workplaces and schoolrooms. In that sense, this pandemic period marks the time when the rest of society began to catch up with postmillennials. Whether Gen Zers will have been better placed—given their fluidity with technology—and prepared to deal with the loneliness that comes, for some at least, from working at home remains to be seen.[54]

CONCLUSION

Social change rarely comes easily, and Gen Zers are already experiencing conflicts between their deeply felt values and expectations and the reality of what they experience. They are wrestling with how to bring about change, and whether and how to do that within or outside the institutions they have inherited. These issues are not unique to them; across the generations, there is speculation about the future of representative democracy, privacy, capitalism, and free speech in a digital age.

Knowing when and how to prioritize certain of their own values over others is still a subject of experimentation for Gen Zers. So, too, is the process of answering deep questions about whether—or how—older ideas and values remain meaningful in the digital age. Developing new social structures for the digital age will require a process of finding compromises, yet to be determined and tested, between competing values, and as societies, we are only at the beginning of that difficult process.

Gen Zers are further along in the process of adaptation to the digital age than those who predate them and are therefore poised to lead the way on so many of the issues we have discussed. Just as younger people reshaped institutions and social norms when they left rural areas to move to the cities during the Industrial Revolution, so Gen Zer citizens of today are working out how best to respond to the challenges of the digital age. They are trying to figure out what to carry forward from the past, what to leave behind, and how to build some entirely new social structures and conventions. In that regard, they may well be the heralds of new attitudes and expectations about how individuals and institutions can change for the better. Their shared understandings about how work should be carried out, what constitutes a family, and what it means to be a friend both reflect and stimulate wider changes. As we have seen with regard to identity and belonging, these changes are producing social forms that are often more fluid, more flexible, and more fully participatory than those of the past.

7

Conclusion: The Art of Living in a Digital Age

In the early years of technological development, what we might call the decades of "techno-optimism," pundits predicted a bright digital future. Such predictions included unprecedented economic growth, unprecedented leisure and convenience (provided by such inventions as driverless cars and refrigerators that could order more milk from the grocery), and unprecedented democratic health resulting from widely accessible broadcast media. In those days, it was easy to predict that the Digital Revolution would be relatively pain-free.[1]

We now know that those predictions were false. As a society, we are confronting issues of "surveillance capitalism," autocratic and populist threats to democracy, concentrations of global wealth, and the effects of climate change, artificial intelligence, and genetic engineering—all created or exacerbated by the digital age. We know that the future is always uncertain, but because of the Digital Revolution, it seems more uncertain than ever. History teaches us that big technological revolutions bring about big social revolutions—think about the previously unimaginable social changes in the workplace, schools, and governments ultimately brought about by the Industrial Revolution—and so we should not be surprised by the social turmoil we are now experiencing. Nonetheless, it is an unnerving, disquieting time in which to be living. We are experiencing the birth pains of a new social era, the contours of which remain very blurry.

Drawn into a world of change and uncertainty from early childhood, Gen Zers have discovered new routes to identity and trusted community by exploring the opportunities offered by the online networks that are so much a part of their daily lives. In that regard, they are no different from their pioneering ancestors who had to adapt to prior technological revolutions. They have wonderful opportunities to be brave and creative, but, as we have highlighted, they have a hard road ahead and, for the most part, they seem to know that.

This book has explored how Gen Zers' lives are shaped by digital technology and how they are constantly adapting and responding to the fast-paced change that the digital age presents to all of us. Although it is easy to dismiss their somewhat paradoxical hopes and disillusionments as those of "youth" who will change as they move further into adulthood, it may be that they will help to lead the way during coming social changes. Yes, some of their idealism will undoubtedly fade as they continue to encounter value conflicts and limits to change, both internal and external. Yes, not all Gen Zers have these hopes and aims—but surprisingly many do. And, yes, some members of their generation will become so disillusioned that they will retreat from the battle. Nevertheless, we have seen and heard from many Gen Zers who, we believe, will not give up their fight for human autonomy and respect and for new kinds of flatter, more equitable, more humane social institutions in the face of the increasing speed, scale, and scope of networks, massive accumulations of personal data, robots using artificial intelligence, the so-called Internet of Things, and genetic engineering.

One of the Lancaster interviewees, speculating on how he might see things at the age of sixty, talked about the importance to his generation of being able to question everything, without simply accepting a prescribed understanding handed down from family, religion, or other authority:

There was far less information available back sixty years ago, and people didn't question things. I hear this a lot from—well, I heard it from my grandparents a lot, that when you were a child you didn't question things, you just went along with it. . . . When my grandma was ten years old, you weren't allowed to question the authority or you get a slap. You go to church. You pray. You do what your parents say. Whereas nowadays if you're ten, the internet can maybe make you question things. You don't need your mum there. You can look at information. So . . . I guess we'll have the answer to that when you see people our age when we're sixty, how much do we change? . . . I don't know how much we're going to change. [Nigel]

With that in mind, we set forth ten attributes of Gen Zers that have emerged from this study and provide some suggestions as to how broader society may change over the coming decades.

1. THEY ARE SELF-DRIVERS WHO CARE ABOUT OTHERS.

Evidence that our interviewees and survey respondents are self-reliant permeates this book. Beginning with their drive to define their own identities, overriding limitations imposed by family or societal ascription, a sense of personal agency is foundational to Gen Zers' behavior, values, and worldviews. With the ubiquity and richness of online resources, they learned at a very early age how to find their own answers to questions, meet and talk with others from across the globe, and navigate networks and use tools that confounded their elders. They became adept at self-curating their public and private images and self-managing the fragmented pieces of their daily lives. As adults, they turn to others for advice and comfort but, ultimately, trust their own judgment most of all.

Although an orientation to self can suggest narcissism, such is not the case for these young people. They are self-identified and self-reliant but markedly not self-centered, egotistical, or selfish. They may exude confidence, but they are not arrogant. On the contrary, many seem quite burdened by the recognition that they live in troubled times and have uncertain futures. Unlike the "rugged individualists" sometimes lauded in Western cultures, they are, as we describe later, very community oriented and social. They are strong in their individuality and strong in their sense of community, which is an interesting combination of traits.

They also care about others. Although some worry that the post-millennial generation lacks empathy, our study suggests the opposite. This age group was exposed to considerable human suffering from a very early age, both IRL and online. Although some were hardened by this exposure, it caused many more to appreciate diversity and deepen their commitment to having a positive impact on the lives of others.

As we look ahead to the future, we can expect to continue to see individual approaches to any number of activities, given the wide range of information and experiences available to any person with internet access. We can also expect that this strong orientation to self-agency will continue to force changes in all areas of social life, something we are already observing in the workplace and in the political sphere, where young people are less willing than their elders have been to subscribe to a comprehensive "party" line. They prefer to make a "personal" difference in any number of arenas.

2. THEY ARE INVESTED IN THEIR COMMUNITIES OF IDENTITY.

One of the more interesting findings of our research is that, in the digital age, self and community are tightly interwoven in a chicken-and-egg relationship. Individuals discover their uniquely personal, fine-grained identities largely by becoming familiar with various communities, and, once they accept a particular attribute of identity as their own, they also accept that they have become members of the "tribe" associated with that attribute.

Attributes of identity are, of course, always group attributes. Even when identity was strictly a matter of family background or religion, the association was with the group. Now that individuals have more freedom to claim attributes of identity for themselves, however, they are often even more invested in honoring and protecting the related communities of belonging. They are also more understanding of others who are advocating for their own communities of belonging, as we saw in the comments of the cisgender students who embraced the practice of "announcing their pronouns" because they wanted to support their transgender peers. While not all Gen Zers see themselves as activists, it appears that many who do are directing their activism toward advancing the interests of their self-claimed communities of identity, and there is a widespread sense among them that they must protect and care for others with different identities.

We believe the new orientation to modular identities is going to continue to be very important to digital age citizens, whose experience of other ways of living is no longer limited by geography and whose need for finding places of belonging has become more acute in a digitally connected world of billions of humans. Already society is changing to reflect the new understandings about modular identities—beyond the growing number of all-gender bathrooms and the increasing use of gender-neutral pronouns. While identity has always had political significance, new technologies have made identity politics all the more possible and visible, and we can expect to see more changes in our civic structures as a range of identity groups push to participate in new ways.

3. THEY STRIVE FOR DIVERSE COMMUNITY.

As a result of Gen Zers' experiences IRL and online, the "free to be" ethic of the 1960s has been expanded. Gen Zers' belief that every person should be free to self-define attributes of identity and have the privilege of equitable treatment in society is perhaps their most widely shared worldview. This belief explains why postmillennials are so adamant about highlighting issues of gender and sexuality, care so much about tackling racism while also acknowledging and addressing white privilege and implicit bias, and feel a need to protect and support minority identities. It also is a factor in their dismay about their elders, many of whom still hold traditional opinions about assigned identity. This orientation to freedom and respect for others serves as a guide, compass, and inspiration; it is at the heart of their wish for a better human future.

However, they also struggle with how to bring about the pluralistic society they extol. They are trying to figure out how to bridge differences with others, particularly in the highly partisan political environments of today. They want to tighten the bonds within their communities of belonging, but that can come at the cost of good relations with those who do not belong. They recognize that they do not yet have good models for how to bring about the better society they envision, but many are experimenting. The student body at Georgetown University, for example, recently voted to tax themselves to create a reparations fund for descendants of slaves owned by the university in the 1800s.[2] Others are taking responsibility for finding new ways to promote civil dialogue on campuses.[3]

This is one area in which postmillennials will bear the greatest brunt of the social change battle. It is where their idealism and hopefulness are most likely to be tested, for, indeed, these are dynamic issues of self, community, and conflict that have never been fully or permanently resolved. Some people like to compare postmillennial idealism about equitable pluralism to that espoused by the baby boomers in the 1960s (and then smugly remind the listener that the baby boomers lost their idealism in the 1970s and 1980s), but the comparison misses some critical distinctions: the baby boomers were rebelling against social institutions that were strong and more or less intact, while Gen Zers are facing a world of social institutions that appear to be weak and even, in some cases, crumbling. And postmillennials are citizens of a world that is increasingly characterized by so-called minority-majority demographics.

4. AUTHENTICITY IS VERY IMPORTANT.

Gen Zers look for authenticity, by which they mean integrity, in people, products, and relationships. As a synonym for honesty, the term *authentic* has moral force. Having grown up in a world of pervasive advertising, both online and off, they are practiced at recognizing exaggeration and dissembling, and they will only tolerate misrepresentation in defined contexts. In areas that truly matter to them, they want to be able to trust the truth of who and what they are dealing with.

Examples of contexts in which authenticity is not expected are advertising, certain social media and news sites known for hyperbole or subjectivity, and TV reality shows. But in contexts where someone has a reasonable expectation of truthful representation, lies and distortions constitute breaches of trust. The violation is especially egregious when an assertion of truth is subsequently discovered to be false. A claim of inauthenticity is a serious matter, precisely because it connotes a lack of integrity and a breach of trust. Members of this generation can be quick to denounce inauthenticity or cultural appropriation forcefully.

This attribute is one that will be crucial as the digital age continues to bring us technologies that can manipulate, distort, and in general undermine "reality." Fake news is rife, affecting political life and democracies. We are already seeing new audio tools that can credibly make a person appear to be saying something they never said, and new video tools that put the head of one person on the body of another who is engaging in offensive behaviors. Every digital age citizen will have to become good at sniffing out what is authentic from what is not if humanity is going to continue to operate on a basis of trust.

5. THEY ARE HIGHLY COLLABORATIVE AND SOCIAL.

Gen Zers generally prefer to work collaboratively rather than in solitude. Even when they must work alone, they like to be in social settings, such as a coffee shop, a library with communal "nesting" areas, or a common room in a dorm. They have grown up engaging in joint problem solving and group work products in school, and they are familiar with online collaborative efforts, such as Wikipedia and GoFundMe. They do not view group efforts as compromising their individuality; rather, they see collaborations as opportunities to take advantage of diverse skills and ideas, leading to a better result. Moreover, they do not necessarily seek public recognition for their specific contributions to a collaborative endeavor.

Beyond enjoying collaborative work, Gen Zers are socially engaged. Thanks to email, texting, and social media, they can stay in touch with many people during the course of a day—a significant change from the past, when communications at a distance were limited by the lesser scale, scope, and velocity of telephones and snail mail. They interact with parents, siblings, and cherished friends throughout the day, and they can check in with more distant family and acquaintances periodically. They take pride in being able to move smoothly from one social context to another, and from offline to online and back seamlessly. Finally, and perhaps most importantly, they want to connect with people in depth, a factor in their preference for face-to-face communication and the emphasis they place on authenticity in people and relationships.

Gen Zers' orientation to collaboration is increasingly becoming the model for doing work. We need not elaborate on this point, for it is clear that collaborative effort is already a new norm, evident not just in online settings (Wikipedia being the obvious example) but in offline settings as well. Workplaces build projects around teams, and students do much of their work in groups. Similarly, social media encourage multiple ways to engage socially, offering some new opportunities to interact that would be impossible without online connectivity. Gen Zers place a high value on face-to-face, IRL engagements, and we anticipate that this attribute will persist into the future.

6. THEY ARE EXPLORING CONSENSUAL MODELS OF LEADERSHIP.

Many Gen Zers have had positive experiences of working in leaderless groups. They recognize that some groups may require leadership to avoid chaos, but in those situations, their preference is for shared or temporary leadership to the extent possible. Flexible leadership might entail having all members of the group hold the role on a rotating basis, or asking a member to lead when that person's skills particularly suit the need at hand. In all cases, though, the leader is expected to help the group accomplish its tasks rather than be an authority figure. The orientation is to leadership that reflects consensus, and skillful moderators of social media sites have been cited as exemplars: the best moderators are "guides" who serve rather than "bosses" who oversee. Many Gen Zers continue to disregard or have left organized religions because the associated leadership structures, which they found too hierarchically rigid and directive, are unappealing.

This attitude about consensual authority, combined with their orientation to self-reliance, helps explain why many postmillennials are leery of "experts." They like communal learning, in which teachers and professors are guides rather than authorities, and they often view parents as helpful assistants, advisers, or facilitators. Nevertheless, they are not hesitant to seek advice on an as-needed basis from those whom they respect for their specific expertise. This perspective about experts can be disconcerting to educators and other elders who are accustomed to being seen as authority figures in general, but it is deeply held. And yet, one paradox that has resulted is that as parents have come to be more like friends, so some of them have simultaneously acted as project managers for their children's lives, and the impact of that is yet to be seen.

As we look to the future, it seems evident that the "factory model" of the industrial age is not appropriate for the digital age, but how organizations can function with light or no leadership is not yet clear. Tech startups and new family structures that are intentionally less hierarchical have provided some examples, but, as with their vision of a pluralistic society, their orientation to collaborative leadership will likely be another front in the Gen Zers' social change battles that proves difficult, requiring considerable innovation and experimentation.

7. THEY ARE ORIENTED TO MODULAR AND FLUID STRUCTURES.

Modularity is prevalent throughout postmillennial life. Fragmentation is an essential feature of digital technologies, where information is broken into bits and bytes of 1s and 0s for easier manipulation and transmission. Those bits and bytes are then reconstituted into various modular wholes. With that orientation in mind, it is not surprising to find that Gen Zers see themselves as a composite whole of separate attributes—the fine-grained identities—and that they similarly identify with multiple communities—fine-grained belonging. In the context of social structures, working in collaboration translates into modular work groups that are fluid; they form to address specific needs and then disband when the needs are met.

Gen Zers no longer assume that the household family means a husband, a wife, and their children but instead recognize that a family can take a variety of forms and be subject to change at any time; moreover, close friends now see themselves as "fam." Similarly, they no longer assume that they will have lifelong professions or employers but rather expect that they will have to move from job to job, or gig to gig, in the coming decades, hoping that their flexibility will lead to financial stability for themselves and their children. They generally do not see a college degree as the end of their academic experience but rather see it as a gateway to a future of "lifelong learning," necessary to stay on top of ever-changing tools and social demands. They are uncertain about how and where they will obtain adequate health care over the course of their lives. Even in the realms of religion and politics, many foresee increasing modularity and fluidity. Unhappy with traditional religious structures, some are gravitating to a variety of new, more flexible forms of spiritual practice and community, and in the political sphere, many are eschewing traditional structures and practices, and engaging in "participatory politics" and other new forms of single-cause or locally relevant civic activity.

It is quite possible that short-term, fluid social structures—including those that pertain to the family, the workplace, and the civic sphere—will become a digital age norm. If so, this will represent a significant change from industrial age expectations about such institutions. Social institutions that are more temporary than permanent and more malleable than rigid present big questions about the future.

8. THEY ARE DISILLUSIONED BY THE PAST AND HAVE
A NO-NONSENSE ATTITUDE ABOUT THE PRESENT.

Gen Zers believe they are inheriting a difficult legacy. They do not expect to do better than their parents, in contrast to the expectations of prior generations, and they worry about climate change, racism, injustice, and gun violence—issues they believe their elders should have addressed. They are for the most part disappointed or, in some cases, angered by the hypocrisy, racism, misogyny, and homophobia of the past. They believe that, thanks to the errors of predecessor generations, they are facing a future of hard work to repair damaged social institutions. And because they do not see the future as resembling the past, they are not generally interested in looking backward for guidance, especially in light of all the social changes they have already experienced in their lives, not to mention the increasing prevalence and power of digital tools and networks that did not exist in the past.

They are oriented to the present partly out of necessity. Using digital tools all day long means they are constantly dealing with a flood of data. They work hard to be efficient and productive, focusing on that which is immediately relevant. They use moments of "free" time to call or text, check social media, or watch videos on their smartphones; there is no risk of boredom with so many opportunities to stay connected. They intermix work time and leisure time throughout the day, and they advocate a balanced lifestyle. They do not want to be so immersed in work that they have no time for self-care activities that address mental and physical well-being.

Their practical orientation to the present also factors into their views of dating. They expect to marry but, for many (especially the university students), marriage is something that will occur at a later time, after they are better established, and so they feel no urgency—indeed may even feel some resistance—to becoming emotionally involved (*catching feelings*) for the present. Emotional involvement can take time away from other activities that are viewed as more immediately relevant, especially when sexual activities are no longer seen as tied to romantic relationships. These views about romance and marriage are bolstered by their awareness that people their age have longer life expectancies than do their elders.

There is no question that postmillennials expect to create new social structures and orientations as they confront problems they believe they are inheriting from the past. In that regard, we found it telling that, when the *New York Times* asked readers in 2018 to pick a name for the generation, they received many suggestions but ultimately found the best one to be the "Delta" generation, a name suggested by a twenty-two-year-old who explained why:

> Delta is used to denote change and uncertainty in mathematics and the sciences, and my generation was shaped by change and uncertainty. . . . We take nothing for granted. . . . We are also a generation of demographic shift—we are more diverse than any in American history. We generally see it as something to embrace, and welcome changes that could make for a more inclusive and just America. . . . We are not passive products of circumstance, but active members of society with agency to affect the course of history, and will to build each other up to make things better. . . . We know all too well that adults aren't doing so today.[4]

In other words, marked and shaped by change, this age cohort now sees a need to change society.

<u>9. THEY USE EDGY HUMOR IN MEMES TO LIFT THEIR SPIRITS
AND AFFIRM THEIR COMMUNITIES OF BELONGING.</u>

Memes have become a creative and popular way for Gen Zers to express their frustrations and disappointments, softened by humor and group solidarity. The in-joke nature of memes strengthens communal ties by highlighting shared experience and values. In addition to providing communal glue, memes can be an outlet for expressing very personal feelings. In the mental health context, memes provide a self-deprecating way to show fears, stresses, and vulnerabilities to others who might understand and provide comfort. In the relationship context, memes can be a way to express friendship: tagging someone with a meme means not only that you are thinking of them, but that you know what they will find funny or meaningful. Memes provide a useful way of dealing with the many pressures and paradoxes of digital age life.

One colleague, noting that her college-age kids and their friends are always laughing together, suggested to us that laughter is the defining feature of the generation. Our interviewees, however, clarified that it is not laughter per se that connects them; rather, it is their generational need for an outlet that both acknowledges difficult truths and provides some comedic relief in the face of those truths. The humor in memes is almost always edgy; in that regard, it is what one of our interviewees called "existential" humor, reflecting underlying skepticism, cynicism, and even, in some cases, feelings of nihilism or fatalism.

We fully expect memes and subsequent forms of short multimedia humor will continue into the future. They are but one example of new kinds of entertaining communications that can become readily viral in the digital age.

10. THEY ARE FIGHTING FOR OUR HUMANITY.

To prepare for the major changes that they believe will be the backdrop to their futures, Gen Zers embrace new technologies and foster habits and values of flexibility and self-reliance. At the same time, they carry what can appear to be a contradictory yearning for security and stability. They fervently desire lasting and stable jobs, friendships, marriages, and communities.

A similar push/pull dynamic is evident in other areas of their lives. They champion the values of diversity and freedom that they learned from their parents and grandparents but are disillusioned by the older generations' hypocrisy and frustrated by their own inabilities to address interpersonal and intergroup conflicts. They highly value authenticity but expect and accept inauthenticity and curation in certain contexts. They primarily communicate via networked media but state a clear preference for face-to-face interaction. They call parents "friends" and friends "family." They share private thoughts and feelings in public settings, and when they work alone, they like to do so surrounded by others. They value individual freedom and self-reliance, on the one hand, and mutuality, collaboration, and communal membership on the other. They think globally but are most likely to act locally. Their humor embeds serious truths. They are practical and realistic about the present but idealistic about the future.

Although some might criticize Gen Zers for these apparent contradictions and ambiguities, they are illustrating the challenge of being at the intersection of old and new. They actually might be characterized as the "back to the future" generation: while they are adopting the digital technologies of the future, they are also embracing cherished human values relating to individual freedom and social belonging. Our research has made obvious to us that, contrary to what many have said about them, Gen Zers want to ensure that the social changes of the future celebrate, rather than override, those human values.

Julie Lythcott-Haims spoke of this attribute, and of the need for elders to appreciate it, in the article she wrote for our Gen Z series in *Pacific Standard*, titled "Why Boomers and Gen X'ers Are Wrong to Bash Gen Z." Although her 2015 book, *How to Raise an Adult*, had admonished parents not to become helicopter parents overinvolved in the lives of their children, in the article she expressed a new perspective:

> Instead of criticizing them for failing to measure up, maybe it's on us to accept that both despite us, and because of us, this [postmillennial] generation is very different from any set of humans we've ever known. Maybe being born on a planet facing potentially cataclysmic climate change instills a voice that will not be silenced. Maybe when elders seem incapable of ending senseless violence, the young learn that they can only count on each other. Maybe being thrust ill-equipped into the real world with all its challenges forces a human to sink or swim. Maybe Charles Darwin is smiling. Maybe precisely because of their environment they're not wimps but warriors who will

be capable of saving themselves. Maybe, then, we should be interested in how they've adapted to this changed world, and in how to join them.[5]

IN CONCLUSION: THE PATH FROM HERE
TO THE FUTURE IS YET TO BE BUILT.

During the course of our study, we could see more clearly the turbulence Gen Zers have grown up with, as well as the huge challenges that are ahead for them. We also came to understand how much they, consciously or not, have been fighting to ensure that humans, messy and emotive as we are, can tame and not be tamed by the increasingly "intelligent" machines of the digital age. Their passions for identity, freedom, agency, authenticity, belonging, collaboration, diversity, equity, and inclusion are part of that fight, as are their beliefs in the importance of mental and emotional health and the possibility of a better, fairer society.

Gen Zers' path for getting from their passions and beliefs to the world they envision, however, is not yet clear, and that lack of clarity is not confined to Gen Zers. Their questions, and the patterns of their daily living and being, nevertheless crystallize the issues. How does effective collaboration on a wide scale occur in an era of identity politics? Can the flexible but often fleeting online communities provide sufficient support and security over time? Is there a viable model for tackling complex problems without the more traditional kinds of institutions and leaders that postmillennials reject as outdated? Can modular, fluid collaborations be an effective substitute? And will organizations that are kinder, gentler, and more participatory than those of the past be sufficiently durable and productive? Answering these and other questions will take innovation and experimentation, not just by Gen Zers but by other age groups as well.

Gen Zers hold on to a hope that their different vision and values, and their clear-eyed recognition of what is wrong with society, will lead to something radically new and better than before. With added understanding of how and why they experience the world as they do, and with appreciation for the challenges they face, those of us who are in different generations might learn from that hope and join them as they work to build a better digital age future for themselves and the generations that follow. "OK Boomer" need not remain words of disappointment and disillusion. With more understanding, they can also morph into words of intergenerational connection, cooperation, and collaboration.

Acknowledgments

First and foremost, we thank Sam Gill and the Knight Foundation for funding our research, and Margaret Levi and her team at Stanford's Center for Advanced Study in the Behavioral Sciences (CASBS) for their exceptional support. We are so grateful for Sam and Margaret's belief in the project and for their kindness throughout.

We thank our student research assistants. Angela Lee, from Stanford, has been exceptional in every way: conducting so many of the interviews with students; doing many pieces of research for us; and being an excellent interlocutor throughout the project. Emily Winter from Lancaster conducted the interviews there and was also a splendid conversation partner, sparking ideas for us in the early stages of the project. We thank all our other research assistants who conducted interviews: Astha Khanal at Foothill Community College and Tony Hackett and Anna-Marie Springer at Stanford.

We are so grateful to all the interviewees at Lancaster, Foothill, and Stanford who so generously took time to answer our questions and whose words form the heart of this book.

To all those who helped with the iGen Corpus and the Survey, we are most grateful. We thank Robert Fromont at the University of Canterbury in New Zealand who worked tirelessly with Sarah to create the iGen Corpus, along with Stanford research assistants Max Farr, Jacob Kupperman, Amelia Leland, Anna-Marie Springer, and Simon Todd. We are grateful for the generous advice and expertise of colleagues at the Stanford Natural Language Processing Group, especially David Jurgens, who is now at the University of Michigan; Will Hamilton, who is now at McGill University; and Chris Manning. In addition, the corpus benefited from the advice and kindness of Arto Anttila, Alex Chekholko, Patrick Hanks, Danny Hernandez, Dan Jurafsky, Margaret Levi, Ruth Marinshaw, Nic Mockler, Byron Reeves, and Mike Scott. We thank Sir Bernard Silverman, who worked with Linda to compile and analyze the survey, and with whom we all had some inspiring and highly enjoyable conversations about our research.

Many colleagues and friends have discussed the ideas in this book along the way. We have Ruby Rich to thank for the title of the book, and we are grateful for her creativity. We thank those who generously shared their thoughts with us at two seminars at CASBS in the preliminary stages of the project. We offer our warm thanks to those who took the time to read a draft of the manuscript and provided vital feedback at a workshop at Harris Manchester College, Oxford, in November 2019, which improved the book immeasurably: Margaret Levi, Julie Lythcott-Haims, Nicole Mockler, Elenie Poulos, Betsy Rajala, and Maya Tudor. And we thank, also, all those who wrote pieces for our Gen Z series in *Pacific Standard*, as well as Betsy Rajala for her editorial work on that series.

We are all deeply appreciative of the wisdom and kindness of three wonderful champions of the book: our superb editor at University of Chicago Press, Elizabeth Branch Dyson, and our literary agents, Rebecca Carter in London and Emma Parry in New York. Thank you, Elizabeth, Rebecca, and Emma for your support.

Many friends and family members have cheered us collectively and individually along the way. Roberta warmly thanks her husband Charles Katz, her Gen X children Sarah, Sydney, and Tim, and her Gen Z grandchildren Rory and Aven, for their unfailing love and support and for all they have taught her over the years. She also thanks her friends and colleagues who offered valuable insights as this study proceeded; Judy Estrin was particularly kind to engage about it during many long walks. Linda thanks her husband Sandy for his constant support, even when the project took her abroad and involved their being apart for such long periods. Sarah is grateful to her Gen Z family members, James Olsen and Grace, Angus, Phoebe, and Ben Ogilvie, as well as her millennial niece Jeanne Ogilvie, for help with a number of questions. She also thanks her colleague at Stanford Gabriella Safran for helpful conversations about the language of Gen Zers. Jane thanks her colleagues Fred Turner at Stanford and Adam Guy at Oxford for conversations about technology and communications in the twentieth century; and her colleagues at Stanford Harry Elam (now president of Occidental College) and Michele Elam for inspiring conversations about undergraduate education and much more. Sarah and Jane thank the Walpole Carro family—spanning the generations from boomers to Gen Zers—who cooked them a splendid lunch one autumn day in 2019 and engaged in a lively intergenerational discussion about the ideas in this book.

This book is dedicated to Margaret Levi: a remarkable friend and colleague, a brilliant political scientist, and a visionary leader of CASBS.

Methodological Appendix

The open-mindedness of our funders, the Knight Foundation, and the support of our institutional host, the Center for Advanced Study in the Behavioral Sciences at Stanford, gave us the freedom to work collaboratively and to grow this project organically, adjusting our approach as findings questioned some of our initial ideas and introduced new themes. Our topic spilled over disciplinary boundaries and required the expertise we each brought to the project (anthropology, linguistics, history, and sociology). We learned from colleagues in social psychology and communication studies, too.

INTERVIEWS

In 2017, we began with a series of interviews with eighteen- to twenty-five-year-old postmillennial students, mostly but not only undergraduates, whose words are central to the texture and narrative of this book. We trained student research assistants to do the interviews, on the grounds that we—and they—thought that such peer-to-peer conversations would elicit more interesting and more honest responses. The student interviewers asked their peers questions about their use of technology, how they see themselves in the world, their values, and how they relate to their families and friends (as described below), keeping the questions as broad and open as possible. We ensured that we had a cross-section of students from a diverse range of socioeconomic backgrounds, cultures, races and ethnicities, and religions. We also supplemented the interviews with some focus groups, engendering conversation among students from different groups across each campus. We should note here that when we quote from the students, we deliberately do not use their identity markers (e.g., ethnicity, gender, sexual orientation, nationality), nor do we note which campus they came from, unless relevant to the topic being discussed. We do so to protect those identities and ensure anonymity.

The interviews were generally conducted on three campuses: Stanford University, Lancaster University, and Foothill Community College. Each represents a distinctive type of higher education institution. Stanford, a private university founded in Palo Alto in Northern California in the late nineteenth century by Jane and Leland Stanford with their railroad fortune, was radical for its time in being both coeducational and nonsectarian, and it brought a practical bent and solution-oriented perspective to undergraduate education, which it has always retained. It is now one of the leading research and teaching universities in the US and internationally. It helped gestate and form many of the tech companies that have come to create the digital age, so that Silicon Valley grew up around it. Since it was obvious for us to ask in our research whether the rise of the internet and mobile communications technology might help explain the changes we were seeing, Stanford seemed a good place to conduct some of our interviews. Its students are in full-time degree programs, and the university has a total of just under 17,000 students, of whom about 7,000 are undergraduates. The majority of our interviewees from this campus were undergraduates, with a small number of graduate students who were still in the Gen Zer cohort.

Lancaster University is a research university and, like almost all universities in the UK, a public university. It was founded in the 1960s along with a number of other universities such as Sussex, on a tidal wave of postwar optimism about higher education and its ability to rejuvenate local areas. Like Stanford, it brought excellent higher education to an area that was growing in population but underserved by colleges and universities at the time of its founding. Its geographical location today forms a deep contrast, however: while Stanford is at the heart of the growing digital technological world, Lancaster is located in the north of England, where the decline of the manufacturing industries has been sharply felt in the past few decades. Lancaster's overall student population is a little smaller than Stanford's, though its undergraduate population is greater, totaling about 11,400 out of its total number of 13,300 students (meaning that its graduate student population is quite small). About two-thirds of that total student body is from the UK, and the rest from abroad (in 2019–2020, 11 percent were from the European Union, and 26 percent the rest of the world). Our interviewees on this campus were almost all undergraduates.

For different reasons, Foothill Community College also offered opportunities for comparisons: it was founded in the late 1950s in the Los Altos Hills in Northern California and is therefore, like Stanford, located in Silicon Valley. However, it caters largely to students seeking two-year associate degrees rather than four-year bachelor's degrees, some of whom take their Foothill course credits and go on to complete four-year bachelor's degrees at universities (often in California). Its campus student population is about 15,300, but only a quarter of those are full-time, with most of the rest part-time and a small percentage taking courses for no credit. Unlike Stanford and Lancaster, it also has a large number (47,000) enrolled in some kind of distant learning. Our interviews here were conducted with undergraduates engaged in full-time or part-time education on the campus.[1]

A total of 120 interviews were conducted over a two-year period at each of Lancaster University, Stanford University, and Foothill Community College. The interviews were all conducted by research assistants who were mainly the same age as the interviewees; we had one research assistant each from Lancaster (Emily Winter) and Foothill (Astha Khanal) and three research assistants from Stanford (Tony Hackett, Angela Lee, and Anna-Marie Springer). They were all instrumental in helping us frame the interview questions. Several of the research assistants had helped us during a "pilot" period in which we were determining the kinds of questions that would best encourage students to tell us about their lives; it was during this pilot period that we learned that the students were especially eager to talk about their values and to be able to speak for themselves rather than be described as "snowflakes" who were unwilling to become adults.

The interviewees were generally selected through word of mouth and personal networking, though the Foothill students were participants in a formal program that solicits students to participate in social science research at Stanford and elsewhere. We did not try to produce a randomized group of interviewees, recognizing that the interview numbers would not allow for that; instead, we relied on the corpus and the survey for a randomized sample of participants in the relevant age group. As noted in the book, we nonetheless found remarkable similarity in the views of the interviewees and the survey respondents, regardless of whether they were in the US or the UK. Also, despite the fact that our interviewees were all enrolled in higher education, they reflected considerable demographic diversity. Not only were Lancaster, Foothill, and Stanford somewhat different in character, but the students themselves came from many diverse backgrounds. Though Stanford is viewed as an "elite" institution, it has a robust scholarship program that attracts many students from low-income households. Similarly, although somewhat different in origin and purpose, Foothill and Lancaster attract many students from abroad and various walks of life.

The interviews opened with an icebreaker exercise, either one that asked students what they would put in a starter pack for themselves (a *starter pack* internet meme is a collage of photos that describe a person and their interests) or one that asked students to place different colored pegs in a game board to illustrate how they spent their time during the preceding day. Following the icebreaker, the students were asked a series of open-ended questions about their online and offline behaviors and affiliations; about their relationships with family, friends, romantic interests, and acquaintances; about their own values and those of their generation; and their thoughts about religion and spirituality and about gender, sexuality, leadership, political/social activism, and work. They were also asked questions about whom or what they could trust and where they would turn for support, advice, and knowledge, including how they would deal with feelings of loneliness, frustration, and sadness. The interviews concluded with the students' thoughts about the future, for themselves and humanity in general. In general, the interviews took about one hour, and we offered the students token gift cards to thank them for their time.

In addition to these interviews, the research assistants facilitated a few focus groups that allowed students to talk with one another about their lives. The focus group questions were similar in character to those in the interviews, though fewer in number to allow time for the students to interact with one another. Interestingly enough, the students seemed equally open to expressing their views in both the interviews and the focus groups, but that may have been due to the composition of the focus groups: for the most part, they were groups of friends.

IGEN LANGUAGE CORPUS

We can't think of many jobs where "Let's get all the cuck you can get" is a phrase you'd reasonably hear from your boss.

MAX FARR, STUDENT RESEARCH ASSISTANT
ON THE IGEN CORPUS (MAY 12, 2017)

An important part of our study was the language of Gen Zers (referred to as iGen-ers in connection with our language corpus). We believe that language is a key to culture and that by investigating Gen Zer language we could access their mindsets, their attitudes, and their values. Young people are the driving force behind linguistic innovation and the most influential transmitters of language change.[2] By studying their language, we gain insight into not only their view of the world but also what is new, where language is heading in the future, and how it might affect the wider population over time.

While our interviews with Gen Zers at Stanford, Foothill, and Lancaster formed the basis of this book, we also gathered information on the general postmillennial population from two important sources: a large collection of general language called the iGen Corpus to which we applied computational analysis, and surveys of American and British Gen Zers (discussed below).

The iGen Corpus is a 70-million-word digital repository of spoken and written language of people aged sixteen to twenty-five years taken from a variety of natural contexts, including transcripts of the focus groups and interviews conducted by the research team at Stanford, Foothill, and Lancaster; data from social media platforms representing different types of engagement online such as social (Twitter), discussion (Reddit), gaming (Twitch), imageboards (4chan), and video (YouTube); and memes, emoji, and copypastas from Facebook and Instagram.

- Twitter: 16,001,261 tokens (1,069,598 distinct word types)
- Reddit: 36,884,918 tokens (415,257 distinct word types)
- Twitch: 10,075,603 tokens (527,798 distinct word types)
- 4chan: 6,110,549 tokens (292,922 distinct word types)
- YouTube: 24,382 tokens (3,022 distinct word types)
- interviews: 891,882 tokens (18,013 distinct word types)
- memes: 11,701 tokens (3,126 distinct word types)

We applied machine-learning algorithms where necessary to extract the language of people within our target age group (sixteen to twenty-five years old). The Twitter data comprised the language of 367,721 users aged sixteen to twenty-five years in March 2016. Their age was determined using a series of automatic heuristics and filtered to be between fourteen and fifty-nine years; we had roughly 900,000 users to start with, from which we extracted the language of 367,721 high-confidence users. The Reddit data was drawn from subreddits for which age surveys had been taken and were therefore high-confidence users, e.g., leagueoflegends, sjwhate, religion, memes, funny, dankmemes, fanfiction, frankocean, beyonce, drizzy, gatekeeping, sex, horizon, nintendoswitch, gaming, nsfw [not safe for work], realgirls, vaporwave, shitpost, addiction, holdthemoan, microdosing, indieheads, westworld, strangerthings, anime_irl, undertale, frat, politics, legalteens, crappyart, crappydesign, highschool, thesilphroad, overwatchcustomgames. In order to ensure that the language from Twitch was uncensored and taken from users within the desired age group, we extracted data from February 2016, before the platform introduced the "auto mod" moderation. The 4chan platform is for users over the age of eighteen years, and our 4chan data was chosen for the demographic aged eighteen to twenty-five years according to the age statistics of 4chan, and extracted from six boards: /a/ anime and manga; /co/ comics and cartoons; /v/ video games; /pol/ politically incorrect; /lgbt/; and /b/ random. The YouTube videos were manually transcribed and time-aligned using ELAN, so that searching the corpus for a word in a video takes a user directly to that place in the video. The sound recordings of the interviews of students from Lancaster, Foothill, and Stanford were transcribed, anonymized, and ingested into the corpus between 2017 and 2019. The memes and copypastas were manually chosen to represent a balanced selection of types for this age group: mostly image posts of varied genres and formats, e.g., Expanding Brain, Drake Yes/No, The Floor Is, Wholesome memes, Relatable memes, Absurd/Ironic memes, Rare Steak, Kermit/Evil Kermit; as well as a few original image macros in Impact font.

The iGen Corpus allows us to apply computational methods to analyze patterns in language use and lexical innovation among the general Gen Z population and to compare it with two corpora of language of the general population (non-Gen Z specific) in the UK and US (British National Corpus and the Corpus of Contemporary American English, respectively). In particular, this kind of comparison enabled us to determine whether certain words and concepts had more salience, or "keyness," to Gen Zers than the general population. Keyness, a measure of the statistical significance of a word's frequency in one corpus relative to another corpus, tells us whether a word occurs in a text more often than we would expect it to occur by chance alone. The higher the keyness value, the more significant is the difference between two frequency scores. We calculated keyness values using log likelihood (LL). The threshold for significance is conventionally at LL = 6.63 (p < .01). Hence, throughout our book we use a log likelihood of 6.63 or above as a reference value for being significantly more frequent among Gen Zers. For example, if a keyword has a log likelihood of 1,000, which is much higher than 6.63, it occurs with *unusual frequency* in the iGen Corpus when compared with corpora of broader language use. Conversely, if a keyword has a negative value, e.g., −10,000, it is *unusually infrequent* in the iGen Corpus when compared with corpora of broader language use.

Our linguistic analysis using the iGen Corpus allows us to build on previous sociolinguistic and variationist studies of the language of young people, such as Penny Eckert's study "Adolescent Social Structure and the Spread of Linguistic Change" in *Language and Society* (1988); Connie Eble's work on college slang, *Slang and Sociability: In-Group Language among College Students* (1996); Maciej Widawski's *African American Slang* (2015); and Sali Tagliamonte's *Teen Talk* (2016).

Sarah Ogilvie created the iGen Corpus with Robert Fromont (University of Canterbury), using his LaBB-CAT platform, and assistance from students Max Farr, Jacob Kupperman, Angela Lee, Amelia Leland, Anna-Marie Springer, and Simon Todd. We benefited from the generous advice and expertise of colleagues Will Hamilton, David Jurgens, Margaret Levi, Chris Manning, Arto Anttila, Dan Jurafsky, Danny Hernandez, Byron Reeves, Alex Chekholko, and Ruth Marinshaw. We are grateful to the Stanford Natural Language Processing Group and David Jurgens for the Twitter data; Will Hamilton for the Reddit data; and Danny Hernandez for the Twitch data. Our work would not have been possible without funding and support from the Knight Foundation and Stanford's Center for Advanced Study in the Behavioral Sciences. Upon completion of our research, we will release the iGen Corpus for public access to allow others to use it for their own research or to replicate the study in languages other than English, thereby creating a large global network of corpora.

SURVEYS

The two surveys discussed in the book were designed by Linda Woodhead in consultation with the project team, Professor Bernard Silverman FRS, and Rebecca Manning at YouGov. They were administered in the UK and the US by the internet polling companies YouGov UK and YouGov USA. They were analyzed by Linda Woodhead in consultation with Bernard Silverman, whose invaluable assistance is gratefully noted.

Fieldwork for the British survey took place February 18–22, 2019. It was completed by a representative sample of 1,002 young Great Britain (excluding Northern Ireland) adults aged eighteen to twenty-five years. Fieldwork for the US survey took place between February 13 and February 21, 2019. It was completed by a representative sample of 1,000 young US adults aged eighteen to twenty-five years. Apart from a few small variations to account for national differences (e.g., names of political figures and parties), the same 28 questions were asked of both the UK and US samples.

To assemble the representative samples, YouGov applied its standard methodology. This involved drawing a subsample of its UK standing panel and a subsample of its US standing panel. These were representative of UK and US eighteen- to twenty-five-year-olds, respectively, in terms of age, gender, social class, education, ethnicity, and political commitment. These subsamples were invited to complete the surveys. Only the subsamples have access to the questionnaire via their username and password, and respondents can only ever answer each survey once.

Once the surveys were complete, the final data were statistically weighted to the national profile of eighteen- to twenty-five-year-olds in the UK and the US (including people without internet access). The initial sampling ensures that the right people are invited in the right proportions; in combination with the statistical weighting, this ensures that the results are representative of eighteen- to twenty-five-year-olds in each country—not just those with internet access, but everyone.

We deliberately left the design of the surveys until the later stages of the interview process. This meant that our questions could be crafted in light of what had been suggested by the preceding qualitative research and could be used to test how representative those findings were. This allowed us to compare what we had found on campus at Lancaster with the attitudes of eighteen- to twenty-five-year-olds as a whole, in Great Britain; and to compare what we had found on campus at Stanford and Foothill with the attitudes of eighteen- to twenty-five-year-olds as a whole, in the US.

Notes

1   We quote from quite a number of these articles, and all of them can be found on the *Pacific Standard* website here: https://psmag.com/ideas/special-projects /generation-z.

CHAPTER ONE

1   W. Joseph Campbell, *1995: The Year the Future Began* (Berkeley: University of California Press, 2015).
2   danah boyd, *It's Complicated: The Social Lives of Networked Teens* (New Haven, CT: Yale University Press, 2014), 41.
3   BBC, "Generation Z and the Art of Self Maintenance," September 30, 2019, https://www.bbc.co.uk/sounds/play/m0008wnn.
4   In our iGen Corpus, the use of *lol* was more salient on the gaming platform Twitch than the other platforms. The threshold for significance is conventionally a keyness or log likelihood score (LL) of 6.63. In this instance, the word *lol* in the iGen Corpus has a keyness score on Twitch of LL = 111,242.14; YouTube, LL = −55.94; Twitter, LL = −3,518.09; 4chan, LL = −8,390.61; and Reddit, LL = −39,035.59.
5   Conversation with kindergarten teacher after presentation by Sarah Ogilvie on "The Effect of Technology on Human Interactions," Center for Advanced Study in the Behavioral Sciences, Stanford University, March 6, 2018.
6   The word *collab* is more common than the words *collaboration* or *collaborate* in our data bank of iGen language, especially in reference to music and video collaborations. It is also unusually frequent when compared with general corpora of language usage that covers all age groups. The threshold for significance is conventionally a keyness or log likelihood score (LL) of 6.63. In this instance, the

word *collaboration* in the iGen Corpus has a keyness score LL = −16.77 against BNC and LL = −703.83 against COCA; the word *collaborate* in the iGen Corpus has a keyness score LL = none against BNC and LL = −86.78 against COCA; the word *collab* in the iGen Corpus has a keyness score LL = 22.19 against BNC and LL = 3,335.48 against COCA.

7   Bianca Bosker, "Crowdsourcing the Novel," *Atlantic*, December 2018, 18.

8   Henry Jenkins, *Fans, Bloggers and Gamers: Exploring Participatory Culture* (New York: New York University Press, 2006).

9   Roberta Katz conversation with Robert Chun, March 2019.

10 "Lunch with the FT: Opal Tometi," *Life and Arts* section of the *Financial Times*, August 15, 2020, 3.

11 On the significance and usefulness of online life for Gen Zers with disabilities, see Sonia Livingstone and Alicia Blum-Ross, *Parenting for a Digital Future* (New York: Oxford University Press), chap. 5.

12 For a recent discussion of this tension, see George Dyson, *Analogia: The Entangled Destinies of Nature, Human Beings and Machines* (London: Allen Lane, 2020).

13 Sarah Ogilvie conversation with RARV, February 2017.

14 Thomas H. Davenport and John C. Beck, *The Attention Economy* (Cambridge, MA: Harvard Business Review, 2002).

15 Byron Reeves, N. Ram, T. N. Robinson, J. J. Cummings, L. Giles, J. Pan, A. Chiatti, M. J. Cho, K. Roehrick, X. Yang, A. Gagneja, M. Brinberg, D. Muise, Y. Lu, M. Luo, A. Fitzgerald, and L. Yeykelis, "Screenomics: A Framework to Capture and Analyze Personal Life Experiences and the Ways That Technology Shapes Them," *Human-Computer Interaction* 36, no. 2 (2021): 150–201.

16 An anecdote from a colleague, who visited another campus to give a lecture there, confirmed this: she gave a guest lecture at University of California, Berkeley, and received extremely high ratings: 100 percent of the students giving feedback said that the lecture was outstanding because it was "so relevant." (Roberta Katz conversation with JE, November 2017).

17 The threshold for significance is conventionally a keyness or log likelihood score (LL) of 6.63 ($p < .01$). In this instance, the word *relatable* in the iGen Corpus has a keyness score LL = 23.89 against BNC and LL = 3,020 against COCA.

18 Nicholas Carr, *The Shallows: What the Internet Is Doing to Our Brains* (New York: W. W. Norton & Co., 2011), 116.

19 Susan Greenfield, *Mind Change: How Digital Technologies Are Leaving their Mark on Our Brains* (London: Random House, 2015), 208.

20 Maryanne Wolf, *Reader, Come Home: The Reading Brain in a Digital World* (San Francisco: HarperCollins, 2018), 70.

21 Sam Wineburg, Sarah McGrew, Joel Breakstone, and Teresa Ortega, "Evaluating Information: The Cornerstone of Civic Online Reasoning," Stanford Digital Repository, 2016, https://purl.stanford.edu/fv751yt5934.

22 Mizuko Ito, Sonja Baumer, Matteo Bittanti, danah boyd, Rachel Cody, Becky Herr Stephenson, Heather A. Horst, Patricia G. Lange, Dilan Mahendran, Katynka Z. Martínez, C. J. Pascoe, Dan Perkel, Laura Robinson, Christo Sims, and Lisa Tripp, *Hanging Out, Messing Around, and Geeking Out* (Cambridge, MA: MIT Press, 2013), 25.

23 See, for example, Tony Wagner, *Creating Innovators* (New York: Scribner, 2012), 154.

24 Rose Macaulay, *Crewe Train* (London: Virago Press, 1926, reprint 2000), 187.

25 See Jean Twenge, *iGen: Why Today's Super-Connected Kids Are Growing Up Less Rebellious, More Tolerant, Less Happy — and Completely Unprepared for Adulthood — and What That Means for the Rest of Us* (New York: Atria Books, 2017).

26 Bell quoted in Ben Rooney, "Women and Children First: Technology and Moral Panic," *Wall Street Journal*, July 11, 2011, https://blogs.wsj.com/tech-europe/2011/07/11/women-and-children-first-technology-and-moral-panic/.

27 Claude S. Fischer, *America Calling: A Social History of the Telephone to 1940* (Berkeley, CA: University of California Press, 1994); and David Trotter, *Literature in the First Media Age: Britain between the Wars* (Cambridge, MA: Harvard University Press, 2013).

28 Franz Kafka, *The Neighbour* (trans. Tanya Ellerbrock, 2021 [1917]), http://www.kafka.org/index.php?aid=163.

29 Safiya Noble, *Algorithms of Oppression: How Search Engines Reinforce Racism* (New York: New York University Press, 2018); and Virginia Eubanks, *Automating Inequality: How High-Tech Tools Profile, Police and Punish the Poor* (New York: St. Martin's Press, 2017).

30 See "A-Levels: Student Foresaw Exam Crisis in Winning Story," *BBC News*, August 17, 2020, https://www.bbc.co.uk/news/uk-england-manchester-53812315; and "University Offer Reinstated for Exam Crisis Author Jessica Johnson," *BBC News*, August 20, 2020, https://www.bbc.co.uk/news/uk-england-manchester-53828077. Jessica Johnson's story can be found here: https://www.orwellfoundation.com/the-orwell-youth-prize/2018-youth-prize/previous-winners-youth/2019-winners/a-band-apart-jessica-johnson/.

31 See Fred Turner, *From Counterculture to Cyberculture: Stewart Brand, the Whole Earth Network, and the Rise of Digital Utopianism* (Chicago: University of Chicago Press, 2006).

32 This statistic comes from Alan Rusbridger, *Breaking News: The Remaking of Journalism and Why It Matters Now* (Edinburgh: Canongate, 2018), xxi.

33 See more on doxing and the dark web in Jamie Bartlett, *The Dark Net: Inside the Digital Underworld* (Brooklyn: Melville House, 2014).

34 S. Craig Watkins, *The Young and the Digital* (Boston: Beacon Press, 2009), 60.

35 For a broader look at how public spaces like libraries can provide social cohesion in contemporary society, see Eric Klinenberg, *Palaces for the People: How Social Infrastructure Can Help Fight Inequality, Polarization, and the Decline of Civic Life* (New York: Crown, 2018).

36 "Under the Hood: TikTok's Rampant Growth Strikes Wrong Note." *FTWeekend*, July 25/26, 2020, 14.

37 See Y Combinator, "Tim Urban of *Wait but Why*," YouTube video, January 3, 2018, https://www.youtube.com/watch?v=7a9lsGtVziM.

CHAPTER TWO

1 Parts of this speech were later published; see Elizabeth Alexander, "How to Make a Life from Scratch," *New York Times*, July 21, 2018.

2   Casper ter Kuile, *The Power of Ritual. Turning Everyday Activities into Soulful Practices* (London: William Collins, 2020), 20. For an older work that describes identity formation as involving processes of both stripping away some elements of identity and welding others together, see Hans Mol, *Identity and the Sacred: A Sketch for a New Social-Scientific Theory of Religion* (New York: The Free Press, 1977).

3   Kwame Anthony Appiah, *The Lies That Bind. Rethinking Identity: Creed, Country, Colour, Class, Culture* (London: Profile Books, 2018), 3.

4   See Leonore Davidoff and Catherine Hall, *Family Fortunes: Men and Women of the English Middle Class 1780–1850* (London: Routledge, 2002).

5   See, for example, Francis Fukuyama, *Identity: Contemporary Identity Politics and the Struggle for Recognition* (London: Profile Books, 2018), 115.

6   "Kimberlé Crenshaw on Intersectionality, more than two decades later," *Columbia Law School News*, June 2017, https://www.law.columbia.edu/news/archive/kimberle-crenshaw-intersectionality-more-two-decades-later. The original article is Kimberlé Williams Crenshaw, "Demarginalizing the Intersection of Race and Sex: A Black Feminist Critique of Antidiscrimination Doctrine, Feminist Theory and Antiracist Politics," *University of Chicago Legal Forum* 1, no. 1 (1989): 139–67.

7   Paul Hond, "Portrait of a Gen Z Activist," *Columbia Magazine*, Fall 2020, https://magazine.columbia.edu/article/portrait-gen-z-activist.

8   Elle Hunt, "Meet the Numtots: The Millennials Who Find Fixing Public Transport Sexy," *Guardian*, July 5, 2018, https://www.theguardian.com/cities/2018/jul/05/meet-the-numtots-the-millennials-who-find-fixing-public-transit-sexy-urbanist-memes.

9   Interview in British *Vogue*, June 2018, 76.

10 Sarah Ogilvie, ed. *Tree Speak: Words of Stanford Dictionary*, Stanford University, 2017, https://words.stanford.edu/.

11 See https://igencorpus.ling-phil.ox.ac.uk/express/transcript?ag_id=190247&threadId=68#ew_0_5289923.

12 "Generation Z Looks a Lot Like Millennials on Key Social and Political Issues," Pew Research Center, January 17, 2019, http://www.pewsocialtrends.org/2019/01/17/generation-z-looks-a-lot-like-millennials-on-key-social-and-political-issues/.

13 Dan Levin, "Young Voters Keep Moving to the Left on Social Issues, Republicans Included," *New York Times*, January 23, 2019, https://www.nytimes.com/2019/01/23/us/gop-liberal-america-millennials.html/.

14 Phillip L. Hammack, "The Future Is Non-binary and Teens are Leading the Way," *Pacific Standard*, April 8, 2019, https://psmag.com/ideas/gen-z-the-future-is-nonbinary.

15 Thomas W. Laqueur, *Making Sex: Body and Gender from the Greeks to Freud* (Cambridge, MA: Harvard University Press, 1992). On the embedding of sexual difference in the nineteenth century, see Cynthia Russett, *Sexual Science: The Victorian Construction of Womanhood* (Cambridge, MA: Harvard University Press, 1991); and Davidoff and Hall, *Family Fortunes*.

16 In a tweet on December 19, 2019. See Aja Romano, "J.K. Rowling's Latest Tweet Seems Like Transphobic BS. Her Fans Are Heartbroken," *Vox*, December 19, 2019, https://www.vox.com/culture/2019/12/19/21029852/jk-rowling-terf-transphobia-history-timeline.

17   Aja Romano, "Harry Potter and the Author Who Failed Us," *Vox*, June 11, 2020, https://www.vox.com/culture/21285396/jk-rowling-transphobic-backlash -harry-potter.

18   See Jamie Raines (Jammidodger), "Responding to JK Rowlings Essay: Is It Anti-Trans?," YouTube video, June 28, 2020, https://www.youtube.com /watch?v=6Avcp-e4bOs. Aja Romano has also made a BBC Radio 4 program on this subject: "Can I Still Read *Harry Potter*?" (broadcast November 13, 2020), https://www.bbc.co.uk/programmes/p08y8x0s.

19   Romano, "Harry Potter and the Author Who Failed Us."

20   We can compare our figures with those of the Office for National Statistics (ONS) in the UK, which found in 2017 that 4.2 percent of people aged between sixteen and twenty-four years were most likely to identify as LGB, compared with the overall population at 2 percent. In terms of methodology, ONS is a phone and doorstep survey, whereas ours is online and therefore more anonymous and impersonal.

21   See Raisa Bruner, "How Halsey's Unflinching Honesty Turned Her into Pop's Most Approachable Star," *Time*, October 8, 2020, https://time.com/collection -post/5896372/halsey-next-generation-leaders/.

22   Rogers Brubaker, *Trans: Gender and Race in an Age of Unsettled Identities* (Princeton, NJ: Princeton University Press, 2016), 141–44.

23   Lauren D. Davenport, *Politics beyond Black and White: Biracial Identity and Attitudes in America* (Cambridge: Cambridge University Press, 2018).

24   We recognize that the acronym BAME has been questioned by some. At the time of publication, it is a term that is in flux. See Rajdeep Sandhu, "Should BAME Be Ditched as a Term for Black, Asian and Minority Ethnic People?" *BBC News*, May 27, 2018, https://www.bbc.co.uk/news/uk-politics-43831279.

25   Lauren D. Davenport, "Beyond Black and White: Biracial Attitudes in Contemporary U.S. Politics," *American Political Science Review* 110, no. 1 (February 2016): 52–67.

26   Thanos Trappelides, Aqsa Ahmed, Tamara Krivskaya, Anca Usurelu, and Jabeel Mahmoud, "Issues of Belonging in the iGeneration," unpublished jointly written student paper, Richardson Institute, Lancaster University, 2019.

27   On the development of white identity in relation to nationalism in the US, see Kathleen Belew, *Bring the War Home: The White Power Movement and Paramilitary America* (Cambridge MA: Harvard University Press, 2018). On the adoption of Norse Gods and rituals as a part of white identity, especially in right-wing groups, see Ethan Doyle White, "Northern Gods for Northern Folk: Racial Identity and Right-Wing Ideology among Britain's Folkish Heathens," *Journal of Religion in Europe*, 10, no. 3 (2017): 241–73; Matthias Gardell, *Gods of the Blood: The Pagan Revival and White Separatism* (Durham, NC: Duke University Press, 2003); and Jennifer Snook, *American Heathens: The Politics of Identity in a Pagan Religious Movement* (Philadelphia: Temple University Press, 2015).

28   Comparing the iGen Corpus with corpora of broader language use such as the British National Corpus (BNC) and the Corpus of Contemporary American English (COCA) allows us to determine whether certain words and concepts have more salience or keyness to iGen-ers than the general population. The threshold for significance is conventionally a keyness, or log likelihood, score (LL) of 6.63 ($p < .01$). In this instance, the word *nation* in the iGen Corpus has

a keyness score LL = −15.17 against BNC and LL = −8,088.26 against COCA. The word *national* in the iGen Corpus has a keyness score LL = −1,191.79 against BNC and LL = −30,057.39 against COCA. The word *nationality* in the iGen Corpus has a keyness score LL = 4.17 against BNC and LL = −23.17 against COCA.

29 Comparing the iGen Corpus with corpora of broader language use such as the BNC and the COCA allows us to determine whether certain words and concepts have more salience or keyness to iGen-ers than the general population. The threshold for significance is conventionally a keyness or log likelihood score (LL) of 6.63 (p < .01). In this instance, the word *class* in the iGen Corpus has a keyness score LL = −26.43 against BNC and LL = −104.16 against COCA. The word *privilege* in the iGen Corpus has a keyness score LL = −7.17 against BNC and LL = −56.84 against COCA. The word *status* in the iGen Corpus has a keyness score LL = −58.53 against BNC and LL = −1,299.46 against COCA.

30 Tim Clydesdale, *The First Year Out: Understanding American Teens after High School* (Chicago: University of Chicago Press, 2007), 39–41.

31 One recent study of how Islam and Muslim students are treated on British campuses finds that implicit and explicit secularism is pervasive on campuses, in the curriculum and academic debate as well as in institutional arrangements. Alison Scott-Baumann, Mathew Guest, Shuruq Naguib, Sariya Cheruvallil-Contractor, and Aisha Phoenix, *Islam on Campus: Contested Identities and the Cultures of Higher Education in Britain* (Oxford: Oxford University Press, 2020).

32 Mathew Guest, Alison Scott-Baumann, Sariya Cheruvallil-Contractor, Shuruq Naguib, Aisha Phoenix, Yenn Lee, and Tarek Al-Baghal, *Islam on Campuses: Perceptions and Challenges*, SOAS University of London, 2020, https://www.soas.ac.uk/representingislamoncampus/publications/file148310.pdf, 15–18.

33 Mathew Guest, Kristin Aune, Sonya Sharma and Rob Warner, *Christianity and the University Experience: Understanding Christian Faith* (London: Bloomsbury Academic, 2012), 39.

34 Mathew Guest, "The 'Hidden Christians' of the UK University Campus," in *Young People and the Diversity of (Non)religious Identities in International Perspective*, ed. Elizabeth Arwick and Heather Shipley (Cham, Switzerland: Springer, 2019), 51–67.

35 Linda Woodhead, "The Rise of 'No Religion' in Britain: The Emergence of a New Cultural Majority," *Journal of the British Academy* 4 (2016): 245–61.

36 Charles Taylor, *Sources of the Self: The Making of Modern Identity* (Cambridge: Cambridge University Press, 1989).

CHAPTER THREE

1 "Apple Martin: Teen Tells Off Her Mum, Gwyneth Paltrow, for Sharing Photo without Permission," BBC *Newsround* (blog), March 27, 2019, https://www.bbc.co.uk/newsround/47718465.

2 On the growing weight and value given to authenticity during the twentieth century and since, see Lionel Trilling, *Sincerity and Authenticity* (Cambridge, MA: Harvard University Press, 1972); and Charles Taylor, *The Ethic of Authenticity* (Cambridge, MA: Harvard University Press, 2002).

3 On the fragmentation of the self, see Anthony Giddens, *The Consequences of Modernity* (Stanford: Stanford University Press, 1990); and *Modernity and Self-Identity: Self and Society in the Late Modern Age* (Stanford: Stanford University Press, 1991). On

plural selves, see Peter L. Berger, Brigitte Berger, and Hansfried Kellner, *The Homeless Mind. Modernization and Consciousness* (New York: Random House, 1973). On the liquid self, see Zygmunt Bauman, *Liquid Life* (Cambridge: Polity Press, 2005).

4   BBC, "Generation Z and the Art of Self Maintenance," September 30, 2019, https://www.bbc.co.uk/sounds/play/m0008wnn, at 5:31.

5   Comparing the iGen Corpus with corpora of broader language use such as the BNC and the COCA allows us to determine whether certain words and concepts have more salience or keyness to iGen-ers than the general population. The threshold for significance is conventionally a keyness or log likelihood score (LL) of 6.63 (p < .01). In this instance, the word *free* in the iGen Corpus has a keyness score LL = 215.31 against BNC and LL = 22,916.4 against COCA.

6   The threshold for significance is conventionally a keyness or log likelihood score (LL) of 6.63 (p < .01). In this instance, the word *real* in the iGen Corpus has a keyness score LL = 145.96 against BNC and LL = 8,839.66 against COCA. The word *true* in the iGen Corpus has a keyness score LL = 168.81 against BNC and LL = 17,339.37 against COCA. The word *honest* in the iGen Corpus has a keyness score LL = 32.58 against BNC and LL = 3286.62 against COCA; and the word *fake* in the iGen Corpus has a keyness score LL = 202.38 against BNC and LL = 13,718.03 against COCA.

7   Erica Bailey, Sandra C. Matz, Wu Youyou, and Sheena S. Iyengar. "Authentic Self-Expression on Social Media Is Associated with Greater Subjective Well-Being," *Nature Communications* 11 (2020), https://doi.org/10.1038/s41467–020 –18539-w.

8   Quoted in Sanam Yar, "Lili Reinhart Is Just Being Honest," *New York Times*, October 8, 2020, https://www.nytimes.com/2020/10/03/style/lili-reinhart -swimming-lessons-riverdale.html/.

9   This statement was made to one of our research assistants, Angela Lee, during her internship at MyDigitalTat2 in the summer of 2018.

10   Gloria Moskowitz-Sweet and Erica Pelavin, "Gen Z's Message to Parents — Put Your Phone Down." *Pacific Standard*, April 22, 2019, https://psmag.com/ideas /put-down-the-phone-and-reconnect-with-your-child; and Jenny Radesky, "What Happens When We Turn to Smartphones to Escape Our Kids?" *Pacific Standard*, April 22, 2019, https://psmag.com/ideas/what-happens-when-parents -cant-put-their-phones-down.

11   Erin McLaughlin, "'On Fleek' Inventor Kayla Newman AKA Peaches Monroee on Her Beauty Line," *Teen Vogue*, March 2017.

12   http://www.pewsocialtrends.org/2019/01/17/generation-z-looks-a-lot-like -millennials-on-key-social-and-political-issues/.

13   https://www.nytimes.com/2019/01/23/us/gop-liberal-america-millennials .html/.

14   http://www.pewsocialtrends.org/2019/01/17/generation-z-looks-a-lot-like -millennials-on-key-social-and-political-issues/.

15   Nicola Madge, Peter J. Hemming, and Kevin Stenson, *Youth on Religion: The Development, Negotiation and Impact of Faith and Non-Faith Identity* (London: Routledge, 2013).

16   However, some older activists have expressed impatience with cancel culture, such as Olivette Otele, the distinguished Black historian at the University of Bristol who said in 2020, "Discussions of cancel culture are very middle-class.

Activists just survive and support each other." Nesrine Malik, "Interview Oli-vette Otele," *Guardian*, October 16, 2020. https://www.theguardian.com/books /2020/oct/16/olivette-otele-discussions-of-cancel-culture-are-very-middle -class-activists-just-survive-and-support-each-other.

17 The threshold for significance is conventionally a keyness or log likelihood score (LL) of 6.63 ($p < .01$). In this instance, the word *cancel* in the iGen Corpus has a keyness score LL = 55.86 against BNC and LL = 2970.21 against COCA; the word *blocking* in the iGen Corpus has a keyness score LL = 18.17 against BNC and LL = 24.47 against COCA; and the word *ghost* in the iGen Corpus has a key-ness score LL = 27.09 against BNC and LL = 2503.48 against COCA.

18 Romano, "Harry Potter and the Author Who Failed Us." https://www.vox.com /culture/21285396/jk-rowling-transphobic-backlash-harry-potter.

19 In that sense, the equity approach has a great deal in common with Martha Albertson Fineman's legal philosophy with its focus on vulnerabilities rather than equality. See, for example, "Vulnerability and Social Justice," *Valparaiso University Law Review* 53 (2019).

20 Sonia Livingstone and Alicia Blum-Ross, *Parenting for a Digital Future* (New York: Oxford University Press, 2020).

CHAPTER FOUR

1 Sarah Ogilvie and David Martin, "Oxford English Dictionary: Building Dictio-naries with Crowdsourcing" podcast, January 2019, https://www.youtube.com /watch?v=ZmoyLCftpAs.

2 Cara Delevingne, "Girl Up Hero Awards Interview," October 13, 2019, at 1:21, https://www.eonline.com/videos/297220/cara-delevingne-gushes-over-ashley -i-m-the-luckiest-girl-in-the-world.

3 Mizuko Ito, Crystle Martin, Rachel Cody Pfister, Matthew H. Rafalow, Katie Salen, and Amanda Wortman, *Affinity Online: How Connection and Shared Interest Fuel Learning* (New York: New York University Press, 2018), 5.

4 See Kat Lin, "The Story of the Subtle Asian Traits Facebook Group," *New Yorker*, December 22, 2018. https://www.newyorker.com/culture/culture-desk/the -story-of-the-subtle-asian-traits-facebook-group; Nicholas Wu and Karen Yuan, "The Meme-ification of Asianness," *Atlantic*, December 27, 2018. https:// www.theatlantic.com/technology/archive/2018/12/the-asian-identity-accord ing-to-subtle-asian-traits/579037/.

5 Lin, "The Story of the Subtle Asian Traits Facebook Group."

6 Wu and Yuan, "The Meme-ification of Asianness."

7 See BBC, "Generation Z and the Art of Self-Maintenance," September 30, 2019, https://www.bbc.co.uk/sounds/play/m0008wnn, at 8:21.

8 See Angela Nagel, *Kill All Normies: The Online Culture Wars from 4chan and Tumblr to Trump and the Alt-Right* (Winchester, UK: Zero Books, 2017). See also boyd, *It's Complicated*, 42–43.

9 The incel movement is the most virulently woman-hating example of these kinds of negative communities. It is a community devoted to hatred of women. Begun in Canada in the mid-1990s by a woman called Alana, it was originally a small and generally supportive online community where men and women shared their sexual fears, frustrations, and unhappiness. She called it *invcels*—

"involuntary celibates." It was this, long after Alana had drifted away, that morphed into something vastly different—the *incels*—a community made up of a sprawling network of websites, blogs, forums, podcasts, YouTube channels, and chatrooms devoted to misogyny. Laura Bates, in her book *Men Who Hate Women*, describes the different paths new recruits take to finding their way to the incel community: "Some stumble across it while looking for answers to life problems or loneliness. Some segue into its path from other areas of the Internet, like more general message boards or websites. Some are pushed toward it by algorithms with video platforms such as YouTube recommending incel content, even though the user didn't go looking for it. Some are sucked in through more sinister means, groomed by messages in private gaming chatrooms or on forums frequented by teenage boys." See Laura Bates, *Men Who Hate Women: From Incels to Pickup Artists, the Truth about Extreme Misogyny and How It Affects Us All* (London: Simon and Schuster, 2020), 13. Like other internet subcommunities we have looked at, incels also develop their own language, and it is through their language that we glimpse their culture. The man-hating world, which they believe promotes women over men, is called *gynocracy*; the *red pill* refers to the moment when an incel wakes up from a "normal" life of ignorance in which men and women are considered equal; a *roastie* is a woman who has had too much sex (so that the genitals resemble roast beef); a *foid* is short for "female humanoid," their name for a woman (because the word *woman* connotes too much humanity); and *rapecel* for an incel who rapes a woman to resolve his sexual frustration.

10   8chan was taken off the clearnet (the public internet, as opposed to the deep web and dark web) in August 2019 after two mass shootings in Texas and Ohio were filmed live on the platform, only to rebrand and reappear in November 2019 as "8kun" through a Russian "bulletproof" hosting provider called Media Land.

11   Casey Newton, "Facebook will pay $52 million in settlement with moderators who developed PTSD on the job," *Verge*, May 12, 2020, https://www.theverge .com/2020/5/12/21255870/facebook-content-moderator-settlement-scola -ptsd-mental-health.

12   See Ito et al., *Affinity Online*, 214.

13   BBC, "Generation Z and the Art of Self-Maintenance," at 9:32.

14   Keywords are words that occur more often than we would expect to occur by chance alone, and they are calculated by carrying out a loglinear statistical test that compares the word frequencies in a subcorpus (e.g., 4chan, Reddit, Twitter) against their expected frequencies in a much larger corpus (the entire iGen Corpus).

15   Ogilvie and Martin, "Oxford English Dictionary."

16   See Henry Jenkins, Shangita Shresthova, Liana Gamber-Thompson, Neta Kligler-Vilenchik, and Arrely Zimmerman, *By Any Media Necessary: The New Youth Activism* (New York: New York University Press, 2016), 49.

17   Sometimes, however, as with the notorious "Pro-ana" sites, which build community for people with anorexia and other eating disorders, that support can be a mixed blessing, such as when it discourages recovery efforts that would result in a person leaving the community. Web MD, "Pro Anorexia Sites: The Thin Web Line," accessed April 28, 2019, https://www.webmd.com/mental-health/eating

-disorders/anorexia-nervosa/features/pro-anorexia-web-sites-thin-web-line; Angela Lee, "Tumblr Helped Me Plan My Eating Disorder. Then It Helped Me Heal," *Pacific Standard*, April 29, 2019, https://psmag.com/ideas/tumblr-helped -me-plan-my-eating-disorder-then-it-helped-me-heal.

18 BBC, "Generation Z and the Art of Self-Maintenance."

19 This is a reference to Robert Putnam's book *Bowling Alone* (New York: Simon & Schuster, 2001), which argues that Americans and Brits are becoming less community minded and more isolated from one another. In his 2020 book, *The Upswing*, co-authored with Shaylyn Romney Garrett, Putnam reiterates this argument, charting the rise of me-centered culture, greater independence and egoism, from the 1960s to the present. Our research suggests a rather different pattern among postmillennials, in which "me" and "we" are combined. See Robert Putnam with Shaylyn Romney Garrett, *The Upswing: How We Came Together a Century Ago and How We Can Do It Again* (New York: Simon and Schuster, 2020).

20 This is a reference to Jean Twenge's book *Generation Me* (New York: Atria Books, 2014), which argues that young people are becoming more narcissistic, self-consumed, and individualistic.

21 Michel Maffesoli, *Time of the Tribes: The Decline of Individualism in Mass Society* (London: Sage, 1996), 147.

CHAPTER FIVE

1 Bernadine Evaristo, *Girl, Woman, Other* (London: Penguin, 2019), 41–42.

2 See BBC, "Generation Z and the Art of Self-Maintenance," September 30, 2019, https://www.bbc.co.uk/sounds/play/m0008wnn, at 25:55.

3 David Brooks, "A Generation Emerging from the Wreckage," *New York Times*, February 26, 2018, https://www.nytimes.com/2018/02/26/opinion/millennials -college-hopeful.html/.

4 The threshold for statistical significance is conventionally a keyness or log likelihood score (LL) of 6.63. In this instance, the first person pronoun *I* in the iGen Corpus has a keyness score LL = 10,785.32 against BNC and LL = 986,003.19 against COCA.

5 See Henry Jenkins, Mizuko Ito, and danah boyd, *Participatory Culture in a Networked Era: A Conversation on Youth, Learning, Commerce and Politics* (London: Polity Press, 2016); and Daniel Kreiss, Megan Finn, and Fred Turner, "The Limits of Peer Production: Some Reminders from Max Weber for the Network Society," *New Media & Society* 13, no. 2 (2011): 243–59.

6 For an overview of the history of the family in the twentieth century, see Mary Abbot, *Family Affairs: A History of the Family in Twentieth-Century England* (London: Routledge, 2002); and Marilyn Coleman, *Family Life in Twentieth-Century America* (Westport, CT: Greenwood, 2007). On more recent changes to the family, see Susan Golombok, *Modern Families: Parents and Children in New Family Forms* (Cambridge: Cambridge University Press, 2015).

7 Laura T. Hamilton, *Parenting to a Degree: How Family Matters for a College Degree* (Chicago: University of Chicago Press, 2016).

8 Julie Lythcott-Haims, among others, has been trying to help parents break that habit. See her book *How to Raise an Adult: Break Free of the Overparenting Trap and Prepare your Kid for Success* (New York: Henry Holt, 2015).

9 *New Yorker*, August 20, 2018, 39.

10 Madeline Levine, *Ready or Not: Preparing Our Kids to Thrive in an Uncertain and Rapidly Changing World* (San Francisco: Harper, 2020).

11 Sonia Livingston and Alicia Blum-Ross, in their study of parenting in the digital age, note that children often misperceive or exaggerate the extent of their parents' technological incompetence, while some parents exaggerate the competence of their children. See Sonia Livingstone and Alicia Blum-Ross, *Parenting for a Digital Future* (New York: Oxford University Press, 2020). However, see also chap. 6 of Elisabeth Gee, Lori Takeuchi, and Ellen Wartella, *Children and Families in the Digital Age: Living Together in a Media-Saturated Culture* (London: Routledge, 2018), which describes how children of Latinx immigrants play an expanded information-brokering role in their families due to their greater experience in using digital technology.

12 See BBC, "Generation Z and the Art of Self-Maintenance."

13 Kristina Sepetys, "Have Headphones Made Gen Z More Insular?" *Pacific Standard*, April 29, 2019, https://psmag.com/ideas/have-headphones-made-gen -z-more-insular.

14 See Ron Lesthaeghe, "The Unfolding Story of the Second Demographic Transition," *Population and Development Review* 36, no. 2 (2010): 211–51.

15 Elisabeth Beck-Gernsheim, "On the Way to a Post-familial Family: From a Community of Need to Elective Affinities," *Theory Culture and Society*, 15 no. 3–4 (August 1998): 53–70.

16 Livingstone and Blum-Ross, *Parenting for a Digital Future*, 17.

17 Susan Golombok, *We Are Family: What Really Matters for Parents and Children* (London: Scribe, 2020). Golombok's 2015 book, *Modern Family*, documents the changing nature of family in recent decades.

18 Claire Haug, "What's a Normal Family, Anyway?" *New York Times*, February 5, 2019, https://www.nytimes.com/2019/02/05/style/the-edit-normal-unconven tional-family.html/.

19 See Pew Research Center, "The American Family Today," December 17, 2015, https://www.pewsocialtrends.org/2015/12/17/1-the-american-family-today/. The report also discusses how ethnicity affects these percentages; for example, children of Asian parents are the most likely to be living in a household with both of their parents.

20 Euromonitor International, "Households in 2030: Rise of the Singletons," March 20, 2017, https://blog.euromonitor.com/households-2030-singletons/.

21 Julie Beck, "It's 10 p.m. Do You Know Where Your Friends Are?" *Atlantic*, August 20, 2019.

22 The threshold for significance is conventionally a keyness or log likelihood score (LL) of 6.63. In this instance, the word *friend* in the iGen Corpus has a keyness score LL = 65.85 against BNC and LL = 9,386.18 against COCA.

23 "Gamers Meet in Real Life at Bedside of Terminally-Ill Friend," *BBC News*, September 29, 2018, https://www.bbc.co.uk/news/world-us-canada-45651739.

24 C. J. Pascoe, "Intimacy," in *Hanging Out, Messing Around and Geeking Out: Living and Learning with the New Media*, ed. Mizuko Ito et al. (Cambridge, MA: MIT Press, 2009), 129.

25 Lisa Wade, *American Hookup: The New Culture of Sex on Campus* (New York: W. W. Norton & Co., 2017).

26 For an insightful and humorous look at this shift driven by technology, see Aziz Ansari with Eric Klinenberg, *Modern Romance* (New York: Penguin, 2015).

27 See BBC, "Generation Z and the Art of Self-Maintenance," at 20:15.

28 See BBC, "Generation Z and the Art of Self-Maintenance," at 24:18.

29 This comports with what Christel J. Manning found: "My own experience suggests that far more young people are simply indifferent to faith. They don't ever think or talk about religion unless it's a topic at school or bad news about religious zealotry in the Middle East or Florida." Manning, "Gen Z Is the Least Religious Generation. Here's Why That Could Be a Good Thing." *Pacific Standard*, May 6, 2019, https://psmag.com/ideas/gen-z-is-the-least-religious-generation -heres-why-that-could-be-a-good-thing.

30 Linda Woodhead, "The Rise of 'No Religion': Towards an Explanation," *Sociology of Religion* 78, no. 3 (Autumn 2017).

31 After reviewing recent surveys from around the world, the Pew Research Center concludes that "younger adults are far less likely than older generations to *identify with a religion*, believe in God or engage in *a variety of religious practices*. But this is not solely an American phenomenon: Lower religious observance among younger adults is common around the world." Pew Research Center, "The Age Gap in Religion around the World," June 13, 2018, https://www.pewforum.org /2018/06/13/the-age-gap-in-religion-around-the-world/.

32 For Europe as a whole, see Stephen Bullivant's analysis of the European Social Survey 2014–2016 in Bullivant, "Europe's Young Adults and Religion: Findings from the European Social Survey (2014–16) to Inform the 2018 Synod of Bishops," https://www.stmarys.ac.uk/research/centres/benedict-xvi/docs/2018 -mar-europe-young-people-report-eng.pdf.

33 See Barna Group, "Atheism Doubles among Generation Z," *Millennials and Generations*, January 24, 2018, https://www.barna.com/research/atheism-doubles -among-generation-z/.

34 Mathew Guest, "The 'Hidden Christians' of the UK University Campus," in *Young People and the Diversity of (Non)religious Identities in International Perspective*, ed. Elizabeth Arwick and Heather Shipley (Cham, Switzerland: Springer, 2019), 51–67. Discussed in more detail in chap. 2.

35 Christel J. Manning, *Losing Our Religion. How Unaffiliated Parents Are Raising Their Children* (New York: New York University Press, 2016), 6.

36 Nellie Bowles, "These Millennials Got New Roommates. They're Nuns," *New York Times*, May 31, 2019, https://www.nytimes.com/2019/05/31/style/millennial -nuns-spiritual-quest.html/.

37 Angie Thurston and Casper ter Kuile, "How We Gather," Sacred Design Lab, 2019, https://sacred.design/wp-content/uploads/2019/10/How_We_Gather _Digital_4.11.17.pdf; Casper ter Kuile and Angie Thurston, "Something More," Sacred Design Lab, 2019, https://sacred.design/wp-content/uploads/2019/10 /SomethingMore_F_Digital_Update.pdf.

38 Manning, "Gen Z Is the Least Religious Generation."

39 David Brooks, "The Age of Aquarius, All Over Again: Belief in Astrology and the Occult Is Surging," *New York Times*, June 10, 2019, https://www.nytimes.com /2019/06/10/opinion/astrology-occult-millennials.html/.

40 Michael Schulman, "The Force Is with Them," *New Yorker*, September 16, 2019, 26.

41 The threshold for significance is conventionally a keyness or log likelihood

score (LL) of 6.63. In this instance, the word *stuck* in the iGen Corpus has a key-ness score LL = 18.55 against BNC and LL = 1,717.19 against COCA. The word *stagnant* in the iGen Corpus has a keyness score LL = 7.93 against BNC and LL = 88.97 against COCA.

42   Sophia Pink, "'Stagnancy Is Scarier Than Change': What I Learned from My Road Trip in Search of Gen Z," *Pacific Standard*, April 8, 2019, https://psmag .com/ideas/road-tripping-to-understand-gen-z.

43   45 percent in the US and 49 percent in the UK.

44   Pink, "'Stagnancy Is Scarier Than Change.'"

45   Among British respondents the equivalent top six were as follows: having a happy marriage or life partnership, having a positive impact on the world, having good friends, having fun, having significant life experiences, and having career success. The option "having significant life experiences" was offered on the British survey but not the US survey. In all other respects the question was identical. The added option means that the US and UK results for this question are not directly comparable.

CHAPTER SIX

1   Ziad Ahmed, quoted in Li Cohen, "From TikTok to Black Lives Matter, How Gen Z Is Revolutionizing Activism," *CBS News*, July 20, 2020, https://www.cbs news.com/news/from-tiktok-to-black-lives-matter-how-gen-z-is-revolution izing-activism/. In 2020, Ziad Ahmed was named a Top 15 Young Prodigy Changing the World by *Business Insider* due to his creation (at the age of thirteen years) of Redefy, a social justice nonprofit for young people "to defy stereotypes and embrace acceptance." See https://www.redefy.org/.

2   See Ann M. Pendleton-Jullian and John Seely Brown, *Design Unbound: Designing for Emergence in a White Water World* (Cambridge, MA: MIT Press, 2018).

3   See especially Jean Twenge, *iGen: Why Today's Super-Connected Kids Are Growing Up Less Rebellious, More Tolerant, Less Happy—and Completely Unprepared for Adulthood—and What That Means for the Rest of Us* (New York: Atria Books, 2017).

4   See Greg Lukianoff and Jonathan Haidt, *The Coddling of the American Mind: How Good Intentions and Bad Ideas Are Setting Up a Generation for Failure* (London: Penguin, 2018).

5   Kevin Quealy and Claire Cain Miller, "Young Adulthood in America: Children Are Grown, but Parenting Doesn't Stop," *New York Times*, March 13, 2019.

6   Janet Adamy, "Gen Z Is Coming to Your Office. Get Ready to Adapt," *Wall Street Journal*, September 6, 2018.

7   Quoted in Nosheen Iqbal, "Generation Z: 'We Have More to Do than Drink and Take Drugs,'" *The Guardian*, July 21, 2018.

8   "Retirement & Survivors Benefits: Life Expectancy Calculator," Social Security Administration, https://www.ssa.gov/cgi-bin/longevity.cgi.

9   See Lynda Gratton and Andrew Scott, *The 100-Year Life: Living and Working in an Age of Longevity* (London: Bloomsbury, 2017).

10   The threshold for statistical significance is conventionally a keyness or log like-lihood score (LL) of 6.63. In this instance, the word *stressful* in the iGen Corpus has a keyness score LL = 16.36 against BNC and LL = 69.25 against COCA.

11   American Psychological Association, "APA Stress in America™ Survey: Gen-

eration Z Stressed About Issues in the News but Least Likely to Vote," press release, October 30, 2018, https://www.apa.org/news/press/releases/2018 /10/generation-z-stressed.

12   Amy Orben and Andrew K. Przybylski, "The Association Between Adolescent Well-Being and Digital Technology," *Nature Human Behaviour* 3 (2019): 173–82. See similar findings in Andrew K. Przybylski and Netta Weinstein, "A Large-Scale Test of the Goldilocks Hypothesis: Quantifying the Relations between Digital-Screen Use and the Mental Well-Bring of Adolescents," *Psychological Science*, 28 (2017): 204–15.

13   Sophie Bethune, "Gen Z More Likely to Report Mental Health Concerns," *Monitor on Psychology* 50, no. 1 (January 2019), 1–20, https://www.apa.org/monitor /2019/01/gen-z.

14   Reported to research assistant Angela Lee by a summer intern at MyDigital Tat2.

15   The impact of racism on mental health has been the subject of significant research for some time. As examples of the literature over the past five decades, see Charles Willie, ed., *Racism and Mental Health: Essays* (Pittsburgh: University of Pittsburgh Press, 1973); David R. Williams and Ruth Williams-Morris, "Racism and Mental Health: The African American Experience," *Ethnicity and Health* 200, no. 5 (3/4): 243–68; Alex L. Pieterse, Helen A. Neville, Nathan R. Todd, and Robert T. Carter, "Perceived Racism and Mental Health among Black American Adults: A Meta-Analytic Review," *Journal of Counseling Psychology* 59, no. 1 (2012): 1–9. The Royal College of Psychiatrists in the UK produced a report in 2018, with recommendations: "Racism and Mental Health," https://www.rcpsych .ac.uk/pdf/PS01_18a.pdf.

16   "Racism and Mental Health" (web page), Young Minds, https://youngminds .org.uk/find-help/looking-after-yourself/racism-and-mental-health/.

17   Wes, "Black Mental Health Matters," June 18, 2020, Young Minds, https:// youngminds.org.uk/blog/black-mental-health-matters/.

18   The online learning platform StuDoc conducted a very small-sample survey with *Business Insider* between June 5 and June 8, 2020, asking how the recent racial tensions in the United States might have had an effect on the mental health of 108 currently enrolled US students between the ages of eighteen and thirty-two years (thereby including both postmillennials and young millennials). Sixty percent of those who responded said that the recent racial tensions have had an impact on their overall mental health, while 64 percent were nevertheless hopeful about the future because of the widespread support the Black Lives Matter movement has received. Dominic-Madori Davis, "The Action Generation: How Gen Z Really Feels about Race, Equality, and Its Role in the Historic George Floyd Protests, Based on a Survey of 39,000 Young Americans," *Business Insider*, June 10, 2020, https://www.businessinsider.com/how-gen-z -feels-about-george-floyd-protests-2020-6.

19   Bethune, "Gen Z More Likely to Report Mental Health Concerns."

20   Richard A. Friedman, "Teenagers Aren't Losing Their Minds," *New York Times*, September 7, 2018, https://www.nytimes.com/2018/09/07/opinion/sunday /teenager/anxiety-phones-social-media.html.

21   This is consistent with the SIA survey of the American Psychological Association referred to above.

22 danah boyd, *It's Complicated: The Social Lives of Networked Teens* (New Haven, CT: Yale University Press, 2014), 86.

23 Sarah Ogilvie, ed., *Tree Speak: Words of Stanford Dictionary*, Stanford University, 2017, https://words.stanford.edu/.

24 Lily Zheng, "When Ducks Drown: Shifting Paradigms of Mental Health," *Stanford Daily*, February 1, 2016.

25 Tiger Sun, "Duck Syndrome and a Culture of Misery," *Stanford Daily*, January 31, 2018; Karen Kurosawa, "Stanford 'Places I've Cried' Gains Over 1000 Members," *Stanford Daily*, January 22, 2018.

26 Zheng, "When Ducks Drown."

27 Raisa Bruner, "How Halsey's Unflinching Honesty Turned Her into Pop's Most Approachable Star," *Time*, October 8, 2020, https://time.com/collection-post/5896372/halsey-next-generation-leaders/.

28 Umair Akram, Jennifer Drabble, Glhenda Cau, Frayer Hershaw, Ashileen Rajenthran, Mollie Lowe, Carissa Trommelen, and Jason G. Ellis, "Exploratory Study on the Role of Emotion Regulation in Perceived Valence, Humour, and Beneficial Use of Depressive Internet Memes in Depression," *Scientific Reports* 10 (2020): 899, https://doi.org/10.1038/s41598-020-57953-4.

29 Cary Funk and Alec Tyson, "Millennial and Gen Z Republicans Stand Out from Their Elders on Climate and Energy Issues," Pew Research Center, June 24, 2020, https://www.pewresearch.org/?p=302449.

30 "Leadership Team," American Conservation Coalition, https://www.acc.eco/leadership-team.

31 Jeff Brady, "'Light Years Ahead' of Their Elders, Young Republicans Push GOP on Climate Change," NPR, September 25, 2020, https://www.npr.org/2020/09/25/916238283/light-years-ahead-of-their-elders-young-republicans-push-gop-on-climate-change.

32 Bruner, "How Halsey's Unflinching Honesty Turned Her Into Pop's Most Approachable Star."

33 Between June 5 and June 7, 2020, Yubo polled 38,919 US-based postmillennials (regarded as aged thirteen to twenty-five years, thus also including younger teenagers, aged thirteen to eighteen years) and found that 88 percent of respondents believe Black Americans are treated differently than others. Of those who participated in the Yubo poll, 36 percent identified as white, 19 percent as Black/African American, 18 percent as Hispanic/Latinx, 12 percent as mixed race, 4 percent as Asian, and 1 percent as Native American. Nearly 90 percent of those who responded to the Yubo poll said that they support Black Lives Matter, and 83 percent said that they feel the police use too much force in the US; 77 percent of respondents had already attended a protest to support equality for Black Americans, and 62 percent said they were willing to get arrested during a peaceful protest to support this equality. See Davis, "The Action Generation."

34 See, for example, Charlie Warzel, "GenZ Will Not Save Us," *New York Times*, June 22, 2020, https://www.nytimes.com/2020/06/22/opinion/trump-protest-gen-z.html/.

35 Cathy J. Cohen and Joseph Kahne, *Participatory Politics: New Media and Youth Political Action* (Oakland, CA: Youth and Participatory Politics Research Network, June 2012), vi.

36 Henry Jenkins, Sangita Shresthova, Liana Gamber-Thompson, Neta Kligler-Vilenchik, and Arely Zimmerman, *By Any Media Necessary: The New Youth Activism* (New York: New York University Press, 2016), 272.

37 John Palfrey and Urs Gasser, *Born Digital* (New York: Basic Books, 2016), 230.

38 See Veronica Terriquez and May Lin, "Yesterday They Marched, Today They Mobilized the Vote: A Developmental Model for Civic Leadership among the Children of Immigrants," *Journal of Ethnic and Migration Studies* 46, no. 4 (2019): 747–69.

39 The June 2020 Yubo survey cited previously found that postmillennials are using social media to express their support for Black Lives Matter and equality and justice for African Americans, with 73 percent using Instagram, 26 percent using TikTok, 25 percent using Twitter, and 13 percent using Facebook. Davis, "The Action Generation."

40 Taylor Lorenz, "The Political Pundits of TikTok," *New York Times*, February 27, 2020, https://www.nytimes.com/2020/02/27/style/tiktok-politics-bernie -trump.html. Researchers at the Technical University of Munich discovered that Republican users of TikTok generated more political content and their videos received more responses than Democrats, and that Democrats engaged significantly more in cross-partisan discussions. It is not clear which percentage of these users were Gen Z. See Juan Carlos Medina Serrano, Orestis Papakyriakopoulos, and Simon Hegelich, "Dancing to the Partisan Beat: A First Analysis of Political Communication on TikTok," *Southampton'20: 12th ACM Conference on Web Science*, July 7–10, 2020, https://arxiv.org/pdf/2004.05478.pdf.

41 Taylor Lorenz, Kellen Browning, and Sheera Frankel, "TikTok Teens and K-Pop Stans Say They Sank Trump Rally," *New York Times*, June 21, 2020, https://www .nytimes.com/2020/06/21/style/tiktok-trump-rally-tulsa.html.

42 "Meet the TikTok Grandma behind the 'No-Show Protest' Campaign," *BBC News*, June 22, 2020, https://www.bbc.co.uk/news/av/world-us-canada-53145618.

43 Kellen Browning, "TikTok Grandma Who Helped Tank Trump Rally Now Works for Biden," *New York Times*, June 26, 2020, https://www.nytimes.com/2020/06 /26/technology/tiktok-grandma-trump-biden.html/.

44 Bruner, "How Halsey's Unflinching Honesty Turned Her Into Pop's Most Approachable Star."

45 Gallup, Inc., "The First Amendment on Campus 2020 Report: College Students' Views of Free Expression," https://www.knightfoundation.org/reports/free -expression-college-campuses.

46 *The First Amendment on Campus 2020 Report: College Students' Views of Free Expression* (Chicago: Gallup, 2020), 1.

47 Eschwar Chandraseharan, Umashanthi Pavalanathan, Anirudh Srinivasan, Adam Glynn, Jacob Eisenstein, and Eric Gilbert, "You Can't Stay Here: The Efficacy of Reddit's 2015 Ban Examined through Hate Speech," *Proceedings of the ACM on Human-Computer Interaction 2017* 1, no. 2: 31–53.

48 Rusbridger discusses free speech and its significance in the arena of journalism in *Breaking News: The Remaking of Journalism and Why It Matters Now* (Edinburgh: Canongate, 2018).

49 Henry Jenkins, Mizuko Ito, and danah boyd, *Participatory Culture in a Networked Era: A Conversation on Youth, Learning, Commerce and Politics* (London: Polity Press, 2016), 25.

50 Francis Fukuyama, *Identity: Contemporary Identity Politics and the Struggle for Recognition* (London: Profile Books, 2018), 183.

51 See, for example, Veronica Terriquez, Tizoc Brenes, and Abdiel Lopez, "Intersectionality as a Multipurpose Collective Action Frame: The Case of the Undocumented Youth Movement," *Ethnicities* 18, no. 2 (2018): 260–76.

52 Nathan Gardels (citing the work of Jim Fishkin), "The Antidote of Deliberative Democracy Is Gaining Ground," *World Post*, January 31, 2020, https://www.berggruen.org/the-worldpost/articles/weekend-roundup-peak-populism-is-approaching/.

53 Claire Cain Miller and Sanam Yar, "Young People Are Going to Save Us All from Office Life," *New York Times*, September 17, 2019, https://www.nytimes.com/2019/09/17/style/generation-z-millennials-work-life-balance.html/.

54 On loneliness in the twenty-first century, including in relation to work, see Noreena Hertz, *The Lonely Century: Coming Together in a World That's Pulling Apart* (London: Sceptre, 2020).

CHAPTER SEVEN

1 For the optimistic origins of the internet, amid the hippie culture of California's Bay Area, see Fred Turner, *From Counterculture to Cyberculture* (Chicago: University of Chicago Press, 2006).

2 Susan Svriuga, "Georgetown Students Vote in Favor of Reparations for Enslaved People," *Washington Post*, April 12, 2019, https://www.washingtonpost.com/education/2019/04/12/georgetown-students-vote-favor-reparations-slaves/.

3 Amy Binder and Jeffrey Kidder, "If You Think Campus Speech Is All Angry Confrontation, You're Looking in the Wrong Places," *Washington Post*, October 30, 2018, https://www.washingtonpost.com/news/monkey-cage/wp/2018/10/30/if-you-think-campus-speech-is-all-angry-confrontation-youre-looking-in-the-wrong-places/.

4 Jonah Engel Bromwich, "We Asked Generation Z to Pick a Name. It Wasn't Generation Z," *New York Times*, January 31, 2018, https://www.nytimes.com/2018/01/31/style/generation-z-name.html/.

5 Julie Lythcott-Haims, "Why Boomers and Gen X'ers Are Wrong to Bash Gen Z," *Pacific Standard*, April 22, 2019, https://psmag.com/ideas/why-boomers-and-gen-xers-are-wrong-to-bash-gen-z.

APPENDIX

1 Information about the three campuses, including student numbers (for the academic year 2018–2019), comes from their respective websites.

2 See Paul Kerswill, "Children, Adolescents, and Language Change," *Language Variation and Change* 8 (1996): 177–202; J. K. Chambers, *Sociolinguistic Theory: Linguistic Variation and Its Social Significance* (Oxford: Blackwell, 2003); Penny Eckert, *Language Variation as Social Practice* (Oxford: Blackwell, 2000); and S. Tagliamonte, *Teen Talk: the Language of Adolescents* (Cambridge: Cambridge University Press, 2016).

Bibliography

Abbot, Mary. *Family Affairs: A History of the Family in Twentieth-Century England*. London: Routledge, 2002.

Adamy, Janet. "Gen Z Is Coming to Your Office. Get Ready to Adapt." *Wall Street Journal*, September 6, 2018.

Akram, Umair, Jennifer Drabble, Glhenda Cau, Frayer Hershaw, Ashileen Rajenthran, Mollie Lowe, Carissa Trommelen, and Jason G. Ellis. "Exploratory Study on the Role of Emotion Regulation in Perceived Valence, Humour, and Beneficial Use of Depressive Internet Memes in Depression." *Scientific Reports* 10 (2020): 899. https://doi.org/10.1038/s41598-020-57953-4.

Alexander, Elizabeth. "How to Make a Life from Scratch." *New York Times*, July 21, 2018, 18.

Ansari, Aziz, with Eric Klinenberg. *Modern Romance*. London: Penguin Books, 2015.

Appiah, Kwame Anthony. *The Lies That Bind. Rethinking Identity: Creed, Country, Colour, Class, Culture*. London: Profile Books, 2018.

Bailey, Erica, Sandra C. Matz, Wu Youyou, and Sheena S. Iyengar. "Authentic Self-Expression on Social Media Is Associated with Greater Subjective Well-Being." *Nature Communications* 11, 4889 (2020). https://doi.org/10.1038/s41467-020-18539-w.

Barna Group. "Atheism Doubles among Generation Z." *Millennials and Gen-*

erations, January 24, 2018. https://www.barna.com/research/atheism
-doubles-among-generation-z/.

Bartlett, Jamie. *The Dark Net: Inside the Digital Underworld*. New York: Melville House, 2014.

Bates, Laura. *Men Who Hate Women: From Incels to Pickup Artists, the Truth about Extreme Misogyny and How It Affects Us All*. London: Simon and Schuster, 2020.

Bauman, Zygmunt. *Liquid Life*. Cambridge: Polity Press, 2005.

Baym, Nancy K. *Personal Connections in a Digital Age*. London: Polity Press, 2015.

BBC. "Apple Martin: Teen Tells Off Her Mum, Gwyneth Paltrow, for Sharing Photo without Permission," March 27, 2019. https://www .bbc.co.uk/newsround/47718465.

BBC. "Gamers Meet in Real Life at Bedside of Terminally-Ill Friend," September 29, 2018. https://www.bbc.co.uk/news/world-us-canada -45651739.

BBC. "Generation Z and the Art of Self-Maintenance," September 30, 2019. https://www.bbc.co.uk/sounds/play/m0008wnn.

Beck, Julie. "It's 10 p.m. Do You Know Where Your Friends Are?" *Atlantic*, August 20, 2019.

Beck-Gernsheim, Elisabeth. "On the Way to a Post-familial Family: From a Community of Need to Elective Affinities." *Theory, Culture & Society* 15, no. 3–4 (August 1998): 53–70.

Belew, Kathleen. *Bring the War Home: The White Power Movement and Paramilitary America*. Cambridge, MA: Harvard University Press, 2018.

Berger, Peter, Brigitte Berger, and Hansfried Kellner. *The Homeless Mind: Modernization and Consciousness*. New York: Random House, 1973.

Bethune, Sophie. "Gen Z More Likely to Report Mental Health Concerns." *Monitor on Psychology* 50, no. 1 (January 2019), 1–20. https://www.apa .org/monitor/2019/01/gen-z.

Bosker, Bianca. "Crowdsourcing the Novel." *Atlantic*, December 2018.

Bowles, Nellie. "These Millennials Got New Roommates. They're Nuns." *New York Times*, May 31, 2019. https://www.nytimes.com/2019/05/31 /style/milliennial-nuns-spiritual-quest.html/.

boyd, danah. "Friendship." In *Hanging Out, Messing Around, and Geeking Out: Kids Living and Learning with New Media*. Edited by Mizuko Ito,

Sonja Baumer, Matteo Bittanti, danah boyd, Rachel Cody, Becky Herr Stephenson, Heather A. Horst, Patricia G. Lange, Dilan Mahendran, Katynka Z. Martínez, C. J. Pascoe, Dan Perkel, Laura Robinson, Christo Sims, and Lisa Tripp, 79–116. Cambridge, MA: MIT Press, 2010.

boyd, danah. *It's Complicated: The Social Lives of Networked Teens.* New Haven, CT: Yale University Press, 2014.

Bromwich, Jonah Engel. "We Asked Generation Z to Pick a Name. It Wasn't Generation Z." *New York Times,* January 31, 2018. https://www .nytimes.com/2018/01/31/style/generation-z-name.html/.

Brooks, David. "The Age of Aquarius, All Over Again: Belief in Astrology and the Occult Is Surging." *New York Times,* June 10, 2019. https://www .nytimes.com/2019/06/10/opinion/astrology-occult-millennials.html/.

Brooks, David. "A Generation Emerging from the Wreckage." *New York Times,* February 26, 2018. https://www.nytimes.com/2018/02/26 /opinion/millennials-college-hopeful.html/.

Brown, Callum G. *Religion and the Demographic Revolution.* Suffolk, UK: Boydell Press, 2012.

Browning, Kellen. "TikTok Grandma Who Helped Tank Trump Rally Now Works for Biden." *New York Times,* June 26, 2020. https://www.nytimes .com/2020/06/26/technology/tiktok-grandma-trump-biden.html/.

Brubaker, Rogers. *Trans: Gender and Race in an Age of Unsettled Identities.* Princeton, NJ: Princeton University Press, 2016.

Bruner, Raisa. "How Halsey's Unflinching Honesty Turned Her into Pop's Most Approachable Star." *Time,* October 8, 2020. https://time.com /collection-post/5896372/halsey-next-generation-leaders/.

Bullivant, Stephen. "Europe's Young Adults and Religion: Findings from the European Social Survey (2014–16) to Inform the 2018 Synod of Bishops." https://www.stmarys.ac.uk/research/centres/benedict-xvi /docs/2018-mar-europe-young-people-report-eng.pdf.

Byron, Ellen. "20-Somethings Embrace Clean Living." *Wall Street Journal,* March 12, 2018.

Campbell, W. Joseph. *1995: The Year the Future Began.* Berkeley: University of California Press, 2015.

Carr, Nicholas. *The Shallows: What the Internet Is Doing to Our Brains.* London: W. W. Norton & Co., 2011.

Case, Anne, and Angus Deaton. *Deaths of Despair and the Future of Capitalism*. Princeton, NJ: Princeton University Press, 2020.

Chambers, J. K. *Sociolinguistic Theory: Linguistic Variation and Its Social Significance*. Oxford: Blackwell, 2003.

Chandraseharan, Eschwar, Umashanthi Pavalanathan, Anirudh Srinivasan, Adam Glynn, Jacob Eisenstein, and Eric Gilbert. "You Can't Stay Here: The Efficacy of Reddit's 2015 Ban Examined through Hate Speech." *Proceedings of the ACM on Human-Computer Interaction 2017* 1, no. 2: 31–53.

Clydesdale, Tim. *The First Year Out: Understanding American Teens after High School*. Chicago: University of Chicago Press, 2007.

Coates, Ta-Nehisi. *Between the World and Me*. New York: Spiegel & Grau, 2015.

Cohen, Cathy J., and Joseph Kahne. *Participatory Politics: New Media and Youth Political Action*. Oakland, CA: Youth and Participatory Politics Research Network, 2012. https://www.researchgate.net/publication/255702744 _Participatory_Politics_New_Media_and_Youth_Political_Action.

Cohen, Li. "From TikTok to Black Lives Matter, How Gen Z is Revolutionizing Activism." *CBS News*, July 20, 2020. https://www.cbsnews.com /news/from-tiktok-to-black-lives-matter-how-gen-z-is-revolution izing-activism/.

Coleman, Marilyn. *Family Life in Twentieth-Century America*. Westport, CT: Greenwood, 2007.

Craig, Shelley L., Lauren McInroy, Lance T. McCready, and Ramona Alaggia. "Media: A Catalyst for Resilience in Lesbian, Gay, Bisexual, Transgender, and Queer Youth," *Journal of LGBT Youth* 12, no. 3 (2015): 254–75.

Crenshaw, Kimberlé Williams. "Demarginalizing the Intersection of Race and Sex: A Black Feminist Critique of Antidiscrimination Doctrine, Feminist Theory and Antiracist Politics," *University of Chicago Legal Forum*, no. 1 (1989): 139–67.

Davenport, Lauren D. "Beyond Black and White: Biracial Attitudes in Contemporary U.S. Politics." *American Political Science Review* 110, no. 1 (February 2016): 52–67.

Davenport, Lauren D. *Politics Beyond Black and White: Biracial Identity and Attitudes in America*. Cambridge: Cambridge University Press, 2018.

Davenport, Thomas H., and John C. Beck. *The Attention Economy*. Cambridge, MA: Harvard Business Review, 2002.

Davidoff, Leonore, and Catherine Hall. *Family Fortunes: Men and Women of the English Middle Class 1780–1850*. London: Routledge, 2002.

Davis, Dominic-Madori. "The Action Generation." *Business Insider*, June 10, 2020. https://www.businessinsider.com/how-gen-z-feels-about -george-floyd-protests-2020-6.

Delevingne, Cara. "Cara Delevingne: 9 Moments That Changed My Life." *British Vogue*, June 2018.

Delevingne, Cara. "Cara Delevingne Gushes Over Ashley: 'I'm the Luckiest Girl in the World.'" Interview at Girl Up Hero Awards. October 13, 2019. https://www.eonline.com/videos/297220/cara-delevingne -gushes-over-ashley-i-m-the-luckiest-girl-in-the-world.

Dyson, George. *Analogia: The Entangled Destinies of Nature, Human Beings and Machines*. London: Allen Lane, 2020.

Eckert, P. *Language Variation as Social Practice*. Oxford: Blackwell, 2000.

Eddo-Lodge, Reni. *Why I'm No Longer Talking to White People about Race*. London: Bloomsbury Circus, 2017.

Eubanks, Virginia. *Automating Inequality: How High-Tech Tools Profile, Police, and Punish the Poor*. New York: St Martin's Press, 2017.

Evans, Claire L. *Broad Band: The Untold Story of the Women Who Made the Internet*. New York: Portfolio, 2018.

Evaristo, Bernadine. *Girl, Woman, Other*. London: Penguin, 2019.

Fineman, Martha Albertson. "Vulnerability and Social Justice." *Valparaiso University Law Review* 53, no. 2 (2019): 341–69.

Fischer, Claude S. *America Calling: A Social History of the Telephone to 1940*. Berkeley: University of California Press, 1994.

Fiske, Susan T., and Hazel Rose Markus. *Facing Social Class: How Societal Rank Influences Interaction*. New York: Russell Sage Foundation, 2012.

Frankenberg, Ruth. *White Women/Race Matters*. Minneapolis: University of Minnesota Press, 1998.

Friedman, Richard A. "Teenagers Aren't Losing Their Minds." *New York Times*, September 7, 2018. https://www.nytimes.com/2018/09/07 /opinion/sunday/teenager/anxiety-phones-social-media.html/.

Fukuyama, Francis. *Identity: The Demand for Dignity and the Politics of Resentment*. New York: Farrar, Straus and Giroux, 2018.

Fukuyama, Francis. *Identity: Contemporary Identity Politics and the Struggle for Recognition.* London: Profile Books, 2018.

Funk, Cary, and Alec Tyson. "Millennial and Gen Z Republicans Stand Out from Their Elders on Climate and Energy Issues." Pew Research Center, June 24, 2020. https://www.pewresearch.org/?p=302449.

Gallup, Inc. "The First Amendment on Campus 2020 Report: College Students' Views of Free Expression." https://www.knightfoundation.org/reports/free-expression-college-campuses.

Gardell, Matthias. *Gods of the Blood: The Pagan Revival and White Separatism.* Durham, NC: Duke University Press, 2003.

Gardels, Nathan. "The Antidote of Deliberative Democracy Is Gaining Ground." *World Post,* January 31, 2020. https://www.berggruen.org/the-worldpost/articles/weekend-roundup-peak-populism-is-approaching/.

Gardner, Howard, and Katie Davis. *The App Generation: How Today's Youth Navigate Identity, Intimacy, and Imagination in a Digital World.* New Haven, CT: Yale University Press, 2013.

Gawande, Atul. "The Blight: How Our Economy Has Created an Epidemic of Despair." *New Yorker,* March 23, 2020.

Gee, Elisabeth, Lori Takeuchi, and Ellen Wartella. *Children and Families in the Digital Age: Learning Together in a Media Saturated Culture.* London: Routledge, 2018.

George, Madeleine J., and Candice L. Odgers. "Seven Fears and the Science of How Mobile Technologies May Be Influencing Adolescents in the Digital Age." *Perspectives on Psychological Science* 10, no. 6, (2015): 832–51.

Giddens, Anthony. *The Consequences of Modernity.* Stanford, CA: Stanford University Press, 1990.

Giddens, Anthony. *Modernity and Self-Identity: Self and Society in the Late Modern Age.* Stanford, CA: Stanford University Press, 1991.

Golombok, Susan. *Modern Families: Parents and Children in New Family Forms.* Cambridge: Cambridge University Press, 2015.

Golombok, Susan. *We Are Family: What Really Matters for Parents and Children.* London: Scribe, 2020.

Gratton, Lynda, and Andrew Scott. *The 100-Year Life: Living and Working in an Age of Longevity.* London: Bloomsbury, 2017.

Greenfield, Susan. *Mind Change: How Digital Technologies are Leaving their Mark on Our Brains*. New York: Random House, 2015.

Guest, Mathew. "The 'Hidden Christians' of the UK University Campus." In *Young People and the Diversity of (Non)religious Identities in International Perspective*, edited by Elizabeth Arweck and Heather Shipley Cham, Switzerland: Springer, 2019.

Guest, Mathew, Kristin Aune, Sonya Sharma and Rob Warner, *Christianity and the University Experience: Understanding Christian Faith*. London: Bloomsbury Academic, 2012.

Guest, Mathew, Alison Scott-Baumann, Sariya Cheruvallil-Contractor, Shuruq Naguib, Aisha Phoenix, Yenn Lee, and Tarek Al-Baghal. *Islam on Campuses: Perceptions and Challenges*. SOAS University of London, 2020. https://www.soas.ac.uk/representingislamoncampus/publications/file148310.pdf.

Hamilton, Laura. *Parenting to a Degree: How Family Matters for College Women's Success*. Chicago: University of Chicago Press, 2016.

Hammack, Phillip L. "The Future Is Non-binary and Teens Are Leading the Way." *Pacific Standard*, April 8, 2019. https://psmag.com/ideas/gen-z-the-future-is-nonbinary.

Harris, Malcolm. *Kids These Days: Human Capital and the Making of Millennials*. New York: Little, Brown, 2017.

Haug, Claire. "What's a Normal Family, Anyway?" *New York Times*, February 5, 2019. https://www.nytimes.com/2019/02/05/style/the-edit-normal-unconventional-family.html/.

Hertz, Noreena. *The Lonely Century: Coming Together in a World That's Pulling Apart*. London: Sceptre, 2020.

Hond, Paul. "Portrait of a Gen Z Activist." *Columbia Magazine*, Fall 2020. https://magazine.columbia.edu/article/portrait-gen-z-activist.

Hunt, Elle. "Meet the Numtots: The Millennials Who Find Fixing Public Transport Sexy." *Guardian*, July 5, 2018. https://www.theguardian.com/cities/2018/jul/05/meet-the-numtots-the-millennials-who-find-fixing-public-transit-sexy-urbanist-memes.

Iqbal, Nosheen. "Generation Z: 'We Have More to Do Than Drink and Take Drugs.'" *Guardian*, July 21, 2018. https://www.theguardian.com/society/2018/jul/21/generation-z-has-different-attitudes-says-a-new-report.

Ito, Mizuko. "Contributors versus Leechers: Fansnubbing, Ethics and a Hybrid Public Culture." In *Fandom Unbound*, edited by Mizuko Ito, D. Okabe, and I. Tsuji. New Haven, CT: Yale University Press, 2012.

Ito, Mizuko, Sonja Baumer, Matteo Bittanti, danah boyd, Rachel Cody, Becky Herr Stephenson, and Heather A. Horst. *Hanging Out, Messing Around, and Geeking Out*. Cambridge, MA: MIT Press, 2013.

Ito, Mizuko, Crystle Martin, Rachel Cody Pfister, Matthew H. Rafalow, Katie Salen, and Amanda Wortman. *Affinity Online: How Connection and Shared Interest Fuel Learning*. New York: New York University Press, 2018.

Jenkins, Henry. *Fans, Bloggers and Gamers: Exploring Participatory Culture*. New York: New York University Press, 2006.

Jenkins, Henry, Mizuko Ito, and danah boyd. *Participatory Culture in a Networked Era: A Conversation on Youth, Learning, Commerce, and Politics*. Cambridge: Polity Press, 2016.

Jenkins, Henry, Shangita Shresthova, Liana Gamber-Thompson, Neta Kligler-Vilenchik, and Arrely Zimmerman. *By Any Media Necessary: The New Youth Activism*. New York: New York University Press, 2016.

Kafka, Franz. *The Neighbour*, trans. Tanya Ellerbrock. The Kafka Project, 2021 [1917]. http://www.kafka.org/index.php?aid=163.

Kahne, Joseph, Nam-Jin Lee, and Jessica T. Feezell. "The Civic and Political Significance of Online Participatory Cultures among Youth Transitioning to Adulthood." *Journal of Information Technology & Politics* 10, no. 1 (2013): 1–20.

Kaplan, Bruce Eric. "He's Less of a Parent and More of a Fixer" (cartoon). *New Yorker*, August 20, 2018: 39.

Kelly, Kevin. *The Inevitable: Understanding the 12 Technological Forces that Will Shape Our Future*. New York: Penguin, 2017.

Kerswill, Paul. "Children, Adolescents, and Language Change." *Language Variation and Change* 8 (1996): 177–202.

Klinenberg, Eric. *Palaces for the People: How Social Infrastructure Can Help Fight Inequality, Polarization, and the Decline of Civic Life*. New York: Crown, 2018.

Kreiss, Daniel, Megan Finn, and Fred Turner. "The Limits of Peer Production: Some Reminders from Max Weber for the Network Society." *New Media & Society* 13, no. 2 (2011): 243–59.

Kurosawa, Karen. "Stanford 'Places I've Cried' Gains Over 1000 Members." *Stanford Daily*, January 22, 2018.

Lantos, Eva. "TikTok: Fears Videos May 'Trigger Eating Disorders.'" *BBC News*, June 22, 2020. https://www.bbc.co.uk/news/uk-wales-52919914.

Lasch, Christopher. *Haven in a Heartless World*. New York: Basic Books, 1977.

Laqueur, Thomas. *Making Sex: Body and Gender from the Greeks to Freud*. Cambridge, MA: Harvard University Press, 1992.

Lauricella, Alexis, Drew Cingel, Leanne Beaudoin-Ryan, Michael B. Robb, Melissa Saphir, and Ellen Wartella. *The Common Sense Census: Plugged-In Parents of Tweens and Teens*. San Francisco: Common Sense Media, 2016.

Lee, Angela. "A Day in the Loop: A Look into Teen Media Lifestyles." Unpublished paper, 2020.

Lee, Angela. "Generation Z and Collective Online Communities: On 'Subtle Asian Traits.'" Unpublished paper, 2019.

Lee, Angela. "Tumblr Helped Me Plan My Eating Disorder. Then It Helped Me Heal." *Pacific Standard*, April 29, 2019. https://psmag.com/ideas/tumblr-helped-me-plan-my-eating-disorder-then-it-helped-me-heal.

Lenhart, Amanda, and Mary Madden. *Teen Content Creators and Consumers*. Washington, DC: Pew Research Center, 2005.

Lesthaeghe, Ron. "The Unfolding Story of the Second Demographic Transition." *Population and Development Review* 36, no. 2 (2010): 211–51.

Levin, Dan. "Young Voters Keep Moving to the Left on Social Issues, Republicans Included." *New York Times*, January 23, 2019. https://www.nytimes.com/2019/01/23/us/gop-liberal-america-millennials.html/.

Levine, Madeline. *Ready or Not: Preparing Our Kids to Thrive in an Uncertain and Rapidly Changing World*. San Francisco: Harper, 2020.

Lin, Kat. "The Story of the Subtle Asian Traits Facebook Group." *New Yorker*, December 22, 2018. https://www.newyorker.com/culture/culture-desk/the-story-of-the-subtle-asian-traits-facebook-group.

Livingstone, Sonia, and Alicia Blum-Ross. *Parenting for a Digital Future: How Hopes and Fears about Technology Shape Our Children's Lives*. New York: Oxford University Press, 2020.

Lorenz, Taylor. "The Political Pundits of TikTok." *New York Times*, February 27, 2020. https://www.nytimes.com/2020/02/27/style/tiktok-politics-bernie-trump.html/.

Lukianoff, Greg, and Jonathan Haidt. *The Coddling of the American Mind: How*

Good Intentions and Bad Ideas are Setting Up a Generation for Failure. London: Penguin, 2018.

Luthar, Suniya S., and Shawn J. Latendresse. "Children of the Affluent: Challenges to Well-Being." *American Psychological Science* 14, no. 1 (2005): 49–53.

Lythcott-Haims, Julie. *How to Raise an Adult: Break Free of the Overparenting Trap and Prepare your Kid for Success*. New York: Henry Holt, 2015.

Lythcott-Haims, Julie. "Why Boomers and Gen X'ers Are Wrong to Bash Gen Z." *Pacific Standard*, April 22, 2019. https://psmag.com/ideas/why-boomers-and-gen-xers-are-wrong-to-bash-gen-z.

Macaulay, Rose. *Crewe Train*. London: Virago Press, 1926; repr. 2000.

Madge, Nicola, Peter J. Hemming, and Kevin Stenson. *Youth on Religion: The Development, Negotiation and Impact of Faith and Non-Faith Identity*. London: Routledge, 2013.

Maffesoli, Michel. *Time of the Tribes: The Decline of Individualism in Mass Society*. London: Sage, 1996.

Malik, Nesrine. "Interview Olivette Otele," *Guardian*, October 16, 2020. https://www.theguardian.com/books/2020/oct/16/olivette-otele-discussions-of-cancel-culture-are-very-middle-class-activists-just-survive-and-support-each-other.

Manning, Christel J. *Losing Our Religion. How Unaffiliated Parents Are Raising Their Children*. New York: New York University Press, 2016.

Manning, Christel J. "Gen Z Is the Least Religious Generation. Here's Why That Could Be a Good Thing." *Pacific Standard*, May 6, 2019. https://psmag.com/ideas/gen-z-is-the-least-religious-generation-heres-why-that-could-be-a-good-thing.

Markus, Hazel Rose, and Paula M. L. Moya, eds. *Doing Race: 21 Essays for the 21st Century*. New York: W. W. Norton & Co., 2010.

Markus, Hazel Rose, and Alana Conner. *Clash!: How to Thrive in a Multicultural World*. New York: Plume, 2014.

McCulloch, Gretchen. *Because Internet*. New York: Riverhead Books, 2019.

McGonigal, Jane. *Reality Is Broken: Why Games Make Us Better and How They Can Change the World*. London: Vintage, 2012.

McLaughlin, Erin. "'On Fleek' Inventor Kayla Newman AKA Peaches Monroe on Her Beauty Line." *Teen Vogue*, March 9, 2017.

Miller, Claire Cain, and Sanam Yar. "Young People Are Going to Save Us

All from Office Life." *New York Times*, September 17, 2019. https://www
.nytimes.com/2019/09/17/style/generation-z-millennials-work-life
-balance.html.

Milroy, Lesley, and Matthew Gordon. *Sociolinguistics: Method and Interpreta-tion*. Oxford: Blackwell, 2003.

Mol, Hans. *Identity and the Sacred: A Sketch for a New Social-Scientific Theory of Religion*. New York: The Free Press, 1977.

Moskowitz-Sweet, Gloria, and Erica Pelavin. "Gen Z's Message to Parents — 'Put Your Phone Down.'" *Pacific Standard*, April 22, 2019. https://psmag.com/ideas/put-down-the-phone-and-reconnect-with -your-child.

Nagel, Angela. *Kill All Normies: The Online Culture Wars from 4chan and Tumblr to Trump and the Alt-Right*. Winchester, UK: Zero Books, 2017.

Noble, Safiya. *Algorithms of Oppression: How Search Engines Reinforce Racism*. New York: New York University Press, 2018.

Ogilvie, Sarah, ed. "Tree Speak: Words of Stanford Dictionary." Stanford University, 2017. https://words.stanford.edu/.

Ogilvie, Sarah, and Dave Martin. "Oxford English Dictionary: Building Dictionaries with Crowdsourcing." Podcast recorded January 2019. https://www.youtube.com/watch?v=ZmoyLCftpAs.

Ogilvie, Sarah, ed. "iGen Corpus." Electronic resource accessed October 2020. https://igencorpus.ling-phil.ox.ac.uk/.

O'Neil, Cathy. *Weapons of Math Destruction: How Big Data Increases Inequality and Threatens Democracy*. New York: Broadway Books, 2017.

Orben, Amy, and Andrew K. Przybylski. "The Association between Ado-lescent Well-Being and Digital Technology." *Nature Human Behaviour* 3 (January 14, 2019): 173–82.

Painter, Nell Irvin. *The History of White People*. New York: W. W. Norton & Co., 2010.

Palfrey, John, and Urs Gasser. *Born Digital*. New York: Basic Books, 2016.

Parker, Kim, Nikki Graf, and Ruth Igielnik. "Generation Z Looks a Lot Like Millennials on Key Social and Political Issues." Pew Research Center. http://www.pewsocialtrends.org/2019/01/17/generation-z -looks-a-lot-like-millennials-on-key-social-and-political-issues/.

Pendleton-Jullian, Ann M., and John Seely Brown. *Design Unbound: Design-ing for Emergence in a White Water World*. Cambridge, MA: MIT Press, 2018.

Perrin, Andrew, and Monica Anderson. "Share of U.S. Adults Using Social Media, Including Facebook, Is Mostly Unchanged since 2018." Pew Research Center. https://www.pewresearch.org/fact-tank/2019/04/10/share-of-u-s-adults-using-social-media-including-facebook-is-mostly-unchanged-since-2018.

Pew Research Center. "The Age Gap in Religion around the World." June 13, 2018. https://www.pewforum.org/2018/06/13/the-age-gap-in-religion-around-the-world/.

Pew Research Center. "The American Family Today." December 17, 2015. https://www.pewsocialtrends.org/2015/12/17/1-the-american-family-today/.

Pink, Sophia. "'Stagnancy Is Scarier Than Change': What I Learned from My Road Trip in Search of Gen Z." *Pacific Standard*, April 8, 2019. https://psmag.com/ideas/road-tripping-to-understand-gen-z.

Przybylski, Andrew K., and Netta Weinstein. "A Large-Scale Test of the Goldilocks Hypothesis: Quantifying the Relations between Digital-Screen Use and the Mental Well-Being of Adolescents." *Psychological Science* 28 (January 13, 2017): 204–15.

Putnam, Robert. *Bowling Alone*. New York: Simon & Schuster, 2001.

Putnam, Robert, with Shaylyn Romney Garrett. *The Upswing: How America Came Together a Century Ago and How We Can Do It Again*. New York: Simon and Schuster, 2020.

Quealy, Kevin, and Claire Cain Miller. "Young Adulthood in America: Children Are Grown, but Parenting Doesn't Stop." *New York Times*, March 13, 2019.

Radesky, Jenny. "What Happens When We Turn to Smartphones to Escape Our Kids?" *Pacific Standard*, April 22, 2019. https://psmag.com/ideas/what-happens-when-parents-cant-put-their-phones-down.

Reeves, B., N. Ram, T. N. Robinson, J. J. Cummings, L. Giles, J. Pan, A. Chiatti, M. J. Cho, K. Roehrick, X. Yang, A. Gagneja, M. Brinberg, D. Muise, Y. Lu, M. Luo, A. Fitzgerald, and L. Yeykelis. "Screenomics: A Framework to Capture and Analyze Personal Life Experiences and the Ways That Technology Shapes Them." *Human-Computer Interaction* 36, no. 2 (2021): 150–201.

Romano, Aja. "Harry Potter and the Author Who Failed Us," *Vox*, June 11,

2020. https://www.vox.com/culture/21285396/jk-rowling-transphobic-backlash-harry-potter.

Roof, Wade Clark. *Spiritual Marketplace. Baby Boomers and the Remaking of American Religion*. Princeton, NJ: Princeton University Press, 1999.

Rooney, Ben. "Women and Children First: Technology and Moral Panic." *Wall Street Journal*, July 11, 2011. https://blogs.wsj.com/tech-europe/2011/07/11/women-and-children-first-technology-and-moral-panic/.

Rusbridger, Alan. *Breaking News. The Remaking of Journalism and Why It Matters Now*. Edinburgh: Canongate, 2018.

Russett, Cynthia. *Sexual Science: The Victorian Construction of Womanhood*. Cambridge, MA: Harvard University Press, 1991.

Sandhu, Rajdeep. "Should BAME Be Ditched as a Term for Black, Asian and Minority Ethnic People?" *BBC News*, May 27, 2018. https://www.bbc.co.uk/news/uk-politics-43831279.

Schulman, Michael. "The Force Is with Them." *New Yorker*, September 16, 2019.

Scott-Baumann, Alison, Mathew Guest, Shuruq Naguib, Sariya Cheruvallil-Contractor, and Aisha Phoenix. *Islam on Campus: Contested Identities and the Cultures of Higher Education in Britain*. Oxford: Oxford University Press, 2020.

Sepetys, Kristina. "Have Headphones Made Gen Z More Insular?" *Pacific Standard*, April 29, 2019. https://psmag.com/ideas/have-headphones-made-gen-z-more-insular.

Serrano, Juan Carlos Medina, Orestis Papakyriakopoulos, and Simon Hegelich. "Dancing to the Partisan Beat: A First Analysis of Political Communication on TikTok." *Southampton '20: 12th ACM Conference on Web Science*, July 7–10, 2020. https://arxiv.org/pdf/2004.05478.pdf.

Snook, Jennifer. *American Heathens: The Politics of Identity in a Pagan Religious Movement*. Philadelphia: Temple University Press, 2015.

Sun, Tiger. "Duck Syndrome and a Culture of Misery." *Stanford Daily*, January 31, 2018.

Svriuga, Susan "Georgetown Students Vote in Favor of Reparations for Enslaved People." *Washington Post*, April 12, 2019. https://www.washingtonpost.com/education/2019/04/12/georgetown-students-vote-favor-reparations-slaves/.

Tagliamonte, S. *Teen Talk: the Language of Adolescents*. Cambridge: Cambridge University Press, 2016.

Taylor, Brandon. *Real Life*. New York: Riverhead Books, 2020.

Taylor, Charles. *Sources of the Self: The Making of Modern Identity*. Cambridge, MA: Cambridge University Press, 1989.

Taylor, Charles. *The Ethic of Authenticity*. Cambridge, MA: Harvard University Press, 2002.

ter Kuile, Casper. *The Power of Ritual: Turning Everyday Activities into Soulful Practices*. London: William Collins, 2020.

ter Kuile, Casper, and Angie Thurston. "Something More." Sacred Design Lab, 2019. https://sacred.design/wp-content/uploads/2019/10/SomethingMore_F_Digital_Update.pdf.

Terriquez, Veronica, Tizoc Brenes, and Abdiel Lopez. "Intersectionality as a Multipurpose Collective Action Frame: The Case of the Undocumented Youth Movement." *Ethnicities* 18, no. 2 (2018): 260–76.

Terriquez, Veronica, and May Lin. "Yesterday They Marched, Today They Mobilized the Vote: A Developmental Model for Civic Leadership among the Children of Immigrants." *Journal of Ethnic and Migration Studies* 46, no. 4 (2019): 747–69.

Thompson, Becky, and Sangeeta Tyagi, eds. *Names We Call Home: Autobiography of Racial Identity*. New York: Routledge, 1996.

Thurston, Angie, and Casper ter Kuile. "How We Gather." Sacred Design Lab, 2019. https://sacred.design/wp-content/uploads/2019/10/How_We_Gather_Digital_4.11.17.pdf.

Trappelides, Thanos, Aqsa Ahmed, Tamara Krivskaya, Anca Usurelu, Jabeel Mahmoud. "Issues of Belonging in the iGeneration." Unpublished manuscript, Richardson Institute, Lancaster University, 2019.

Trilling, Lionel. *Sincerity and Authenticity*. Cambridge, MA: Harvard University Press, 1972.

Trotter, David. *Literature in the First Media Age: Britain between the Wars*. Cambridge, MA: Harvard University Press, 2013.

Turkle, Sherry. *Alone Together*. New York: Basic Books, 2011.

Turkle, Sherry. *Reclaiming Conversation: The Power of Talk in A Digital Age*. London: Penguin, 2015.

Turner, Fred. *From Counterculture to Cyberculture: Stewart Brand, the Whole Earth*

Network, and the Rise of Digital Utopianism. Chicago: University of Chicago Press, 2006.

Twenge, Jean. Generation Me. New York: Atria, 2014.

Twenge, Jean. iGen: Why Today's Super-Connected Kids Are Growing Up Less Rebellious, More Tolerant, Less Happy—and Completely Unprepared for Adulthood—and What That Means for the Rest of Us. New York: Atria Books, 2017.

"Under the Hood: TikTok's Rampant Growth Strikes Wrong Note." FTWeekend, July 25/26, 2020, 14.

US Social Security Administration. "Retirement & Survivors Benefits: Life Expectancy Calculator." https://www.ssa.gov/cgi-bin/longevity.cgi.

Wade, Lisa. American Hookup: The New Culture of Sex on Campus. New York: W. W. Norton & Co., 2017.

Wagner, Tony. Creating Innovators. New York: Scribner, 2012.

Ware, Vron. Beyond the Pale: White Women, Racism and History. London: Verso, 1992.

Ware, Vron. Out of Whiteness: Color, Politics, and Culture. Chicago: University of Chicago Press, 2002.

Warzel, Charlie. "Gen Z Will Not Save Us." New York Times, June 22, 2020. https://www.nytimes.com/2020/06/22/opinion/trump-protest-gen-z.html/.

Watkins, S. Craig. The Young and the Digital: What the Migration to Social-Network Sites, Games, and Anytime, Anywhere Media Means for Our.Future. Boston: Beacon Press, 2009.

Web MD. "Pro Anorexia Sites: The Thin Web Line." Accessed April 28, 2019. https://www.webmd.com/mental-health/eating-disorders/anorexia-nervosa/features/pro-anorexia-web-sites-thin-web-line.

White, Ethan Doyle. "Northern Gods for Northern Folk: Racial Identity and Right-Wing Ideology among Britain's Folkish Heathens." Journal of Religion in Europe 10, no. 3 (2017): 241–73.

Wilkerson, Isabel. Caste: The Lies That Divide Us. London: Allen Lane, 2020.

Williams, Patricia J. The Alchemy of Race and Rights: Diary of a Law Professor. Cambridge, MA: Harvard University Pres, 1991.

Wineburg, Sam, Sarah McGrew, Joel Breakstone, and Teresa Ortega. "Evaluating Information: The Cornerstone of Civic Online Reasoning.'" Stanford Digital Repository, 2016. https://purl.stanford.edu /fv751yt5934.

Wolf, Maryanne. Reader, Come Home: The Reading Brain in a Digital World. New York: HarperCollins, 2018.

Woodhead, Linda. "The Rise of 'No Religion' in Britain: The Emergence of a New Cultural Majority." Journal of the British Academy 4 (2016): 245–61.

Woodhead, Linda. "The Rise of 'No Religion': Towards an Explanation." Sociology of Religion 78, no. 3 (Autumn 2017): 247–62.

Wu, Nicholas, and Karen Yuan. "The Meme-ification of Asianness." Atlantic, December 27, 2018. https://www.theatlantic.com/technology /archive/2018/12/the-asian-identity-according-to-subtle-asian-traits /579037.

Wuthnow, Robert. Sharing the Journey. Support Groups and America's New Quest for Community. New York: The Free Press, 1994.

Zheng, Lily. "When Ducks Drown: Shifting Paradigms of Mental Health." Stanford Daily, February 1, 2016.

Zuckerman, Ethan. Digital Cosmopolitans: Why We Think the Internet Connects Us, Why It Doesn't, and How to Rewire It. New York: W. W. Norton & Co., 2014.

Index

activism, 3, 20, 64, 176–77, 213; and Black Lives Matter (BLM) movement, 181; boomer, 154; forms of, 179–80; Gen Z, 160, 178–79, 193; and identity, 85; immigrant, 179; and mental health, 165, 169–70; and participatory politics, 178–79; political, 173; among postmillennials, 2, 176–79; by queer women of color, 169–70; racial disparities in, 85; social media, as central to, 179–80; student, 4, 20 admins, 119. See also moderators/moderation, online
adulting, 161
affinity networks, 94
African Americans, 44, 126, 181, 233n33, 234n39; appropriation of language and culture of, 82; Black activism, 55, 64, 177, 179, 183–84; Black evangelicals, 148; Black female culture, appropriation of, 81; Black identity, 53–54, 56, 60, 64, 83, 166; English of, 82, 86, 109; Gen Zers, 53, 58–59, 62, 66, 104; and Juneteenth, 180; police violence against, 174, 178; and racism, 84–85, 165; unfair treatment of, 84; as vulnerable, 165. See also Black; Black Lives Matter (BLM) movement
Ahmed, Ziad, 231n1

Alexander, Elizabeth, 39
algorithms, 7, 28–30, 70, 101–2, 214, 226–27n9
allyship, 49
alt-right, 61, 100, 178, 183, 226n8
Amazon, 11, 31; Echo, 17
American Conservation Coalition (ACC), 173
American Psychological Association, Stress in America (SIA) survey, 162, 164
anime, 100, 102, 215
Anonymous, 100
anorexia, 227–28n17
Apple Homepod, 17
appropriation, 55; of African American culture, 82; and authenticity, 81, 118; cultural, 81–82, 118, 195; denouncing of, 195; of Native American culture, 81–82; as taboo among Gen Zers, 118; of traditional Japanese culture, 82
artificial intelligence, 26, 30, 38, 101, 124, 127, 189
Asian, 40, 44, 59, 61–62, 96–97, 119, 174
Asian Americans, 57–59, 81, 96, 104
Asian-British, 40, 41
Asian immigrants, 57, 95–96, 155
astrology, 153
atheism, 148, 151–52